CLIFFSCOMPLETE

Shakespeare's

The Merchant of Venice

Edited by Sidney Lamb

Associate Professor of English

Sir George Williams University, Montreal

Complete Text + **Commentary** + **Glossary**

Commentary by David Nicol

IDG BOOKS WORLDWIDE

IDG Books Worldwide, Inc.

An International Data Group Company

Foster City, CA • Chicago, IL • Indianapolis, IN • New York, NY

CLIFFSCOMPLETE

Shakespeare's

The Merchant of Venice

About the Author
David Nicol received his M.A. from the Shakespeare Institute (University of Birmingham) in Stratford-upon-Avon. He is currently teaching and researching Renaissance Drama at the University of Central England in Birmingham.

Publisher's Acknowledgments
Editorial
Project Editor: Elizabeth Netedu Kuball
Acquisitions Editor: Gregory W. Tubach
Editorial Director: Kristin A. Cocks
Special Help: Michelle Hacker
Production
Indexer: Sherry Massey
Proofreader: Nancy L. Reinhardt
Illustrator: DD Dowden.
IDG Books Indianapolis Production Department

CliffsComplete The Merchant of Venice
Published by
IDG Books Worldwide, Inc.
An International Data Group Company
919 E. Hillsdale Blvd.
Suite 400
Foster City, CA 94404
www.idgbooks.com (IDG Books Worldwide Web site)
www.cliffsnotes.com (CliffsNotes Web site)

Library of Congress Catalog Card No.: 00-01093

ISBN: 0-7645-8575-4

Printed in the United States of America

10 9 8 7 6 5 4 3 2 1

1O/SQ/QU/QQ/IN

Distributed in the United States by IDG Books Worldwide, Inc.

Distributed by CDG Books Canada Inc. for Canada; by Transworld Publishers Limited in the United Kingdom; by IDG Norge Books for Norway; by IDG Sweden Books for Sweden; by IDG Books Australia Publishing Corporation Pty. Ltd. for Australia and New Zealand; by TransQuest Publishers Pte Ltd. for Singapore, Malaysia, Thailand, Indonesia, and Hong Kong; by Gotop Information Inc. for Taiwan; by ICG Muse, Inc. for Japan; by Norma Comunicaciones S.A. for Colombia; by Intersoft for South Africa; by Eyrolles for France; by International Thomson Publishing for Germany, Austria and Switzerland; by Distribuidora Cuspide for Argentina; by Livraria Cultura for Brazil; by Ediciones ZETA S.C.R. Ltda. for Peru; by WS Computer Publishing Corporation, Inc., for the Philippines; by Contemporanea de Ediciones for Venezuela; by Express Computer Distributors for the Caribbean and West Indies; by Micronesia Media Distributor, Inc. for Micronesia; by Grupo Editorial Norma S.A. for Guatemala; by Chips Computadoras S.A. de C.V. for Mexico; by Editorial Norma de Panama S.A. for Panama; by American Bookshops for Finland. Authorized Sales Agent: Anthony Rudkin Associates for the Middle East and North Africa.

For general information on IDG Books Worldwide's books in the U.S., please call our Consumer Customer Service department at **800-762-2974**. For reseller information, including discounts and premium sales, please call our Reseller Customer Service department at **800-434-3422**.

For information on where to purchase IDG Books Worldwide's books outside the U.S., please contact our International Sales department at 317-596-5530 or fax 317-572-4002.

For consumer information on foreign language translations, please contact our Customer Service department at **1-800-434-3422**, fax 317-572-4002, or e-mail rights@idgbooks.com.

For information on licensing foreign or domestic rights, please phone +1-650-653-7098.

For sales inquiries and special prices for bulk quantities, please contact our Order Services department at 800-434-3422 or write to the address above.

For information on using IDG Books Worldwide's books in the classroom or for ordering examination copies, please contact our Educational Sales department at **800-434-2086** or fax **317-596-5499**.

For press review copies, author interviews, or other publicity information, please contact our Public Relations department at **650-655-3000** or fax **650-655-3299**.

For authorization to photocopy items for corporate, personal, or educational use, please contact Copyright Clearance Center, 222 Rosewood Drive, Danvers, MA 01923, or fax **978-750-4470**.

 is a registered trademark or trademark under exclusive license to IDG Books Worldwide, Inc. from International Data Group, Inc. in the United States and/or other countries.

CLIFFSCOMPLETE

Shakespeare's

The Merchant of Venice

CONTENTS AT A GLANCE

CLIFFSCOMPLETE

Shakespeare's

The Merchant of Venice

TABLE OF CONTENTS

Shakespeare's

THE MERCHANT OF VENICE

INTRODUCTION TO WILLIAM SHAKESPEARE

William Shakespeare, or the "Bard" as people fondly call him, permeates almost all aspects of our society. He can be found in our classrooms, on our televisions, in our theatres, and in our cinemas. Speaking to us through his plays, Shakespeare comments on his life and culture, as well as our own. Actors still regularly perform his plays on the modern stage and screen. The 1990s, for example, saw the release of cinematic versions of *Romeo and Juliet, Hamlet, Othello, A Midsummer Night's Dream,* and many more of his works.

In addition to the popularity of Shakespeare's plays as he wrote them, other writers have modernized his works to attract new audiences. For example, *West Side Story* places *Romeo and Juliet* in New York City, and *A Thousand Acres* sets *King Lear* in Iowa corn country. Beyond adaptations and productions, his life and works have captured our cultural imagination. The twentieth century witnessed the production of a play about two minor characters from Shakespeare's *Hamlet* in *Rosencrantz and Guildenstern Are Dead* and a fictional movie about Shakespeare's early life and poetic inspiration in *Shakespeare in Love.*

Despite his monumental presence in our culture, Shakespeare remains enigmatic. He does not tell us which plays he wrote alone, on which plays he collaborated with other playwrights, or which versions of his plays to read and perform. Furthermore, with only a handful of documents available about his life, he does not tell us much about Shakespeare the person, forcing critics and scholars to look to historical references to uncover the true-life great dramatist.

Anti-Stratfordians — modern scholars who question the authorship of Shakespeare's plays — have used this lack of information to argue that William Shakespeare either never existed or, if he did exist, did not write any of the plays we attribute to him. They believe that another historical figure, such as Francis Bacon or Queen Elizabeth I, used the name as a cover. Whether or not a man named William Shakespeare ever actually existed is ultimately secondary to the recognition that the group of plays bound together by that name does exist and continues to educate, enlighten, and entertain us.

An engraved portrait of Shakespeare by an unknown artist, ca. 1607.
Culver Pictures, Inc./SuperStock

Family life

Though scholars are unsure of the exact date of Shakespeare's birth, records indicate that his parents — Mary and John Shakespeare — baptized him on April 26, 1564, in the small provincial town of Stratford-upon-Avon — so named because it sat on the banks of the Avon River. Because common practice was to baptize infants a few days after they were born, scholars generally recognize April 23, 1564, as Shakespeare's birthday. Coincidentally, April 23 is the day of St. George, the patron saint of England, as well as the day upon which Shakespeare would die 52 years later. William was the third of Mary and John's eight children and the first of four sons. The house in which scholars believe Shakespeare to have been born stands on Henley Street and, despite many modifications over the years, you can still visit it today.

Shakespeare's father

Prior to Shakespeare's birth, John Shakespeare lived in Snitterfield, where he married Mary Arden, the daughter of his landlord. After moving to Stratford in 1552, he worked as a glover, a moneylender, and a dealer in agricultural products such as wool and grain. He also pursued public office and achieved a variety of posts including bailiff, Stratford's highest elected position — equivalent to a small town's mayor. At the height of his career, sometime near 1576, he petitioned the Herald's Office for a coat of arms and, thus, the right to be a gentleman. But the rise from the middle class to the gentry did not come right away, and the costly petition expired without being granted.

About this time, John Shakespeare mysteriously fell into financial difficulty. He became involved in serious litigation, was assessed heavy fines, and even lost his seat on the town council. Some scholars suggest that this decline could have resulted from religious discrimination because the Shakespeare family may have supported Catholicism, the practice of which was illegal in England. However, other scholars point out that not all religious dissenters (both Catholics and radical Puritans) lost their posts due to their religion. Whatever the cause of his decline, John did regain some prosperity toward the end of his life. In 1596, the Herald's Office granted the Shakespeare family a coat of arms at the petition of William, by now a successful playwright in London. And John, prior to his death in 1601, regained his seat on Stratford's town council.

Childhood and education

Our understanding of William Shakespeare's childhood in Stratford is primarily speculative because children do not often appear in the legal records from which many scholars attempt to reconstruct Shakespeare's life. Based on his father's local prominence, scholars speculate that Shakespeare most likely attended King's New School, a school that usually employed Oxford graduates and was generally well respected. Shakespeare would have started *petty school* — the rough equivalent to modern pre-school — at the age of four or five. He would have learned to read on a *hornbook,* which was a sheet of parchment or paper on which the alphabet and the Lord's Prayer were written. This sheet was framed in wood and covered with a transparent piece of horn

Shakespeare's birthplace.
SuperStock

for durability. After two years in petty school, he would have transferred to grammar school, where his school day would have probably lasted from 6 or 7 o'clock in the morning (depending on the time of year) until 5 o'clock in the evening, with only a handful of holidays.

While in grammar school, Shakespeare would primarily have studied Latin, reciting and reading the works of classical Roman authors such as Plautus, Ovid, Seneca, and Horace. Traces of these authors' works can be seen in his dramatic texts. Toward his last years in grammar school, Shakespeare would have acquired some basic skills in Greek as well. Thus the remark made by Ben Jonson, Shakespeare's well-educated friend and contemporary playwright, that Shakespeare knew "small Latin and less Greek" is accurate. Jonson is not saying that when Shakespeare left grammar school he was only semi-literate; he merely indicates that Shakespeare did not attend University, where he would have gained more Latin and Greek instruction.

Wife and children

When Shakespeare became an adult, the historical records documenting his existence began to increase. In November 1582, at the age of 18, he married 26-year-old Anne Hathaway from the nearby village of Shottery. The disparity in their ages, coupled with the fact that they baptized their first daughter, Susanna, only six months later in May 1583, has caused a great deal of modern speculation about the nature of their relationship. However, sixteenth-century conceptions of marriage differed slightly from our modern notions. Though all marriages needed to be performed before a member of the clergy, many of Shakespeare's contemporaries believed that a couple could establish a relationship through a premarital contract by exchanging vows in front of witnesses. This contract removed the social stigma of pregnancy before marriage. (Shakespeare's plays contain instances of marriage prompted by pregnancy, and

Measure for Measure includes this kind of premarital contract.) Two years later, in February 1585, Shakespeare baptized his twins Hamnet and Judith. Hamnet died at the age of 11, when Shakespeare was primarily living away from his family in London.

For seven years after the twins' baptism, the records remain silent on Shakespeare. At some point, he traveled to London and became involved with the theatre, but he could have been anywhere between 21 and 28 years old when he did. Though some have suggested that he may have served as an assistant to a schoolmaster at a provincial school, it seems likely that he went to London to become an actor, gradually becoming a playwright and gaining attention.

The plays: On stage and in print

The next mention of Shakespeare comes in 1592 by a University wit named Robert Greene when Shakespeare apparently was already a rising actor and playwright for the London stage. Greene, no longer a successful playwright, tried to warn other University wits about Shakespeare. He wrote:

> For there is an upstart crow, beautified with our feathers, that with his "Tiger's heart wrapped in a player's hide" supposes he is as well able to bombast out a blank verse as the best of you, and, being an absolute Johannes Factotum, is in his own conceit the only Shake-scene in a country.

This statement comes at a point in time when men without a university education, like Shakespeare, were starting to compete as dramatists with the University wits. As many critics have pointed out, Greene's statement recalls a line from *Henry VI, Part 3*, which reads, "O tiger's heart wrapped in a woman's hide!" (I.4.137). Greene's remark does not indicate that Shakespeare was generally disliked. On the contrary, another University wit, Thomas Nashe, wrote of the great theatrical success of *Henry VI,* and Henry Chettle, Greene's publisher, later printed a flattering apology to Shakespeare. What Greene's statement does show us is that Shakespeare's reputation for poetry had reached enough of a prominence to provoke the envy of a failing competitor.

In the following year, 1593, the government closed London's theatres due to an outbreak of the bubonic plague. Publication history suggests that during this closure, Shakespeare may have written his two narrative poems, *Venus and Adonis,* published in 1593, and *The Rape of Lucrece,* published in 1594. These are the only two works that Shakespeare seems to have helped into print; each carries a dedication by Shakespeare to Henry Wriothesley, Earl of Southampton.

A ground plan of London after the fire of 1666, drawn by Marcus Willemsz Doornik.
Guildhall Library, London/AKG, Berlin/SuperStock

Stage success

When the theatres reopened in 1594, Shakespeare joined the Lord Chamberlain's Men, an acting company. Though uncertain about the history of his early dramatic works, scholars believe that by this point he had written *The Two Gentlemen of Verona, The Taming of the Shrew,* the *Henry VI* trilogy, and *Titus Andronicus.* During his early years in the theatre, Shakespeare primarily wrote history plays, with his romantic comedies emerging in the 1590s. Even at this early stage in his career, Shakespeare was a success. In 1597, he was able to purchase New Place, one of the two largest houses in Stratford, and secure a coat of arms for his family.

In 1597, the lease expired on the Lord Chamberlain's playhouse, called The Theatre. Because the owner of The Theatre refused to renew the lease, the acting company was forced to perform at various playhouses until the 1599 opening of the now famous Globe Theatre, which was literally built with lumber from The Theatre. (The Globe, later destroyed by fire, has recently been reconstructed in London and can be visited today.)

Recent scholars suggest that Shakespeare's great tragedy, *Julius Caesar,* may have been the first of Shakespeare's plays performed in the original playhouse. When this open-air theatre on the Thames River opened, financial papers list Shakespeare's name as one of the principal investors. Already an actor and a playwright, Shakespeare was now becoming a "Company Man." This new status allowed him to share in the profits of the theatre rather than merely getting paid for his plays, some of which publishers were beginning to release in quarto format.

Publications

A *quarto* was a small, inexpensive book typically used for leisure books such as plays; the term itself indicates that the printer folded the paper four times. The modern day equivalent of a quarto would be a paperback. In contrast, the first collected works of Shakespeare were in *folio* format, which means that the printer folded each sheet only once. Scholars call the collected edition of Shakespeare's works the *First Folio*. A folio was a larger and more prestigious book than a quarto, and printers generally reserved the format for works such as the Bible.

No evidence exists that Shakespeare participated in the publication of any of his plays. Members of Shakespeare's acting company printed the First Folio seven years after Shakespeare's death. Generally, playwrights wrote their works to be performed on stage, and publishing them was a novel innovation at the time. Shakespeare probably would not have thought of them as books in the way we do. In fact, as a principal investor in the acting company (which purchased the play as well as the exclusive right to perform it), he may not have even thought of them as his own. He would probably have thought of his plays as belonging to the company.

For this reason, scholars have generally characterized most quartos printed before the Folio as "bad" by arguing that printers pirated the plays and published them illegally. How would a printer have received a pirated copy of a play? The theories range from someone stealing a copy to an actor (or actors) selling the play by relating it from memory to a printer. Many times, major differences exist between a quarto version of the play and a folio version, causing uncertainty about which is Shakespeare's true creation. *Hamlet*, for example, is almost twice as long in the Folio as in quarto versions. Recently, scholars have come to realize the value of the different versions. The *Norton Shakespeare,* for example, includes all three versions of *King Lear* — the quarto, the folio, and the *conflated* version (the combination of the quarto and folio).

Prolific productions

The first decade of the 1600s witnessed the publication of additional quartos as well as the production of most of Shakespeare's great tragedies, with *Julius Caesar* appearing in 1599 and *Hamlet* in 1600–1601. After the death of Queen Elizabeth in 1603, the Lord Chamberlain's Men became the King's Men under James I, Elizabeth's successor. Around the time of this transition in the English monarchy, the famous tragedy *Othello* (1603–1604) was most likely written and performed, followed closely by *King Lear* (1605–1606), *Antony and Cleopatra* (1606), and *Macbeth* (1606) in the next two years.

Shakespeare's name also appears as a major investor in the 1609 acquisition of an indoor theatre known as the Blackfriars. This last period of Shakespeare's career, which includes plays that considered the acting conditions both at the Blackfriars and the open-air Globe Theatre, consists primarily of romances or tragicomedies such as *The Winter's Tale* and *The Tempest.* On June 29, 1613, during a performance of *All is True,* or *Henry VIII,* the thatching on top of the Globe Theatre caught fire and the playhouse burned to the ground. After this incident, the King's Men moved solely into the indoor Blackfriars Theatre.

Final days

During the last years of his career, Shakespeare collaborated on a couple of plays with contemporary dramatist John Fletcher, even possibly coming out of retirement — which scholars believe began sometime in 1613 — to work on *The Two Noble Kinsmen* (1613–1614). Three years later, Shakespeare died on April 23, 1616. Though the exact cause of death remains unknown, a vicar from Stratford in the mid-seventeenth-century wrote in his diary that Shakespeare, perhaps celebrating the marriage of his daughter, Judith, contracted a fever during a night of revelry with fellow literary figures Ben Jonson and Michael Drayton. Regardless, Shakespeare may have felt his death was imminent in March of that year, because he altered his will. Interestingly, his will mentions no book or theatrical manuscripts, perhaps indicating the lack of value that he put on printed versions of his dramatic works and their status as company property.

Seven years after Shakespeare's death, John Heminge and Henry Condell, fellow members of the King's Men, published his collected works. In their preface, they claim that they are publishing the true versions of Shakespeare's plays partially as a response to the previous quarto printings of 18 of his plays, most of these with multiple printings. This Folio contains 36 plays to which scholars generally add *Pericles* and *The Two Noble Kinsmen*. This volume of Shakespeare's plays began the process of constructing Shakespeare not only as England's national poet but also as a monumental figure whose plays would continue to captivate imaginations at the end of the millennium with no signs of stopping. Ben Jonson's prophetic line about Shakespeare in the First Folio — "He was not of an age, but for all time!" — certainly holds true.

Chronology of Shakespeare's plays

1590–1591	*The Two Gentlemen of Verona*
	The Taming of the Shrew
1591	*Henry VI, Part 2*
	Henry VI, Part 3
1592	*Henry VI, Part 1*
	Titus Andronicus
1592–1593	*Richard III*
	Venus and Adonis
1593–1594	*The Rape of Lucrece*
1594	*The Comedy of Errors*
1594–1595	*Love's Labour's Lost*
1595	*Richard II*
	Romeo and Juliet
	A Midsummer Night's Dream
1595–1596	*Love's Labour's Won*
	(This manuscript was lost.)
1596	*King John*

1596–1597	*The Merchant of Venice*
	Henry IV, Part 1
1597–1598	*The Merry Wives of Windsor*
	Henry IV, Part 2
1598	*Much Ado About Nothing*
1598–1599	*Henry V*
1599	*Julius Caesar*
1599–1600	*As You Like It*
1600–1601	*Hamlet*
1601	*Twelfth Night,* or *What You Will*
1602	*Troilus and Cressida*
1593–1603	*Sonnets*
1603	*Measure for Measure*
1603–1604	*A Lover's Complaint*
	Othello
1604–1605	*All's Well That Ends Well*
1605	*Timon of Athens*
1605–1606	*King Lear*
1606	*Macbeth*
	Antony and Cleopatra
1607	*Pericles*
1608	*Coriolanus*
1609	*The Winter's Tale*
1610	*Cymbeline*
1611	*The Tempest*
1612–1613	*Cardenio* (with John Fletcher; this manuscript was lost.)
1613	*All Is True,* or *Henry VIII*
1613–1614	*The Two Noble Kinsmen* (with John Fletcher)

This chronology is derived from Stanley Wells' and Gary Taylor's *William Shakespeare: A Textual Companion,* which is listed in the "Works consulted" section later in this introduction.

A note on Shakespeare's language

Readers encountering Shakespeare for the first time usually find Early Modern English difficult to understand. Yet, rather than serving as a barrier to Shakespeare, the richness of this language should form part of our appreciation of the Bard.

One of the first things readers usually notice about the language is the use of pronouns. Like the King James Version of the Bible, Shakespeare's pronouns are slightly different from our own and can cause confusion. Words like "thou" (you), "thee" and "ye" (objective cases of you), and "thy" and "thine" (your/yours) appear throughout Shakespeare's plays. You may need a little time to get used to these changes. You can find the definitions for other words that commonly cause confusion in the glossary column on the right side of each page in this edition.

Iambic pentameter

Though Shakespeare sometimes wrote in prose, he wrote most of his plays in poetry, specifically blank verse. Blank verse consists of lines in unrhymed *iambic pentameter*. *Iambic* refers to the stress patterns of the line. An *iamb* is an element of sound that consists of two beats — the first unstressed (da) and the second stressed (DA). A good example of an iambic line is Hamlet's famous line "To be or not to be," in which you do not stress "To," "or," and "to," but you do stress "be," "not," and "be." *Pentameter* refers to the *meter* or number of stressed syllables in a line. *Penta*meter has five stressed syllables. Thus, Juliet's line "But soft, what light through yonder window breaks?" (II.2.2) is a good example of an iambic pentameter line.

Wordplay

Shakespeare's language is also verbally rich because he, along with many dramatists of his period, had a fondness for wordplay. This wordplay often takes the forms of double meanings, called *puns,* in which a word can mean more than one thing in a given context. Shakespeare often employs these puns as a way of illustrating the distance between what is on the surface — *apparent* meanings — and what meanings lie underneath. Though recognizing these puns may be difficult at first, the glossaries in the far right column of this edition point many of them out to you.

If you are encountering Shakespeare's plays for the first time, the following reading tips may help ease you into the plays. Shakespeare's lines were meant to be spoken; therefore, reading them aloud or speaking them should help with comprehension. Also, though most of the lines are poetic, do not forget to read complete sentences — move from period to period as well as from line to line. Although Shakespeare's language can be difficult at first, the rewards of immersing yourself in the richness and fluidity of the lines are immeasurable.

Works consulted

For more information on Shakespeare's life and works, see the following:

Bevington, David, ed. *The Complete Works of Shakespeare.* New York: Longman, 1997.

Evans, G. Blakemore, ed. *The Riverside Shakespeare.* Boston: Houghton Mifflin Co., 1997.

Greenblatt, Stephan, ed. *The Norton Shakespeare.* New York: W.W. Norton and Co., 1997.

Kastan, David Scott, ed. *A Companion to Shakespeare.* Oxford: Blackwell, 1999.

McDonald, Russ. *The Bedford Companion to Shakespeare: An Introduction with Documents.* Boston: Bedford-St. Martin's Press, 1996.

Wells, Stanley and Gary Taylor. *William Shakespeare: A Textual Companion.* New York: W.W. Norton and Co., 1997.

INTRODUCTION TO EARLY MODERN ENGLAND

William Shakespeare (1564 –1616) lived during a period in England's history that people have generally referred to as the English Renaissance. The term *renaissance,* meaning rebirth, was applied to this period of English history as a way of celebrating what was perceived as the rapid development of art, literature, science, and politics — in many ways, the rebirth of classical Rome.

Recently, scholars have challenged the name "English Renaissance" on two grounds. First, some scholars argue that the term should not be used, because women did not share in the advancements of English culture during this time period; their legal status was still below that of men. Second, other scholars have challenged the basic notion that this period saw a sudden explosion of culture. A rebirth of civilization suggests that the previous period of time was not civilized. This second group of scholars sees a much more gradual transition between the Middle Ages and Shakespeare's time.

Some people use the terms *Elizabethan* and *Jacobean* when referring to periods of the sixteenth and seventeenth centuries. These terms correspond to the reigns of Elizabeth I (1558–1603) and James I (1603–1625). The problem with these terms is that they do not cover large spans of time; for example, Shakespeare's life and career spans both monarchies.

Scholars are now beginning to replace *Renaissance* with the term *Early Modern* when referring to this time period, but people still use both terms interchangeably. The term *Early Modern* recognizes that this period established many of the foundations of our modern culture. Though critics still disagree about the exact dates of the period, in general, the dates range from 1450 to 1750. Thus, Shakespeare's life clearly falls within the Early Modern period.

Shakespeare's plays live on in our culture, but we must remember that Shakespeare's culture differed greatly from our own. Although his understanding of human nature and relationships seems to apply to our modern lives, we must try to understand the world he lived in so we can better understand his plays. This introduction helps you do just that. It examines the intellectual, religious, political, and social contexts of Shakespeare's work before turning to the importance of the theatre and the printing press.

Intellectual context

In general, people in Early Modern England looked at the universe, the human body, and science very differently from the way we do today. But while we do not share their same beliefs, we must not think of people during Shakespeare's time as lacking in intelligence or education. Discoveries made during the Early Modern period concerning the universe and the human body provide the basis of modern science.

Cosmology

One subject we view very differently from Early Modern thinkers is cosmology. Shakespeare's contemporaries believed in the astronomy of Ptolemy, an intellectual from Alexandria in the second century A.D. Ptolemy thought that the Earth stood at the center of the universe, surrounded by nine concentric rings. The celestial bodies circled the earth in the following order: the moon, Mercury, Venus, the Sun, Mars, Jupiter, Saturn, and the stars. The entire system was controlled by the *primum mobile,* or Prime Mover, which initiated and maintained the movement of the celestial bodies. No one had yet discovered the last three planets in our solar system, Uranus, Neptune, and Pluto.

In 1543, Nicolaus Copernicus published his theory of a sun-based solar system, in which the sun stood at the center and the planets revolved around it. Though this theory appeared prior to Shakespeare's birth, people didn't really start to change their minds until 1610, when Galileo used his telescope to confirm Copernicus' theory. David Bevington asserts in the general introduction to his edition of Shakespeare's works that, during most of Shakespeare's writing career, the cosmology of the universe was in question, and this sense of uncertainty influences some of his plays.

Universal hierarchy

Closely related to Ptolemy's hierarchical view of the universe is a hierarchical conception of the Earth (sometimes referred to as the Chain of Being). During the Early Modern period, many people believed that all of creation was organized hierarchically. God existed at the top, followed by the angels, men, women, animals, plants, and rocks. (Because all women were thought to exist below all men on the chain, we can easily imagine the confusion that Elizabeth I caused when she became queen of England. She was literally "out of order," an expression that still exists in our society.) Though the concept of this hierarchy is a useful one when beginning to study Shakespeare, keep in mind that distinctions in this hierarchical view were not always clear and that we should not reduce all Early Modern thinking to a simple chain.

Elements and humors

The belief in a hierarchical scheme of existence created a comforting sense of order and balance that carried over into science as well. Shakespeare's contemporaries generally accepted that four different elements composed everything in the universe: earth, air, water, and fire. People associated these four elements with four qualities of being. These qualities — hot, cold, moist, and dry — appeared in different combinations in the elements. For example, air was hot and moist; water was cold and moist; earth was cold and dry; and fire was hot and dry.

In addition, people believed that the human body contained all four elements in the form of *humors* — blood, phlegm, yellow bile, and black bile — each of which corresponded to an element. Blood corresponded to air (hot and moist), phlegm to water (cold and moist), yellow bile to fire (hot and dry), and black bile to earth (cold and dry). When someone was sick, physicians generally believed that the patient's humors were not in the proper balance. For example, if someone were diagnosed with an abundance of blood, the physician would bleed the patient (using leeches or cutting the skin) in order to restore the balance.

Shakespeare's contemporaries also believed that the humors determined personality and temperament. If a person's dominant humor was blood, he was considered light-hearted. If dominated by yellow bile (or choler), that person was irritable. The dominance of phlegm led a person to be dull and kind. And if black bile prevailed, he was melancholy or sad. Thus, people of Early Modern England often used the humors to explain behavior and emotional outbursts. Throughout Shakespeare's plays, he uses the concept of the humors to define and explain various characters.

For example, in *The Merchant of Venice*, Antonio's melancholic attitude in the opening scene suggests that he has an excess of black bile. In the same scene, Gratiano, the most cheerful character, complains about "peevish" people; he says that they are ignoring the warmth of their blood, and instead creeping "into the jaundice" – that is, allowing their yellow bile to take over their emotions (I.1.83–86).

Religious context

Shakespeare lived in an England full of religious uncertainty and dispute. From the Protestant Reformation to the translation of the Bible into English, the Early Modern era is punctuated with events that have greatly influenced modern religious beliefs.

The Reformation

Until the Protestant Reformation, the only Christian church was the Catholic, or "universal," church. Beginning in Europe in the early sixteenth century, religious thinkers such as Martin Luther and John Calvin, who claimed that the Roman Catholic Church had become corrupt and was no longer following the word of God, began what has become known as the Protestant Reformation. The Protestants ("protestors") believed in salvation by faith rather than works. They also believed in the primacy of the Bible and advocated giving all people access to reading the Bible.

Many English people initially resisted Protestant ideas. However, the Reformation in England began in 1527 during the reign of Henry VIII, prior to Shakespeare's birth. In that year, Henry VIII decided to divorce his wife, Catherine of Aragon, for her failure to produce a male heir. (Only one of their children, Mary, survived past infancy.) Rome denied Henry's petitions for a divorce, forcing him to divorce Catherine without the Church's approval, which he did in 1533.

The Act of Supremacy

The following year, the Pope excommunicated Henry VIII while Parliament confirmed his divorce and the legitimacy of his new marriage through the

A portrait of King Henry VIII, artist unknown, ca. 1542.
National Portrait Gallery, London/SuperStock

Act of Succession. Later in 1534, Parliament passed the *Act of Supremacy,* naming Henry the "Supreme Head of the Church in England." Henry continued to persecute both radical Protestant reformers and Catholics who remained loyal to Rome.

Henry VIII's death in 1547 brought Edward VI, his 10-year-old son by Jane Seymour (the king's third wife), to the throne. This succession gave Protestant reformers the chance to solidify their break with the Catholic Church. During Edward's reign, Archbishop Thomas Cranmer established the foundation for the Anglican Church through his 42 articles of religion. He also wrote the first *Book of Common Prayer,* adopted in 1549, which was the official text for worship services in England.

Bloody Mary

Catholics continued to be persecuted until 1553, when the sickly Edward VI died and was succeeded by Mary, his half-sister and the Catholic daughter of Catherine of Aragon. The reign of Mary witnessed the reversal of religion in England through the restoration of Catholic authority and obedience to Rome. Protestants were executed in large numbers, which earned the monarch the nickname *Bloody Mary.* Many Protestants fled to Europe to escape persecution.

Elizabeth, the daughter of Henry VIII and Anne Boleyn, outwardly complied with the mandated Catholicism during her half-sister Mary's reign, but she restored Protestantism when she took the throne in 1558 after Mary's death. Thus, in the space of single decade, England's throne passed from Protestant to Catholic to Protestant, with each change carrying serious and deadly consequences.

Though Elizabeth reigned in relative peace from 1558 to her death in 1603, religion was still a serious concern for her subjects. During Shakespeare's life, a great deal of religious dissent existed in England. Many Catholics, who remained loyal to Rome and their church, were persecuted for their beliefs. At the other end of the spectrum, the Puritans were persecuted for their belief that the Reformation was not complete. (The English pejoratively applied the term *Puritan* to religious groups that wanted to continue purifying the English church by such measures as removing the *episcopacy,* or the structure of bishops.)

The Great Bible

One thing agreed upon by both the Anglicans and Puritans was the importance of a Bible written in English. Translated by William Tyndale in 1525, the first authorized Bible in English, published in 1539, was known as the Great Bible. This Bible was later revised during Elizabeth's reign into what was known as the Bishop's Bible. As Stephen Greenblatt points out in his introduction to the *Norton Shakespeare,* Shakespeare would probably have been familiar with both the Bishop's Bible, heard aloud in Mass, and

A portrait of Elizabeth I by George Gower, ca. 1588.
National Portrait Gallery, London/SuperStock

the Geneva Bible, which was written by English exiles in Geneva. The last authorized Bible produced during Shakespeare's lifetime came within the last decade of his life when James I's commissioned edition, known as the King James Bible, appeared in 1611.

Political context

Politics and religion were closely related in Shakespeare's England. Both of the monarchs under whom Shakespeare lived had to deal with religious and political dissenters.

Elizabeth I

Despite being a Protestant, Elizabeth I tried to take a middle road on the religious question. She allowed Catholics to practice their religion in private as long as they outwardly appeared Anglican and remained loyal to the throne.

Elizabeth's monarchy was one of absolute supremacy. Believing in the divine right of kings, she styled herself as being appointed by God to rule England. To oppose the Queen's will was the equivalent of opposing God's will. Known as *passive obedience,* this doctrine did not allow any opposition even to a tyrannical monarch because God had appointed the king or queen for reasons unknown to His subjects on earth. However, as Bevington notes, Elizabeth's power was not as absolute as her rhetoric suggested. Parliament, already well established in England, reserved some power, such as the authority to levy taxes, for itself.

Elizabeth I lived in a society that restricted women from possessing any political or personal autonomy and power. As queen, Elizabeth violated and called into question many of the prejudices and practices against women. In a way, her society forced her to "overcome" her sex in order to rule effectively. However, her position did nothing to increase the status of women in England.

One of the rhetorical strategies that Elizabeth adopted in order to rule effectively was to separate her position as monarch of England from her natural body — to separate her *body politic* from her *body natural*. In addition, throughout her reign, Elizabeth brilliantly negotiated between domestic and foreign factions — some of whom were anxious about a female monarch and wanted her to marry — appeasing both sides without ever committing to one.

She remained unmarried throughout her 45-year reign, partially by styling herself as the Virgin Queen whose purity represented England itself. Her refusal to marry and her habit of hinting and promising marriage with suitors both foreign and domestic helped Elizabeth maintain internal and external peace. Not marrying allowed her to retain her independence, but it left the succession of the English throne in question. In 1603, on her deathbed, she named James VI, King of Scotland and son of her cousin Mary, as her successor.

James I

When he assumed the English crown, James VI of Scotland became James I of England. (Some historians refer to him as James VI and I.) Like Elizabeth, James was a strong believer in the divine right of kings and their absolute authority.

Upon his arrival in London to claim the English throne, James made his plans to unite Scotland and England clear. However, a long-standing history of enmity existed between the two countries. Partially as a result of this history and the influx of Scottish courtiers into English society, anti-Scottish prejudice abounded in England. When James asked Parliament for the title of "King of Great Britain," he was denied.

As scholars such as Bevington have pointed out, James was less successful than Elizabeth was in negotiating between the different religious and political factions in England. Although he was a Protestant,

he began to have problems with the Puritan sect of the House of Commons, which ultimately led to a rift between the court (which also started to have Catholic sympathies) and the Parliament. This rift between the monarchy and Parliament eventually escalated into the Civil War that would erupt during the reign of James' son, Charles I.

In spite of its difficulties with Parliament, James' court was a site of wealth, luxury, and extravagance. James I commissioned elaborate feasts, masques, and pageants, and in doing so he more than doubled the royal debt. Stephen Greenblatt suggests that Shakespeare's *The Tempest* may reflect this extravagance through Prospero's magnificent banquet and accompanying masque. Reigning from 1603 to 1625, James I remained the King of England throughout the last years of Shakespeare's life.

Social context

Shakespeare's England divided itself roughly into two social classes: the aristocrats (or nobility) and everyone else. The primary distinctions between these two classes were ancestry, wealth, and power. Simply put, the aristocrats were the only ones who possessed all three.

Aristocrats were born with their wealth, but the growth of trade and the development of skilled professions began to provide wealth for those not born with it. Although the notion of a middle class did not begin to develop until after Shakespeare's death, the possibility of some social mobility did exist in Early Modern England. Shakespeare himself used the wealth gained from the theatre to move into the lower ranks of the aristocracy by securing a coat of arms for his family.

Shakespeare was not unique in this movement, but not all people received the opportunity to increase their social status. Members of the aristocracy feared this social movement and, as a result, promoted harsh laws of apprenticeship and fashion, restricting certain styles of dress and material. These laws dictated that only the aristocracy could wear certain articles of clothing, colors, and materials. Though enforcement was a difficult task, the Early Modern aristocracy considered dressing above one's station a moral and ethical violation.

The status of women

The legal status of women did not allow them much public or private autonomy. English society functioned on a system of patriarchy and hierarchy (see the "Univeral hierarchy" section earlier in this introduction), which means that men controlled society beginning with the individual family. In fact, the family metaphorically corresponded to the state. For example, the husband was the king of his family. His authority to control his family was absolute and based on divine right, similar to that of the country's king. People also saw the family itself differently than today, considering apprentices and servants part of the whole family.

The practice of *primogeniture* — a system of inheritance that passed all of a family's wealth through the first male child — accompanied this system of patriarchy. Thus, women did not generally inherit their family's wealth and titles. In the absence of a male heir, some women, such as Queen Elizabeth, did. But after women married, they lost almost all of their already limited legal rights, such as the right to inherit, to own property, and to sign contracts. In all likelihood, Elizabeth I would have lost much of her power and authority if she had married.

Furthermore, women did not generally receive an education and could not enter certain professions, including acting. Instead, society relegated women to the domestic sphere of the home.

In *The Merchant of Venice*, Portia is the heir to a vast fortune, and the head of her household. She therefore has an unusual amount of power for a woman. But when she marries Bassanio, she must hand over all her money and power to him (see III.2.149–74). Even so, Portia's obvious intellectual superiority over Bassanio raises questions about whether he ought to be her commander.

Daily life

Daily life in Early Modern England began before sunup — exactly how early depended on one's station in life. A servant's responsibilities usually included preparing the house for the day. Families usually possessed limited living space, and even among wealthy families multiple family members tended to share a small number of rooms, suggesting that privacy may not have been important or practical.

Working through the morning, Elizabethans usually had lunch about noon. This midday meal was the primary meal of the day, much like dinner is for modern families. The workday usually ended around sundown or 5:00 p.m., depending on the season. Before an early bedtime, Elizabethans usually ate a light repast and then settled in for a couple of hours of reading (if the family members were literate and could bear the high cost of books) or socializing.

Mortality rates

Mortality rates in Early Modern England were high compared to our standards, especially among infants. Infection and disease ran rampant because physicians did not realize the need for antiseptics and sterile equipment. As a result, communicable diseases often spread very rapidly in cities, particularly London.

In addition, the bubonic plague frequently ravaged England, with two major outbreaks — from 1592–1594 and in 1603 — occurring during Shakespeare's lifetime. People did not understand the plague and generally perceived it as God's punishment. (We now know that the plague was spread by fleas and could not be spread directly from human to human.) Without a cure or an understanding of what transmitted the disease, physicians could do nothing to stop the thousands of deaths that resulted from each outbreak. These outbreaks had a direct effect on Shakespeare's career, because the government often closed the theatres in an effort to impede the spread of the disease.

London life

In the sixteenth century, London, though small compared to modern cities, was the largest city of Europe, with a population of about 200,000 inhabitants in the city and surrounding suburbs. London was a crowded city without a sewer system, which facilitated epidemics such as the plague. In addition, crime rates were high in the city due to inefficient law enforcement and the lack of street lighting.

Despite these drawbacks, London was the cultural, political, and social heart of England. As the home of the monarch and most of England's trade, London was a bustling metropolis. Not surprisingly, a young Shakespeare moved to London to begin his professional career.

The theatre

Most theatres were not actually located within the city of London. Rather, theatre owners built them on the South bank of the Thames River (in Southwark) across from the city in order to avoid the strict regulations that applied within the city's walls. These restrictions stemmed from a mistrust of public performances as locations of plague and riotous behavior. Furthermore, because theatre performances took place during the day, they took laborers away from their jobs. Opposition to the theatres also came from Puritans who believed that they fostered immorality. Therefore, theatres moved out of the city, to areas near other sites of restricted activities, such as dog fighting, bear- and bull-baiting, and prostitution.

The recently reconstructed Globe Theatre.
Chris Parker/PAL

Despite the move, the theatre was not free from censorship or regulation. In fact, a branch of the government known as the Office of the Revels attempted to ensure that plays did not present politically- or socially-sensitive material. Prior to each performance, the Master of the Revels would read a complete text of each play, cutting out offending sections or, in some cases, not approving the play for public performance.

Performance spaces

Theatres in Early Modern England were quite different from our modern facilities. They were usually open-air, relying heavily on natural light and good weather. The rectangular stage extended out into an area that people called the *pit* — a circular, uncovered area about 70 feet in diameter. Audience members had two choices when purchasing admission to a theatre. Admission to the pit, where the lower classes (or *groundlings*) stood for the performances, was the cheaper option. People of wealth could purchase a seat in one of the three covered tiers of seats that ringed the pit. At full capacity, a public theatre in Early Modern England could hold between 2,000 and 3,000 people.

The stage, which projected into the pit and was raised about five feet above it, had a covered portion called the *heavens*. The heavens enclosed theatrical equipment for lowering and raising actors to and from the stage. A trapdoor in the middle of the stage provided theatrical graves for characters such as Ophelia and also allowed ghosts, such as Banquo in *Macbeth,* to rise from the earth. A wall separated the back of the stage from the actors' dressing room, known as the *tiring house.* At each end of the wall stood a door for major entrances and exits. Above the wall and doors stood a gallery directly above the stage, reserved for the wealthiest spectators. Actors occasionally used this area when a performance called for a difference in height — for example, to represent Juliet's balcony or the walls of a besieged city. A good example of this type of theatre was the original Globe Theatre in London in which Shakespeare's company, The Lord Chamberlain's Men (later the King's Men), staged its plays. However, indoor theatres, such as the Blackfriars, differed slightly because the pit was filled with chairs that faced a rectangular stage. Because only the wealthy could afford the cost of admission, the public generally considered these theatres private.

The Merchant of Venice does not use the "heavens" or the trapdoor. However, in Act II, Scene 6, Shakespeare uses the "gallery" to represent a window of Shylock's house. Jessica appears at this "window" and throws down Shylock's treasure to her lover, Lorenzo, who is standing on the stage below. She then leaves the "gallery" and reappears at one of the doors to the tiring-house, which is used to represent the door of Shylock's house.

Actors and staging

Performances in Shakespeare's England do not appear to have employed scenery. However, theatre companies developed their costumes with great care and expense. In fact, a playing company's costumes were its most valuable items. These extravagant costumes were the object of much controversy because some aristocrats feared that the actors could use them to disguise their social status on the streets of London.

Costumes also disguised a player's gender. All actors on the stage during Shakespeare's lifetime were men. Young boys whose voices had not reached maturity played female parts. This practice no doubt influenced Shakespeare's and his contemporary playwrights' thematic explorations of cross-dressing.

Though historians have managed to reconstruct the appearance of the early modern theatre, such as the recent construction of the Globe in London, much of the information regarding how plays were performed during this era has been lost. Scholars of Early Modern theatre have turned to the scant external and internal

Shakespeare in Love shows how the interior of the Globe would have appeared.
Everett Collection

stage directions in manuscripts in an effort to find these answers. Although a hindrance for modern critics and scholars, the lack of detail about Early Modern performances has allowed modern directors and actors a great deal of flexibility and room for creativity.

For example, modern directors of *The Merchant of Venice* can use lighting and sets to emphasize the differences between Venice and Belmont. They could make Venice into a dark, gloomy place, full of stagnant canals and decaying buildings, in order to stress the financial corruption and moral decay that they perceive in Shakespeare's depiction of the city. They could then create a contrast with Belmont, by making Portia's house beautiful, emphasizing its idyllic nature. This type of visual symbolism can help to clarify the play's issues to a modern audience. However, it is important to remember that the original productions would not have been able to use lighting or sets to achieve these effects. Shakespeare created the play's locations in the audience's minds with only words and costumes as his tools.

The printing press

If not for the printing press, many Early Modern plays may not have survived until today. In Shakespeare's time, printers produced all books by *sheet* — a single large piece of paper that the printer would fold in order to produce the desired book size. For example, a folio required folding the sheet once, a quarto four times, an octavo eight, and so on. Sheets would be printed one side at a time; thus, printers had to simultaneously print multiple nonconsecutive pages.

In order to estimate what section of the text would be on each page, the printer would *cast off* copy. After the printer made these estimates, *compositors* would set the type upside down, letter by letter. This process of setting type produced textual errors, some of which a proofreader would catch.

When a proofreader found an error, the compositors would fix the piece or pieces of type. Printers called corrections made after printing began *stop-press* corrections because they literally had to stop the press to fix the error. Because of the high cost of paper, printers would still sell the sheets printed before they made the correction.

Printers placed frames of text in the bed of the printing press and used them to imprint the paper. They then folded and grouped the sheets of paper into gatherings, after which the pages were ready for sale. The buyer had the option of getting the new play bound.

The printing process was crucial to the preservation of Shakespeare's works, but the printing of drama in Early Modern England was not a standardized practice. Many of the first editions of Shakespeare's plays appear in quarto format and, until recently, scholars regarded them as "corrupt." In fact, scholars still debate how close a relationship exists between what appeared on the stage in the sixteenth and seventeenth centuries and what appears on the printed page. The inconsistent and scant appearance of stage directions, for example, makes it difficult to determine how close this relationship was.

We know that the practice of the theatre allowed the alteration of plays by a variety of hands other than the author's, further complicating any efforts to extract what a playwright wrote and what was changed by either the players, the printers, or the government censors. Theatre was a collaborative environment. Rather than lament our inability to determine authorship and what exactly Shakespeare wrote, we should work to understand this collaborative nature and learn from it.

The Merchant of Venice has a comparatively simple textual history. It was first printed in 1600, several years after its original performances. This first publication was a quarto (a small, cheap edition). Textual scholars believe that it might have been printed from a manuscript in Shakespeare's hand-writing, but they cannot tell whether the manuscript represents the play before or after it had been performed in the theatre. The second major printing of the play was its inclusion in the expensive 1623 Folio edition of Shakespeare's collected plays. There are few significant differences between the two editions, although the Folio version contains some extra stage directions, which seem to be the work of a theatre prompter.

Shakespeare wrote his plays for the stage, and the existing published texts reflect the collaborative nature of the theatre as well as the unavoidable changes made during the printing process. A play's first written version would have been the author's *foul papers,* which invariably consisted of blotted lines and revised text. From there, a scribe would recopy the play and produce a *fair copy.* The theatre manager would then copy out and annotate this copy into a playbook (what people today call a *promptbook*).

At this point, scrolls of individual parts were copied out for actors to memorize. (Due to the high cost of paper, theatre companies could not afford to provide their actors with a complete copy of the play.) The government required the company to send the playbook to the Master of the Revels, the government official who would make any necessary changes or mark any passages considered unacceptable for performance.

Printers could have used any one of these copies to print a play. We cannot determine whether a printer used the author's version, the modified theatrical version, the censored version, or a combination when printing a given play. Refer back to the "Publications" section of the Introduction to William Shakespeare for further discussion of the impact printing practices has on our understanding of Shakespeare's works.

Works cited

For more information regarding Early Modern England, consult the following works:

Bevington, David. "General Introduction." *The Complete Works of William Shakespeare.* Updated Fourth edition. New York: Longman, 1997.

Greenblatt, Stephen. "Shakespeare's World." *Norton Shakespeare.* New York: W.W. Norton and Co., 1997.

Kastan, David Scott, ed. *A Companion to Shakespeare.* Oxford: Blackwell, 1999.

McDonald, Russ. *The Bedford Companion to Shakespeare: An Introduction with Documents.* Boston: Bedford-St. Martin's Press, 1996.

INTRODUCTION TO THE MERCHANT OF VENICE

The Merchant of Venice is a controversial and difficult play, in which a modern reader must confront the darker side of Elizabethan culture. The play has been accused of racism, and many people have argued that, because of this, it should no longer be read in schools or performed in the theatre. The accusations of racism are powerful and often justified. Nonetheless, there is another side to *The Merchant of Venice.* It has been staged regularly for over three hundred years and contains a role that many of the most famous actors have longed to play. In addition, its racism has often been reversed in performance, and parts of the play have become viewed as an eloquent plea for human equality. Indeed, in some ways the play has been instrumental in changing people's perceptions of the Jewish community, and it therefore occupies a valuable place in world culture.

Synopsis

The play begins in Venice, a powerful city-state on the coast of what we now call Italy. In the opening scene, we learn the predicament of a young aristocrat named Bassanio. Bassanio has spent all of his inheritance and is now looking for a way to pay off his debts. He thinks he has found one. He has heard that in Belmont, there is a lady whose father has left her a vast fortune. Bassanio has visited her once, and is sure that she loves him. However, he cannot afford to travel to Belmont again.

Fortunately, Bassanio's best friend Antonio is a wealthy merchant and so devoted to Bassanio that he is happy to lend him the money that he requires. However, Antonio has no ready cash, because he is waiting for some ships to return. Therefore, he and Bassanio visit a moneylender.

The moneylender is a Jew named Shylock. He and Antonio have a history of animosity, which revolves around their religious differences and their arguments over the morality of moneylending. Upon meeting, they fall into argument once more, where-upon Shylock devises a "merry bond." He suggests that if Antonio fails to repay the loan, he must be fined; but the fine will not be money. Instead, Shylock will be allowed to cut a pound of flesh from Antonio's body. Antonio is confident that he will be able to repay the loan and signs the bond.

Meanwhile, we meet Portia, the lady in Belmont. She is besieged by suitors who want to marry her. But under the terms of her father's will, a man can only marry Portia if he passes a test first. There are three caskets in Portia's house: gold, silver, and lead. Each has a riddling statement attached to it. If a suitor chooses the correct casket, he will win Portia's hand in marriage. We see two suitors, the Princes of Morocco and Arragon, attempt the test and fail.

Back in Venice, Bassanio prepares for his journey. He invites Shylock to his house for a meal. But the offer is, in fact, a diversion. Shylock has a daughter, Jessica, who loves Lorenzo, one of Bassanio's friends. While Shylock is visiting Bassanio, Lorenzo runs to Shylock's house and helps Jessica to escape. She takes with her some of her father's money. The elopement is assisted by the fact that Shylock's servant, Launcelot, has decided to betray his master and work for Bassanio instead.

When Shylock returns to his house he finds that both his daughter and his money have vanished. At the same time, Bassanio leaves for Belmont. Shylock tries to prevent him, but Lorenzo and Jessica have already escaped by another route. Left alone, Shylock asks another Jewish moneylender, Tubal, to find out where his daughter has

Choosing the caskets, as portrayed in a modern stage production.
Chris Parker/PAL

gone. Tubal observes Jessica and Lorenzo on a spending spree in Genoa, where Jessica swaps Shylock's engagement ring for a monkey. Shylock is furious and thirsts for revenge.

In Belmont, Bassanio arrives at Portia's house in splendid clothes. He attempts the casket test. Realizing that the riddles are describing the difference between appearance and reality, he chooses the lead casket, because it is the least impressive-looking. Bassanio is correct in his choice and wins Portia's hand; they are both delighted, and Bassanio becomes lord of Belmont. Simultaneously, Bassanio's friend Gratiano falls in love with Portia's waiting-woman, Nerissa. However, this happiness is short-lived, as a messenger enters with bad news.

In Venice, Antonio's ships have failed to arrive; every one of them has sunk. Shylock is delighted. He now has the opportunity to get his revenge on one of the Christians who caused his unhappiness. He takes Antonio to court, in order to collect his bond: the pound of flesh. Hearing the news, Bassanio and Gratiano rush to Venice with money given by Portia to repay the loan. Portia and Nerissa remain in Belmont, saying that they will stay in a monastery and pray. But they are lying.

In fact, Portia and Nerissa disguise themselves as male lawyers and follow Bassanio to Venice. There, Antonio and Shylock are in court. The court is trying to find a way of preventing Shylock from claiming his pound of flesh. But the law is on Shylock's side, because the bond has Antonio's signature on it. Shylock refuses to accept Bassanio's money in payment. He wants revenge, not money.

Portia arrives, disguised as a lawyer called Balthazar. She begs Shylock to exercise "mercy" (forgiveness), but he refuses. At the last minute, Portia discovers a loophole: The bond says nothing about blood, only flesh. Portia reasons that Shylock must perform the impossible task of cutting flesh without spilling blood. She also discovers that Venetian law demands the execution of any "alien" who threatens

the death of a Christian. Shylock is defeated and is ordered to bequeath his money to Jessica and become a Christian. He leaves the court a broken man.

Still in disguise, Portia tests her husband. She asks him for his wedding ring as payment for her saving Antonio. With some misgivings, Bassanio agrees. Nerissa does the same to Gratiano. Then the men return to Belmont. There, Portia, free from her disguise, asks Bassanio where the ring is. He is forced to admit that he gave it to a lawyer. Portia pretends to be devastated, and, after making Bassanio repent, she reveals that, in fact, *she* was the lawyer. Having demonstrated their intellectual superiority, the women forgive their husbands, and the play ends.

When read in synopsis form, the story of *The Merchant of Venice* seems extremely silly. The disguises, the casket test, and the bond of a pound of flesh are not remotely realistic. But Elizabethan plays hardly ever try to portray "real life" onstage. An Elizabethan audience did not watch a play thinking of the likelihood of the events actually happening. They watched it thinking of the meaning of the play or what it symbolized. And that is how Elizabethan plays should be read today.

The issue of racism in the play

The character of Shylock is problematic for a modern audience. It is fair to describe him as a racial stereotype of the worst kind: one implying that the bad qualities of a single character are shared by all other members of his race or faith. Not only did Shakespeare stereotypically link Jews with money-lending, but he also drew on the Elizabethan belief that Jews were bloodthirsty murderers. He appears to be condemning the Jewish faith, as well as advocating the conversion (whether voluntary or forced) of all Jews to Christianity. People have found this depiction of Jews offensive for at least three hundred years. Since World War II, in which over six million Jewish people were deliberately massacred,

The Merchant of Venice has come to symbolize for some the origins of the anti-Semitic attitude that eventually culminated in the Holocaust.

However, we must remember that for the same three hundred years, the play has been continually staged, and both readers and actors (many of them Jewish) have found in the play powerful statements against racial and religious hatred. In order to understand the depiction of Shylock, and also to understand some of the arguments against the play's racist qualities, it is necessary to look at Elizabethan culture and the stories on which Shakespeare based his play.

The Elizabethan image of the Jew

Elizabethan England was the home of very few Jews. Officially, the Jews were expelled from England in 1290, but in reality, some sort of Jewish community probably did reside in Britain. This community consisted mostly of Jewish refugees from Spain, who claimed to have converted to Christianity. It is difficult to say how many Jews there were in 1590s London, but in any case, few of them would have been *openly* Jewish. It is quite likely that Shakespeare could have lived his entire life without ever meeting an openly practicing Jew.

Because of this, the Elizabethan image of a Jew was fanciful. Many people, both educated and uneducated, believed Jews to be responsible for all manner of appalling crimes, such as kidnapping children, poisoning wells, mutilation, and even cannibalism. However, this anti-Jewish feeling was not uniform to every Elizabethan person. Many extremist Protestants were adopting Jewish religious rites in an effort to get closer to the traditions of the earliest Christians. Therefore, there was no single image of "Jews" in Elizabethan England; the image of the Jew depended entirely on the individual thinker.

Two stereotypes are especially relevant to *The Merchant of Venice*. The first is the belief that all Jews are moneylenders. The term *moneylending* refers to the business of loaning money and charging very high interest on it. The Elizabethans used the word *usury*; nowadays we tend to call it *loan sharking*. In Elizabethan fiction, Jews are nearly always usurers. The stereotype arose because the Jewish faith did not forbid usury, whereas the Christian faith did. However, in England, usury had been legal since 1571. The Elizabethan audience would, therefore, have known perfectly well that the stereotype of the Jewish usurer was unfair, because nearly all the usurers in London would have been Christians.

The second important stereotype is the idea that a Jew might demand a pound of flesh as repayment for a loan. This story is an ancient one that had been retold in many different ways over the centuries, and it would have been familiar to Shakespeare's audience. The story would have reminded the audience of the recent rumors of Christian travelers being mutilated by Jews. These rumors may have added an element of personal fear to the Elizabethan audience.

The assumption that these appalling prejudices in Elizabethan society meant that any play involving a Jew would be intolerably offensive is not illogical. However, the two most famous Elizabethan plays written about Jews have a far more complex attitude and demonstrate that Elizabethans were capable of thinking critically about their own culture.

Christopher Marlowe's *The Jew of Malta* and its influence on Shakespeare

The original audience of Shakespeare's play would already have a strong image of a Jewish villain in their minds. A play called *The Jew of Malta* by Christopher Marlowe had taken London by storm some years earlier. If you are studying *Merchant* in detail, you will find it very helpful to read Marlowe's play. There now exist several inexpensive, modern-spelling editions of Marlowe's plays; alternatively, you can find a downloadable electronic text at **www.perseus.tufts.edu/texts/marlowe.html**

The Jew of Malta is an outrageous but wickedly funny play. Its central character is Barabas, a Jew whose money is confiscated by the Christian governors of Malta. Barabas gets his revenge on the town by committing all kinds of evil deeds. For example, he murders the nuns by poisoning their porridge, and then chortles, "How sweet the bells ring now the nuns are dead." Barabas is finally killed when the Christians set a trap for him, and he plunges into a boiling cauldron.

Barabas is clearly based on the Elizabethan stereotype of the murderous Jew. Yet the play is much more subversive than it sounds, for three reasons. First, Barabas is very much a parody of the Elizabethan Jewish stereotype. He is more like a cartoon character than a human being; in performance, the actor wore a bright red wig and a false nose.

Second, Marlowe portrays the Christian rulers of Malta not as pious saints, but as ruthless, cold-blooded hypocrites, and he demonstrates that Barabas' killing spree begins when the Christians confiscate his property without any justification. In addition, the play also pokes fun at some Turkish Muslims who arrive on the island. On the few occasions when *The Jew of Malta* has been staged in the twentieth century, audiences have concluded that it is not anti-Jewish, but anti-*religion*, because no faith escapes criticism. The play seems designed to raise awkward questions about Elizabethan culture, which is relevant because the modern justification for continuing to read *The Merchant of Venice* often rests on similar grounds.

The third subversive aspect of *The Jew of Malta* is that the audience *likes* Barabas. Of course they don't approve of his crimes — but he is an extremely entertaining character. Barabas is full of energy and humor, so that the stage comes to life whenever he enters and boasts of his wicked deeds. This recalls an important dramatic technique that Shakespeare uses in *Merchant:* encouraging sympathy for the villain.

Sympathy for the villain

Shylock is a villain, no matter how much he was provoked. But a dramatist can make an audience sympathize with a villain in three ways.

The first way to gain the audience's sympathy for a villain is to make the villain *enjoyably* wicked, by making his crimes funny and thrilling. This technique is the one that Marlowe employed when he created Barabas. Shakespeare used it in his *Richard III,* and there is an element of the technique in Shylock, too.

The second way to create a sympathetic villain is to allow the audience to see the mental anguish of the villain, as his conscience wrestles with his desire to do evil. Shakespeare used this technique in *Macbeth,* but not in *Merchant;* Shylock never seems to grapple with his conscience at all.

Finally, the last method for creating a sympathetic villain is to give the villain a *reason* for wanting to commit his crimes, so that the audience can understand his desire to do evil. This technique is the one that Shakespeare uses most often in his depiction of Shylock. Shylock is given specific reasons for his hatred of Antonio and of Christians in general. He has suffered years of abuse from Antonio and blames him for helping Jessica to betray him.

The most important moment in the story of Shylock is that in which Shylock makes his impassioned speech against inequality: "Hath not a Jew eyes . . ." (III.1.58–72). The speech suggests that the shared humanity of people is more important than religious or racial differences; and it also suggests that Shylock's violence is something he has learned from the Christians who have abused him. Both suggestions transform our understanding of Shylock and make the play's depiction of religious difference much more complex than it may appear at first glance.

Performing Shylock

A valuable tool for understanding Shylock can be a comparison of two productions of the play. For example, one can compare Laurence Olivier's performance in the 1973 video with Bob Peck in Channel 4's 1996 version (on British television). Olivier begins the play as a cheerful, humorous man, who is devastated by Jessica's betrayal and transforms into a twisted but still sympathetic villain. In contrast, Bob Peck begins the play as a despicable and sinister man, but even so, sympathy for him gradually increases as the film progresses.

Shylock can be interpreted in many ways on the stage. He can be seen as a simple comic villain who occasionally reveals sympathetic qualities. Or he can be a tragic hero, a spurned and battered victim of

Sir Laurence Olivier as Shylock.
Everett Collection

oppression, who tries unsuccessfully to challenge the society that oppresses him. Similarly, the Christians can be saintly personifications of charity and mercy, or hypocritical money-grubbers. It may seem strange that a play can produce such divergent readings, but they are, in fact, a result of the *complexity* of Shakespeare's writing. Shakespeare imitated Marlowe in creating a Jewish character whose violent behavior is explained by the way Christians treat him. But Shakespeare also seems concerned with humanizing Shylock, rather than making him into a caricature. The difference can be seen if we contrast the emotional natures of the two characters. When Barabas is accused of fornication, he protests "But that was in another country. / And besides, the wench is dead." His cynical response is pure black comedy, especially because we suspect Barabas was the person who killed her. In contrast, when Shylock hears that Jessica has sold his engagement ring, he says "It was my turquoise. I had it of Leah when I was a bachelor" (III.1.121–123), a line that conjures up a moving image of a happier life that Shylock has lost.

Having said that, we should remember that the play does end with both of its Jewish characters converted to Christianity. We should imagine that the Elizabethan audience would regard this not as a cruel enforcement, but as the saving of their souls. Even so, Shylock does not seem pleased by the ruling. His final lines are "I am not well" (IV.1.395), which suggests a defeated, broken man; and we can hardly imagine he will accept the Christian faith willingly. The final image of Shylock casts a shadow over the jollity of the final act.

Shakespeare and Marlowe lived in a culture that accepted an image of Jewish people that we now find appallingly racist. Perhaps neither dramatist would have thought of Jewish people in a modern way, as unequivocally deserving equality and religious freedom. But both used the stereotype to subvert it; they used it not necessarily to criticize Jews, but to suggest that the causes of the stereotype may be found in the culture that created it. Both plays are fascinating historical artifacts of different cultural attitudes toward race; and with only minor exaggerations of their subversive qualities, they can still be staged today and produce more powerful antiracist effects than their authors could ever have imagined.

The manipulation of Shakespeare's sources

Shakespeare did not invent the story of *The Merchant of Venice*. It is better to say that he "constructed" it, using the work of other writers as building-blocks. Although *The Jew of Malta* was probably Shakespeare's initial inspiration, several other stories were ransacked for ideas to create a very different plot from Marlowe's play.

The plot of *Merchant* comes primarily from an Italian story by Giovanni Fiorentino, who included it in a collection of tales called *Il pecorone*. It is not certain how Shakespeare came upon this story — he may have been able to read Italian, or there may have been a translation of the tale that has not survived the passage of time. In any case, he would have read a strange story with much dramatic potential.

The following section is a summary of Fiorentino's story. As you read it, compare it with the synopsis of *Merchant*, to see how Shakespeare adapted the story. Fiorentino's characters have different names from Shakespeare's, so to avoid confusion, they are referred to by their social positions.

A Young Man of Venice borrows money from a Rich Friend to take a boat trip to Alexandria. On the way, the ship passes Belmont. The Young Man learns of a Lady who rules the land and has promised to give herself and all of her possessions to the first man who sleeps with her. The Young Man lands at Belmont and meets the Lady, who entertains him at her house with a huge feast. When they have eaten, they

go to her bedchamber. The Lady gives the Young Man a drink, but his drink is drugged and he falls asleep until morning. He has failed the test.

The Young Man is forced to give up his ship as a forfeit. He returns shamefacedly to Venice, and pretends he was shipwrecked. But the Young Man decides to try again. His Rich Friend has now run out of money, but he loves the Young Man and generously offers to use his credit to help him. He borrows money from a Jewish Moneylender. The Jew sets a pound of flesh as the penalty if he fails to pay on time. The Young Man sets sail once more. This time, the Lady's Serving-Woman warns the Young Man about the drugged drink. So when the Lady leads him to her bedchamber, he is able to make love to her. He has passed the test.

The Young Man becomes ruler of Belmont, and rules it wisely. However, he is enjoying himself so much that he forgets about his Rich Friend's bond with the Jewish Moneylender. Remembering too late, the Young Man hurries to Venice.

In Venice, the bond has expired. The Jew sues the Rich Friend, demanding his pound of flesh. The Young Man arrives with the money, but the Jew refuses it, insisting on the pound of flesh. But the Lady also arrives, disguised as a lawyer. She successfully defeats the Jew. Still in disguise, she persuades the Young Man to give her his wedding ring, and then, after she is out of her disguise, reveals to him what she has done. Everyone travels to Belmont, and the Rich Friend marries the Lady's Serving-Woman.

The story of *Il pecorone* is broadly the same as the main plot of *The Merchant of Venice*. However, there are important differences. Shakespeare changes the Young Man's Rich Friend into a merchant; he gives the Jew a reason for his cruelty, which Fiorentino leaves unexplained; and he leaves the Rich Friend single at the end of the play, because the Serving-Woman marries a different friend of the Young Man. But of course, the most important change is the nature of the test that the Young Man has to pass. In Fiorentino's story, the Young Man is interested only in money and sex when he attempts to seduce the Lady. Although elements of this remain in Shakespeare's play, Shakespeare romanticizes both characters so that love becomes much more relevant to the story.

Shakespeare makes love more relevant to the story by replacing the sexual test in Fiorentino with a test that he found in another collection of tales, the *Gesta romanum* (Roman Tales), translated by Richard Robinson. The thirty-second story of the *Gesta* describes the adventures of a Princess who must undergo a test before she can marry a Prince. The test involves her choosing between three caskets: gold, silver, and lead. Shakespeare made two changes. First, he reversed the gender of the test, so that the man must choose the casket to win the woman. Second, he altered the inscriptions on the caskets; in the original story, they are religious in their meaning, but Shakespeare removed the overt emphasis on holiness in favor of a moral about the difference between appearance and reality.

Shakespeare did not stop hunting for refinements to the story. From *The Jew of Malta* he borrowed the idea of the Jew having a daughter. He then integrated this idea with a story from yet another story-collection, *Il novellino* by Masuccio Salonitano, in which a Daughter escapes from the house of her Miserly Father, to run off with a Young Man, and also steals all his money. The Miser ends up losing both his daughter and his money.

Some other minor sources for the play do exist, but these are the principal origins of Shakespeare's ideas. *The Merchant of Venice* may have begun as an attempt to emulate the popularity of *The Jew of Malta*, but the end result is a "patchwork," constructed from a neat interweaving of several stories. Comparing source material with the finished play is a very useful method of studying a Renaissance play. Think about the differences between the versions of the stories and how the differences alter their effect on the audience.

The play in Shakespeare's own time

The Merchant of Venice was probably written in 1596–1597. It was first printed in a cheap quarto format in 1600, and then as part of the large, expensive Folio edition of Shakespeare's plays in 1623.

The first performances of *The Merchant of Venice* would have been staged at a theatre called The Theatre. This building, constructed in 1576, was one of the first permanent theatres to be built in London. It was owned by the Lord Chamberlain's Men, a major playing company of which Shakespeare was actor, joint owner, and principal playwright. The Theatre was in Shoreditch, a disreputable part of London beyond its Northern walls. The audience would have been a mixture of people — poor workers, professionals, and some members of the aristocratic classes.

After 1599, the Lord Chamberlain's Men relocated to a new theater called the Globe, on the South Bank of the Thames River in London. The Globe was very similar to The Theatre, and there is now a modern reconstruction of it in London; you can take a guided virtual tour of the new Globe at **www.rdg.ac.uk/globe/**

The title page of the 1600 edition gives us a glimpse of what the original productions may have been like. Its full title is *The most excellent History of the Merchant of Venice. With the extreme cruelty of Shylock the Jew towards the said Merchant, in cutting off a just pound of his flesh: and the obtaining of Portia by the choice of three chests.* The title may be describing the most popular moments in the play, in order to ensure good sales for the publication.

However, *The Merchant of Venice* may not have been especially popular during Shakespeare's lifetime. Apart from a court performance in 1605, no other performances are recorded for some sixty years. Hardly any references to *The Merchant of Venice* have been found in the literature of the day, which is a stark contrast to *The Jew of Malta,* which was one of the most popular plays of the Renaissance and was still being revived forty years after Marlowe wrote it. The lack of popularity of *Merchant* during Elizabethan times also contrasts with the modern opinion of it, as it is now one of Shakespeare's most popular plays.

The play as part of Shakespeare's canon

The Merchant of Venice can be thought of as a stepping stone in Shakespeare's career. It has been suggested that it is the first of Shakespeare's "dark comedies" in which he infused the simple elements of light-hearted romantic comedy with a consideration of the darker possibilities of society. For example, this is one of the first of his comedies to contain a villain. It represents a movement away from the light-hearted fun of *A Midsummer Night's Dream* and *Love's Labour's Lost* and points toward the difficult, questioning, and disturbing "comedy" of *Measure for Measure* and *Troilus and Cressida.*

Critical and general reception

After Shakespeare's death, the play was not staged until the beginning of the eighteenth century, and even then it was in heavily adapted versions. Eighteenth-century productions tended to treat the play as a simple romantic comedy, with Shylock as a manic villain. Shylock was always played with a bright red wig; this tradition did not end until 1814.

During the nineteenth century, audiences became increasingly uncomfortable with the play's anti-Semitic aspects, and by the 1870s, Shylock had become a tragic hero. The play came to be "about" Shylock, and productions often interpolated extra stage business, which intensified audience sympathy for Shylock. Because *Merchant* can so easily be adapted in this way, it has often been used as an argument for religious and racial equality. Many modern productions have rearranged the text somewhat, in order to enhance Shylock's tragic qualities.

World War II has completely altered our attitude to the play. Portrayals of Shylock that appear anti-Semitic can be profoundly upsetting to modern audiences. But *Merchant* has continued to be staged, and the ease with which performances can make Shylock sympathetic has made many people argue that the original productions may not have been as simplistically anti-Semitic as had been thought. Interest is now shifting to the ways in which the play reflects aspects of Renaissance society.

In the twentieth century, audiences have had two basic reactions to the play. Some believe the play to be a simple romantic comedy. Proponents of this view claim that Shylock is simply a comic villain and that the Elizabethan audience would not have found the Jewish stereotype problematic. The second view argues that the play is not simple at all. In this view, *Merchant* is a *questioning* play, highlighting awkward problems in Renaissance society, such as the clash between friendship and marriage or the hypocritical treatment of Jewish people.

A third view argues that we should not read Elizabethan plays in search of ideas that we find in our own society. Instead, we should read them to see what they say about Elizabethan culture. Proponents of this view argue that we *should* be shocked by the play's anti-Semitism, because it reminds us that modern society has changed for the better.

Issues to watch for

The following sections cover some key issues to keep in mind as you read the play.

Venice and Belmont

Venice was an appropriate setting for the play. In the modern world, Venice is a scenic tourist destination, but the Elizabethan audience would have thought of Venice as a powerful trading city with a vast fleet of merchant vessels. The city was believed to have achieved its success by being exceptionally tolerant toward foreigners, who were treated as equals in its laws. This belief is important to the play, because Shakespeare uses it as a plot device at III.4.26–31, although he invents an exception at lines IV.1.346–355.

Venice was also famous for its tolerance toward religions other than Christianity. The audience would have known that Venetian Jews were permitted to practice their religion freely, whereas in London it was illegal. However, Venetian "tolerance" was actually a myth; the Jews were forced to live in a special part of the city, called the *ghetto*. They had to wear a distinctive "uniform," which included the yellow badge later revived by the Nazis. However, Shakespeare does not mention these restrictions in his play, indicating that he may not have known about them. The action of the play would, therefore, have agreed with the Elizabethan audience's image of Venice as a mercantile city that was tolerant of foreigners and non-Christians.

A second setting exists in the play: Belmont. We never learn where Belmont is, and we never see any of it beyond Portia's house. Shakespeare portrays these two settings in very different ways. He gives Venice a dark and murky atmosphere of mercantile dealings and nighttime escapades, but he withholds any description of Belmont. It seems as though Belmont's only inhabitants are an incredibly rich lady and her household. This raises some important points that may illuminate the way the play is structured.

Reality and idealism

The Merchant of Venice is structured partly on the contrast between idealistic and realistic opinions about society and relationships. On the one hand, the play tells us that love is more important than money, mercy is preferable to revenge, and love lasts forever. On the other hand, more cynical voices tell us that money rules the world, mercy alone cannot govern our lives, and love can evaporate after marriage. The play switches abruptly between these different attitudes.

For example, the play often portrays love and marriage in a very romantic light. The fullest expression of this is in Act III, Scene 2, in which Bassanio successfully wins Portia by refusing to judge by appearances. Indeed, the folly of judging by "outward show" is often described as the moral of the play. Yet Shakespeare constantly undermines this romantic depiction of love, by questioning the attitude of the male characters toward it. When Lorenzo and Jessica are eloping, Gratiano and Salerio laugh at them behind their backs, and suggest that once Lorenzo has "caught" his woman, he will lose interest in her (II.6.5–19). Similarly, at the beginning of Act V, Scene 1, Lorenzo and Jessica compare themselves to mythological figures, but the stories they use are those in which lovers are betrayed or doomed. The romance of the scene is undercut by these images of the catastrophes that can befall lovers.

Shakespeare organizes the shifts between idealism and realism by associating the two concepts with the play's two locations. Venice is depicted as a city of merchants, usurers, and cynical young men. Belmont, in contrast, is the land where fairytales come true. Only in Belmont could a woman be won by means of a simple test, and only in Belmont could we be certain that the test will be defeated by the only man she ever loved. Belmont is a land where idealistic love can still exist; Venice is not. We can observe the effect that these differences have on the characters by watching the behavior of Gratiano. In Venice, Gratiano is a cynic who sneers at Lorenzo's love for Jessica. Yet as soon as he arrives in Belmont, Gratiano falls in love with Nerissa and reveals that he has a romantic side after all.

Belmont is a safe, idyllic world where money is limitless and, therefore, irrelevant. Venice is a dark, dangerous world, which is much more similar to the city of London that the Elizabethan audience would have returned to when they left the theatre. When the two worlds clash, it is therefore fascinating to see which will prove stronger. That clash occurs when Portia travels to Venice.

Portia and mercy

If Belmont is a fantasy world, then Portia is an idealized character. Despite the play's title, it is helpful to regard Portia as its main character. There are several reasons for this. The first is that she has more lines than anyone else. People tend to regard Shylock as the main character, but he only appears in five scenes and is entirely absent from the fifth act. Bassanio rarely excites the audience, while Antonio, the title character, does not appear very often and certainly does not dominate the play.

Portia is the only character whom it is difficult to criticize, and Shakespeare appears to use her as a symbol of mercy and forgiveness. The symbolism of Portia becomes most apparent when she travels to Venice, disguised as a lawyer. Because Venice can be thought of as symbolizing the real world, whereas Belmont is the world of idealism, when Portia travels to Venice, she is a character from the fantasy world entering the dangerous city. Her idealistic beliefs must come face to face with reality.

When she arrives in the court, Portia's mission is to prevent Shylock from harming Antonio. She tries to do so by appealing to Shylock's good nature and makes her famous speech about mercy (IV.1.181–202), in which she tries to persuade Shylock to forgive Antonio. She believes that mercy is the only "law" we should follow. But Shylock refuses, arguing that the letter of the law is more important than mercy. Here we see Portia's ideals facing a less admirable human desire: the desire for revenge. Portia has been forced to face reality, and she eventually conquers Shylock by a legal loophole, rather than by sticking to her principles.

However, Portia does manage to bring about some mercy in Venice. When Shylock faces execution for his crimes, Portia persuades the Duke to pardon him. She then persuades Antonio to exercise mercy by not taking all of Shylock's money from him (374–386). Here, Portia's presence turns the proceedings away from violence and toward forgiveness. Portia does, therefore, succeed in transmitting some of her idealism into Venice. Act IV ends with a suggestion that idealism can sometimes survive in the real world.

Marriage and friendship

Portia's story is also a demonstration of Shakespeare's interest in creating a female character with power and intelligence. Elizabethan society was much more oppressive toward women than we can imagine today. Aristocratic women like Portia would rarely be educated, because reading was thought to corrupt the purity of their minds. When they married, they were expected to be completely obedient to their husbands. Women who educated themselves or acted according to their own wills were viewed as dangerous or immoral. Portia appears to fit into the Renaissance ideal of a wife when she formally hands over all her power and wealth to her new husband, Bassanio (III.2.149–171). But shortly afterward, it becomes apparent that Portia will never be content as a subservient wife. Despite her claim to be "unschooled," her intervention in the court scene reveals her to be intelligent and learned. And in Act V, Scene 1, she reveals this intelligence to her husband. The audience is likely to suspect that Bassanio will not be the dominant partner in their marriage.

The reasons for this depiction of Portia are partly due to the way society was changing in England and the way close human relationships were being rethought. One type of close relationship is that of Bassanio and Antonio. Antonio's love for Bassanio is very powerful, as can be seen in the description of their tearful farewell in II.8.35–49. Modern audiences tend to be uncomfortable with such emotional behavior between men, but Medieval and Renaissance society often idealized male friendship above sexual love between men and women. Many writers argued that platonic (non-sexual) love was more noble and admirable than sexual love. The intense friendship between Antonio and Bassanio can be viewed in that light.

However, there were other impulses in Renaissance society. The creation of the Protestant Church of England, and the emergence of the extremist Protestants known as "Puritans" had generated a rethinking of the "hierarchy" of love. These thinkers viewed marriage as a "partnership" in which friendship between the partners was important (although it was not to conflict with the man's supremacy over his wife). These new ideas created an obvious clash with the older ones. For example, it is possible to *imagine* that Antonio might be jealous of Bassanio's love for Portia, and that there might be a kind of "competition" between them. Such an idea is never explicitly stated in the text. However, it helps to explain why Portia plays the ring trick on Bassanio; she is testing him, to see whether he regards her as more important than his friend. When the disguised Portia asks Bassanio to give his wedding ring to the "man" who saved his friend's life, Antonio tells him that his friend's love ought to be more important than his wife's. Bassanio decides that Antonio is right, much to Portia's disappointment. At the end of the play, it is left ambiguous whether Bassanio has successfully changed his mind. But when the play is staged, it becomes obvious that, in Act V, Antonio is left alone while everyone around him gets married. One cannot help but notice that Antonio has become an outsider and that Portia has replaced him as Bassanio's primary companion.

The theatre of questions

The Merchant of Venice asks a lot of questions and doesn't often answer them. Who does Bassanio love the most? Has Antonio's sadness been cured? Will Lorenzo and Jessica's love last forever? Should we feel sorry for Shylock? Should we approve of Portia's domineering nature?

These questions are the ones that the original audience would have been asking themselves as they left the theatre. And we should remember that they may have been *arguing* over the answers, rather than agreeing. *The Merchant of Venice* ends in harmony, but it leaves enough questions unanswered to keep the audience debating the important issues that it raises.

CHARACTERS IN THE PLAY

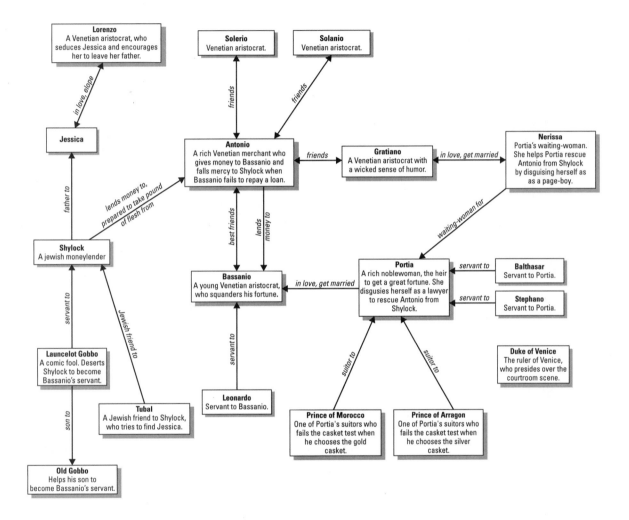

THE MERCHANT OF VENICE

ACT I

Shylock *What should I say to you? Should I not say,*
"Hath a dog money? is it possible
A cur can lend three thousand ducats?" Or
Shall I bend low, and in a bondman's key,
With bated breath and whisp'ring humbleness,
Say this:
"Fair sir, you spit on me on Wednesday last,
You spurned me such a day, another time
You called me dog; and for these courtesies
I'll lend you thus much moneys"?

Act I, Scene 1

Bassanio reveals to his friend Antonio that he plans to marry a rich heiress. Antonio agrees to lend him money to help.

ACT I, SCENE 1.
Venice, a street.

[*Enter* ANTONIO, SALERIO, *and* SOLANIO.]

Antonio In sooth I know not why I am so sad.
  It wearies me, you say it wearies you;
  But how I caught it, found it, or came by it,
  What stuff 'tis made of, whereof it is born,
  I am to learn;   5
  And such a want-wit sadness of me
  That I have much ado to know myself.

Salerio Your mind is tossing on the ocean,
  There where your argosies with portly sail —
  Like signiors and rich burghers on the flood,   10
  Or as it were, the pageants of the sea —
  Do overpeer the petty traffickers
  That cursy to them, do them reverence,
  As they fly by them with their woven wings.

Solanio Believe me, sir, had I such venture forth,   15
  The better part of my affections would
  Be with my hopes abroad. I should be still
  Plucking the grass to know where sits the wind,
  Peering in maps for ports and piers and roads;
  And every object that might make me fear   20
  Misfortune to my ventures, out of doubt
  Would make me sad.

Salerio   My wind cooling my broth
  Would blow me to an ague when I thought
  What harm a wind too great might do at sea
  I should not see the sandy hourglass run   25
  But I should think of shallows and of flats,
  And see my wealthy Andrew docked in sand,
  Vailing her high top lower than her ribs
  To kiss her burial. Should I go to church

NOTES

5. *am to learn:* have yet to learn.

6. *want-wit:* one who lacks wits or common sense.

9. *argosies:* large merchant ships.

   portly: fat, indicating that the ships' sails are puffed out by the wind.

11. *pageants:* large cart or float, used in a procession.

12. *petty traffickers:* small merchant ships.

13. *cursy:* to curtsy, or bow; but in a nautical sense, it can also refer to the smaller ships lowering their topsails to Antonio's larger vessels as a mark of respect.

19. *roads:* anchorage, open harbors where ships may anchor.

23. *ague:* fever.

27. *Andrew:* the name of a ship. The name may have been suggested to Shakespeare by the capture of a Spanish galleon called the Saint Andrew at Cadiz in 1596.

28. *Vailing:* lowering.

And see the holy edifice of stone   30
And not bethink me straight of dangerous rocks,
Which touching but my gentle vessel's side
Would scatter all her spices on the stream,
Enrobe the roaring waters with my silks —
And in a word, but even now worth this,   35
And now worth nothing? Shall I have the thought
To think on this, and shall I lack the thought
That such a thing bechanced would make me sad?
But tell not me! I know Antonio
Is sad to think upon his merchandise.   40

Antonio Believe me, no. I thank my fortune for it
My ventures are not in one bottom trusted,
Nor to one place; nor is my whole estate
Upon the fortune of this present year.
Therefore my merchandise makes me not sad.   45

Solanio Why then you are in love.

Antonio   Fie, fie!

Solanio Not in love neither? Then let us say you
        are sad
Because you are not merry; and 'twere as easy
For you to laugh and leap, and say you are merry
Because you are not sad. Now by two-headed Janus,   50
Nature hath framed strange fellows in her time:
Some that will evermore peep through their eyes
And laugh like parrots at a bagpiper,
And other of such vinegar aspect
That they'll not show their teeth in way of smile   55
Though Nestor swear the jest be laughable.

[*Enter* BASSANIO, LORENZO, *and* GRATIANO.]
Here comes Bassanio your most noble kinsman,
Gratiano, and Lorenzo. Fare ye well;
We leave you now with better company.

Salerio I would have stayed till I had made you   60
        merry,
If worthier friends had not prevented me.

Antonio Your worth is very dear in my regard.
I take it your own business calls on you,
And you embrace th' occasion to depart.

35–36. *but . . . nothing?:* at one moment valuable, and at the next moment worthless.

42. *bottom:* ship.

50. *two-headed Janus:* a Roman god represented with two faces, one smiling and the other frowning. Solanio is suggesting that even a deity may be subject to opposing moods.

53. *laugh . . . bagpiper:* laugh at anything. Bagpipes were supposed to make one melancholy.

56. *Nestor:* an old and serious counselor in the *Iliad;* one not given to laughing.

Salerio Good morrow, my good lords. 65

Bassanio Good signiors both, when shall we laugh?
Say, when?
You grow exceeding strange. Must it be so?

Salerio We'll make our leisures to attend on yours.

[*Exeunt* SALERIO *and* SOLANIO.]

Lorenzo. My Lord Bassanio, since you have found
Antonio,
We two will leave you; but at dinner time 70
I pray you have in mind where we must meet.

Bassanio I will not fail you.

Gratiano You look not well, Signior Antonio.
You have too much respect upon the world;
They lose it that do buy it with much care. 75
Believe me, you are marvelously changed.

Antonio I hold the world but as the world,
Gratiano —
A stage where every man must play a part,
And mine a sad one.

Gratiano   Let me play the fool!
With mirth and laughter let old wrinkles come, 80
And let my liver rather heat with wine
Than my heart cool with mortifying groans.
Why should a man whose blood is warm within
Sit like his grandsire cut in alabaster?
Sleep when he wakes? and creep into the jaundice 85
By being peevish? I tell thee what, Antonio,
I love thee, and 'tis my love that speaks:
There are a sort of men whose visages
Do cream and mantle like a standing pond,
And do a willful stillness entertain 90
With purpose to be dressed in an opinion
Of wisdom, gravity, profound conceit —
As who should say, "I am Sir Oracle,
And when I ope my lips, let no dog bark!"
O my Antonio, I do know of these 95
That therefore only are reputed wise
For saying nothing, when I am very sure

67. *strange:* estranged, distant.

68. *We'll . . . yours:* We'll meet you whenever you wish.

74. *respect upon:* concern for.

81. *let . . . wine:* the Elizabethans considered the liver to be the seat of the passions.

85. *jaundice:* a symptom of violent passion.

89. *cream and mantle:* become solidified, like cream on top of milk, or algae on a stagnant pond.

standing: stagnant.

If they should speak would almost damn those ears,
Which hearing them would call their brothers fools.
I'll tell thee more of this another time.   100
But fish not with this melancholy bait
For this fool gudgeon, this opinion.
Come, good Lorenzo. Fare ye well awhile;
I'll end my exhortation after dinner.

Lorenzo Well, we will leave you then till dinner   105
    time.
I must be one of these same dumb wise men,
For Gratiano never lets me speak.

Gratiano Well, keep me company but two years moe,
Thou shalt not know the sound of thine own tongue.

Antonio Fare you well; I'll grow a talker for this   110
    gear.

Gratiano Thanks i' faith; for silence is only
    commendable
In a neat's tongue dried and a maid not vendible.

[*Exeunt* GRATIANO *and* LORENZO.]

Antonio Is that anything now?

Bassanio Gratiano speaks an infinite deal of nothing, more than any man in all Venice. His reasons   115
are as two grains of wheat hid in two bushels of
chaff: you shall seek all day ere you find them,
and when you have them they are not worth the
search.

Antonio Well, tell me now what lady is the same   120
To whom you swore a secret pilgrimage,
That you today promised to tell me of.

Bassanio 'Tis not unknown to you, Antonio,
How much I have disabled mine estate
By something showing a more swelling port   125
Than my faint means would grant continuance.
Nor do I now make moan to be abridged
From such a noble rate; but my chief care
Is to come fairly off from the great debts
Wherein my time, something too prodigal,   130

98–99. *If . . . fools:* refers to Matthew 5.22, but whoso-ever shall say [to his brother] thou art a fool shall be in danger of hellfire. Gratiano means that if the reputed wise did speak, they would talk nonsense; their hearers would call them fools and risk the danger of damnation.

102. *gudgeon:* a fish.

104. *exhortation:* sermon.

108. *moe:* more.

110. *for this gear:* because of this business; that is, what you have just said.

112. *neat's:* ox's.
vendible: marketable; here, in terms of marriage.

124. *disabled:* reduced.

125. *swelling port:* lavish style of living.

127–128. *make . . . rate:* complain at having to reduce my way of living.

Hath left me gaged. To you, Antonio,
I owe the most in money and in love,
And from your love I have a warranty
To unburden all my plots and purposes
How to get clear of all the debts I owe.   135

Antonio I pray you, good Bassanio, let me know it,
And if it stand as you yourself still do,
Within the eye of honor, be assured
My purse, my person, my extremest means
Lie all unlocked to your occasions.   140

Bassanio. In my schooldays, when I had lost one
    shaft
I shot his fellow of the selfsame flight
The selfsame way, with more advised watch,
To find the other forth; and by adventuring both
I oft found both. I urge this childhood proof   145
Because what follows is pure innocence.
I owe you much, and like a willful youth
That which I owe is lost; but if you please
To shoot another arrow that self way
Which you did shoot the first, I do not doubt,   150
As I will watch the aim, or to find both
Or bring your latter hazard back again
And thankfully rest debtor for the first.

Antonio. You know me well, and herein spend but
    time
To wind about my love with circumstance;   155
And out of doubt you do me now more wrong
In making question of my uttermost
Than if you had made waste of all I have.
Then do but say to me what I should do
That in your knowledge may by me be done,   160
And I am prest unto it. Therefore speak.

Bassanio In Belmont is a lady richly left;
And she is fair, and fairer than that word,
Of wondrous virtues. Sometimes from her eyes
I did receive fair speechless messages.   165
Her name is Portia, nothing undervalued
To Cato's daughter, Brutus' Portia;
Nor is the wide world ignorant of her worth,

---

131. *gaged:* indebted.

139. *extremest means:* all my wealth.

140. *occasions:* needs.

141. *shaft:* arrow.

142. *selfsame flight:* same sort.

143. *advised:* careful.

146. *is pure innocence:* has the same childlike sincerity.

151. *or:* either.

154–155. *spend . . . circumstance:* waste time in persuading me with arguments.

157. *making . . . uttermost:* doubting that I will do all I can.

161. *prest unto it:* re0ady to do it.

162. *richly left:* has inherited wealth.

166. *nothing undervalued:* in no way inferior.

167. *Brutus' Portia:* the wife of Brutus, who conspired against Julius Caesar. Brutus' wife, Portia, was noted for her wisdom and courage.

For the four winds blow in from every coast
Renowned suitors, and her sunny locks   170
Hang on her temples like a golden fleece,
Which makes her seat of Belmont Colchos' strond,
And many Jasons come in quest of her.
O my Antonio, had I but the means
To hold a rival place with one of them,   175
I have a mind presages me such thrift
That I should questionless be fortunate!

Antonio Thou know'st that all my fortunes are
    at sea;
Neither have I money, nor commodity
To raise a present sum. Therefore go forth.   180
Try what my credit can in Venice do;
That shall be racked even to the uttermost
To furnish thee to Belmont, to fair Portia.
Go presently inquire, and so will I,
Where money is; and I no question make   185
To have it of my trust or for my sake. [*Exeunt.*]

172. *Colchos' strond:* the strand, or shore, of Colchis, where Jason sailed to find the Golden Fleece in Greek legend.

179. *commodity:* possessions.

186. *of . . . sake:* on my credit or for my friendship.

COMMENTARY

For any playwright, the beginning of a play must set the scene. For an Elizabethan playwright, setting the scene was especially important. The words "Venice, a street" at the beginning of this scene were not written by Shakespeare; they have been added by the editor of this text. Elizabethan playwrights never specified the locations of their scenes in this way, because their theatres did not use scenery; the actors simply walked onto a bare stage. Because the stage was bare, the opening scene is rich in descriptive language; the words "paint" the stage and help the audience to imagine the world in which the play is set.

Modern audiences think of Venice as a picturesque tourist destination, but Elizabethan audiences knew it as a great trading power, and that is how Shakespeare portrays the city. Salerio's speech (8–14) describes Venice as a seaport. His speech stresses the grandeur and beauty of the huge argosies as they "fly by" the smaller ships. Salerio's speech creates in the audience's minds an image of a bustling harbor filled with different types of merchant vessels. Shakespeare is ensuring that his audience not only imagines Venice as a thriving center of trade but also knows that Antonio, the controller of the argosies, is the biggest fish in the pond.

This scene reveals two things about Antonio: he is rich, and he is sad. But why is he sad? Antonio himself does not know. Shakespeare begins the play with a mystery and never solves it. But this mystery has not prevented actors and critics from trying to find causes for Antonio's sadness.

One thing we do know is that Shakespeare is highlighting the contrast between Antonio's great wealth and his great sadness. As a successful merchant, Antonio should be happy. But, as Salerio points out, wealth can bring problems with it. In Salerio's second long speech (22–40), the argosies are beached on sandbanks, and are broken apart on dangerous rocks, illustrating that wealth can vanish in a matter of seconds. For a merchant, the risky nature of his trade means that he can never stop worrying about his ships, even when he should be praying in church (29–36). Although Antonio denies that concern over his ships is the reason for his sadness, the speech reminds the audience that beneath the beauty and wealth of Venice, dangers lurk, even if Antonio refuses to acknowledge them. This acknowledgment of pending danger also helps set the scene for the events that follow.

Antonio is one of the recurring characters on the Elizabethan stage known as *melancholics*. The melancholic character was excessively serious and usually wore black clothing, because the Elizabethan stage used the color black to symbolize sadness. The most famous example of the use of black in Shakespeare's plays is in *Hamlet*, Act I, Scene 2, where Hamlet's "inky cloak" contrasts with the glamorous attire of the King and Queen's wedding feast.

Antonio's serious behavior and dark clothing are a striking visual contrast with the other characters that enter the scene at this point (Bassanio, Lorenzo, and Gra-

tiano). Like Salerio and Solanio, these characters would almost certainly have been dressed in bright, colorful clothing. The Elizabethan stage made up for its lack of scenery with spectacular costumes. The theatre companies spent most of their budgets on clothing. Sometimes they acquired castoff clothes from their aristocratic patrons. Therefore, at this point in the scene, the stage is filling with glamorous, fashionable young men.

Salerio, Solanio, Bassanio, Gratiano, and Lorenzo are what the Elizabethans would have called *gallants*. A gallant was a rich, aristocratic, unmarried man. Today we call such people "eligible bachelors." Having no occupation, gallants would occupy themselves with pleasurable activities such as drinking, dancing, and playgoing. The carefree, cheerful existence of the aristocratic bachelors is an obvious contrast with the sad sobriety of Antonio, and their attempts to cheer him up (73–101) only demonstrate this further. Gratiano is the most outrageous of the group, and his jovial banter sums up the careless attitude of these young men.

One of the possible explanations for Antonio's sadness suggested by some actors and critics is particularly important to note at this point. Notice that Salerio and Solanio are eager to leave Antonio with Bassanio (57–59). Lorenzo also recognizes that Antonio and Bassanio need to be alone together. (Gratiano, characteristically oblivious, fails to realize this.) The swift departure of the gallants suggests that there is a special friendship between Antonio and Bassanio, which the others are aware of and do not want to intrude upon. In lines 121–123, Antonio reveals that he already knows Bassanio is planning to visit a woman. Some have argued that this is the reason for Antonio's sadness: He is upset that Bassanio has transferred his affections to someone else. It must be stressed that the text never states this explicitly, but the explanation does fit in well with other events that take place later in the play. The clash between friendship and love is a theme of this play, and Antonio's sadness may be the first sign of it.

When Gratiano and Lorenzo exit, Antonio and Bassanio are left alone on stage. Bassanio has said very little until this point. Now, it becomes apparent that he is an important character in the story. When Antonio mentions "a lady" and "a secret pilgrimage," the audience is signalled that there is a romance in the offing.

A gallant, or fashionable gentleman.
Metropolitan Museum of Art, New York City/SuperStock

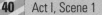

Like the other gallants, Bassanio has a way of life different from Antonio's. Bassanio does not have to work for a living. Instead, his income comes from the estate that he has inherited from his family. However, as Bassanio explains, he has "disabled" his estate by spending too much, and he cannot pay off his debts (128–131). This situation was common for young heirs to fall into in the Renaissance; when they finally inherited their wealth, they found themselves ill-equipped to appreciate the true value of money and spent it too quickly on frivolous things. Bassanio is now searching for a means by which he can regain his wealth. He explains that he has devised "plots and purposes" with which to do so, and he needs Antonio's help to achieve them (133–135).

In lines 141–153, Bassanio begins to explain what he needs from Antonio. Bassanio finds this explanation difficult, because he is in an awkward situation. He has borrowed money from Antonio in the past, and spent it all (146–147). Now he wants to borrow more. Bassanio makes this request by using a long and convoluted metaphor taken from archery. The reason behind this drawn-out manner of speaking seems to be Bassanio's embarrassment; he is hiding the awkwardness of the request beneath a metaphor.

An important question is whether Bassanio is presented by Shakespeare as an admirable character. Many productions portray him as a spoiled young fool. However, although Bassanio has made mistakes in the past, Shakespeare makes it clear that Antonio is entirely committed to helping him. Antonio is devoted to Bassanio and is prepared to open his purse to whatever Bassanio needs (138–140). Antonio's commitment to helping Bassanio seems to indicate that Bassanio should be seen as likeable, even if he has been careless with his money. And when Antonio reassures Bassanio that there is no need to "wind about my love" with arguments (154–155), Shakespeare is stressing that Antonio has no misgivings about Bassanio.

Now, Bassanio explains the route to riches that he has found. Portia, a lady in Belmont has been "richly left." Because Portia has inherited a large amount of money, she is a magnet for impoverished aristocrats. Renaissance law insisted that the husband was the ruler of the wife. Therefore, when a man married a wealthy woman, the money passed into his control. Bassanio's "plot and purpose," therefore, is to marry Portia. But of course, it will not be easy for Bassanio to orchestrate his plot and execute it successfully, because many other noblemen have had the same idea. Bassanio believes that he needs Antonio's financial support if he is to impress Portia.

Of course, this pursuit of Portia for her money sounds odd when coming from a man who is supposedly the play's romantic hero. Shakespeare makes it clear that Bassanio's desire to marry Portia *is* driven primarily by her money, because his "chief care" is to pay off his "great debts" (127–128). Although he says that Portia is beautiful, notice that Bassanio's description of her golden hair swiftly turns into a comparison to the Golden Fleece. In mythology, the Golden Fleece was a fabulous treasure. The Greek hero Jason sailed to Colchis in search of it, just as Bassanio will sail to Belmont in search of Portia's riches. However, some romance is present here, too. When Bassanio recalls that "Sometimes from her eyes / I did receive fair speechless messages" (163–164), it becomes clear that Portia is attracted to Bassanio as well. However, the audience cannot set aside the suspicion that Bassanio's attraction to Portia is somewhat less romantic.

In this opening scene, Shakespeare introduces us to the play's central plotline and to some of the themes of the play as well. Shakespeare brings Antonio and Bassanio on stage and describes Portia to us. In addition, Shakespeare signals the importance of money to the workings of the plot. And, in Antonio's enigmatic melancholy, he has given a small foreshadowing of the conflicts that arise between friendship and love.

Act I, Scene 2

Portia is besieged by suitors. Anyone who wishes to marry her must pass a test first.

ACT I, SCENE 2.
Belmont, a room in Portia's house.

[*Enter* PORTIA *with her Waiting Woman,* NERISSA.]

Portia By my troth, Nerissa, my little body is aweary of this great world.

Nerissa You would be, sweet madam, if your miseries were in the same abundance as your good fortunes are; and yet for aught I see, they are as sick that surfeit with too much as they that starve with nothing. It is no mean happiness, therefore, to be seated in the mean; superfluity comes sooner by white hairs, but competency lives longer.

Portia Good sentences, and well pronounced.

Nerissa They would be better if well followed.

Portia If to do were as easy as to know what were good to do, chapels had been churches, and poor men's cottages princes' palaces. It is a good divine that follows his own instructions; I can easier teach twenty what were good to be done than to be one of the twenty to follow mine own teaching. The brain may devise laws for the blood, but a hot temper leaps o'er a cold decree; such a hare is madness the youth to skip o'er the meshes of good counsel the cripple. But this reasoning is not in the fashion to choose me a husband. O me, the word "choose"! I may neither choose who I would nor refuse who I dislike, so is the will of a living daughter curbed by the will of a dead father. Is it not hard, Nerissa, that I cannot choose one, nor refuse none?

5

10

15

20

25

8. *seated in the mean:* with neither too much nor too little.

comes sooner by: gets sooner.

8–9. *superfluity . . . longer:* a life of excess (superfluity) brings us white hairs quickly, whereas a modest way of life (competency) helps us live longer.

14. *divine:* preacher, religious adviser.

20. *meshes:* nets.

21–22. *not . . . fashion:* not the proper manner.

24. *will:* wish

25. *will:* last will and testament.

Nerissa Your father was ever virtuous, and holy
men at their death have good inspirations. Therefore the lott'ry that he hath devised in these three   30
chests of gold, silver, and lead — whereof who chooses
his meaning chooses you — will no doubt never be
chosen by any rightly but one who you shall rightly
love. But what warmth is there in your affection
towards any of these princely suitors that are al-   35
ready come?

Portia I pray thee overname them; and as thou
namest them I will describe them, and according
to my description level at my affection.

Nerissa First, there is the Neapolitan prince.   40

Portia Ay, that's a colt indeed, for he doth nothing
but talk of his horse, and he makes it a great appropriation to his own good parts that he can shoe him
himself. I am much afeard my lady his mother
played false with a smith.   45

Nerissa Then is there the County Palatine.

Portia He doth nothing but frown — as who should
say, "An you will not have me, choose!" He hears
merry tales and smiles not; I fear he will prove the
weeping philosopher when he grows old, being so   50
full of unmannerly sadness in his youth. I had rather
be married to a death's-head with a bone in his
mouth than to either of these. God defend me from
these two!

Nerissa How say you by the French lord, Mon-   55
sieur Le Bon?

Portia God made him, and therefore let him pass
for a man. In truth, I know it is a sin to be a mocker,
but he — why he hath a horse better than the Neapolitan's, a better bad habit of frowning than the   60
Count Palatine; he is every man in no man. If a
throstle sing, he falls straight a-cap'ring; he will
fence with his own shadow. If I should marry him, I
should marry twenty husbands. If he would de-
spise me, I would forgive him; for if he love me to   65
madness, I shall never requite him.

---

32. *his meaning:* i.e., who chooses correctly.

37. *overname:* name them over.

39. *level at my affection:* try to guess where my affections lie.

42. *appropriation:* addition.

46. *the County:* the Count.

48. *choose:* i.e., have it your own way, choose someone else.

52. *death's-head:* skull.

59. *he . . . than:* i.e., he boasts his horse is better than.

62. *throstle:* thrush

64. *twenty husbands:* i.e., since his character changes so rapidly.

Nerissa What say you then to Falconbridge, the
young baron of England?

Portia You know I say nothing to him, for he
understands not me, nor I him. He hath neither   70
Latin, French, nor Italian; and you will come into
the court and swear that I have a poor pennyworth
in the English. He is a proper man's picture, but
alas! who can converse with a dumb-show? How
oddly he is suited! I think he bought his doublet   75
in Italy, his round hose in France, his bonnet in Germany, and his behavior everywhere.

Nerissa What think you of the Scottish lord, his
neighbor?

Portia That he hath a neighborly charity in him,   80
for he borrowed a box of the ear of the Englishman
and swore he would pay him again when he was
able. I think the Frenchman became his surety and
sealed under for another.

Nerissa How like you the young German, the   85
Duke of Saxony's nephew?

Portia Very vilely in the morning when he is sober,
and most vilely in the afternoon when he is drunk.
When he is best he is a little worse than a man, and
when he is worst he is little better than a beast. An   90
the worst fall that ever fell, I hope I shall make shift
to go without him.

Nerissa If he should offer to choose, and choose
the right casket, you should refuse to perform
your father's will if you should refuse to accept him. 95

Portia Therefore, for fear of the worst, I pray thee
set a deep glass of Rhenish wine on the contrary
casket, for if the devil be within and that temptation
without, I know he will choose it. I will do anything, Nerissa, ere I will be married to a sponge.   100

Nerissa You need not fear, lady, the having any of
these lords. They have acquainted me with their
determinations, which is indeed to return to their

72. *poor pennyworth:* only a small quantity.

76. *hose:* tights.

83–84. *became . . . another:* a reference to the French alliance with Scotland against England.

84. *sealed under for another:* set his seal to an agreement for another box to the ear.

91. *make shift:* be able to, manage.

97. *contrary:* the wrong casket.

home and to trouble you with no more suit, unless
you may be won by some other sort than your   105
father's imposition, depending on the caskets.

Portia If I live to be as old as Sibylla, I will die as
chaste as Diana unless I be obtained by the manner
of my father's will. I am glad this parcel of wooers
are so reasonable, for there is not one among them   110
but I dote on his very absence; and I pray God grant
them a fair departure.

Nerissa Do you not remember, lady, in your father's time, a Venetian, a scholar and a soldier, that
came hither in company of the Marquis of Mont-
ferrat?   115

Portia Yes, yes, it was Bassanio — as I think, so
was he called.

Nerissa True, madam. He, of all the men that
ever my foolish eyes looked upon, was the best   120
deserving a fair lady.

Portia I remember him well, and I remember
him worthy of thy praise.

[*Enter a* Servingman.]
How now? What news?

Servingman The four strangers seek for you,   125
madam, to take their leave; and there is a fore-
runner come from a fifth, the Prince of Morocco,
who brings word the Prince his master will be here
tonight.

Portia If I could bid the fifth welcome with so   130
good heart as I can bid the other four farewell, I
should be glad of his approach. If he have the condition of a saint and the complexion of a devil, I
had rather he should shrive me than wive me.
Come, Nerissa. Sirrah, go before. Whiles we shut   135
the gate upon one wooer, another knocks at the
door. [*Exeunt.*]

107. *Sibylla:* Apollo gave the Sibyl (or prophetess) as many years of life as she had grains of sand in her hand.

108. *Diana:* goddess of the moon, of the hunt, and the protectress of virgins.

125. *four strangers:* there were in fact six. Minor inconsistencies of this sort frequently occur in Shakespeare's plays.

133. *complexion:* black was held to be the devil's color.

134. *shrive me:* hear my confession.

COMMENTARY

Scene 2 begins in Belmont, the home of Portia. Shakespeare offers very little description of Belmont, providing no speeches like Salerio's evocation of the Venetian harbor. Instead, he focuses directly on the character of Portia.

As in Bassanio's speech about her (I.1.162–77), Portia is immediately linked to wealth. But, as Nerissa points out, Portia is living proof that people with "good fortunes" can be just as miserable as those who are starving. In Nerissa's opinion, the best way is to have a "mean" (average), amount of money, because moderation is the secret of long life.

Some people compare Portia's attitude to Antonio's in Act I, Scene 1, but Portia is not melancholy. Rather, she is weary or bored. The cause of Portia's boredom is explained in her dialogue with Nerissa.

Portia has inherited a great fortune after the death of her father. But her father's will has given her the money with a condition: She is not permitted to choose her own husband. Instead, She must marry the man who passes the test that her father has devised. Understandably, Portia herself is not pleased with this situation.

Portia's behavior comes as a surprise to the audience, which has so far only known her from Bassanio's description. In Bassanio's speech, Portia is an idealized image, like a statue on a pedestal; but now Shakespeare shows us the real woman. The most obvious characteristic that comes across from this sequence is Portia's sharp wit. Indeed, Shakespeare suggests that Portia is too intelligent for the situation that she finds herself in. Her speech in lines 12–26 creates images of constraint and its defeat by youthful passion. For the Elizabethans, blood signified passion, because it rises to your face when

An aristocratic lady.
David David Gallery, Philadelphia/ SuperStock

you blush. Portia imagines a conflict within the human mind between the brain and the blood; the brain tries to control the blood, but the blood is too powerful and "leaps over" the instructions of the brain. Similarly, Portia personifies "good counsel" (that is, good advice) as a slow-moving cripple who tries and fails to capture "youth," which is personified as a mad march hare that skips over the "traps" set by good counsel. The effect of this speech is to portray Portia as a passionate and nimble-minded young woman who is frustrated by the restrictions imposed on her, both by Nerissa and by the legacy of her father.

However, despite Portia's frustration and boredom, there seems to be nothing she can do to remedy the situation. Nerissa, in contrast, is making the best of the situation. She acts as a mother-figure to Portia, dampening down her complaints and encouraging her to be less willful.

Portia's description of her suitors is a comic set-piece. She and Nerissa operate as a double act, with Nerissa feeding the lines, and Portia using her quick wit to describe the suitors in the most unflattering light. We never see any of these suitors, but Portia's descriptions build a comic portrait of each one. For each of these portraits, Shakespeare builds on the stereotypical ideas held by Elizabethans about particular nationalities.

Neapolitans were famous for their horsemanship, and so Shakespeare portrays the Neapolitan prince as a man who talks only about horses (39–43). The County Palatine is a middle-European, who were considered to be dour and gloomy. Shakespeare exaggerates this aspect of the stereotype, so that Portia finds him less cheerful than a skull (45–51). The Frenchman is ridiculously changeable, so that Portia finds he has no true identity of his own (54–63). As for the Englishman, Portia's description of him illustrates that the stereotypical English traveler who refuses to learn the local language was alive and well in 1596 (66–74).

For Elizabethan playgoers in 1596, Scots were famous for their hatred of the English. In the wars between England and Scotland, France often sided with the Scots. Shakespeare satirizes this when Portia describes an ungentlemanly squabble between the Englishman and the Scotsman (77–81), which results in a fistfight into which the Frenchman is also drawn. This description creates the impression that the suitors are squabbling amongst themselves, adding further to Portia's disgust.

Finally, the German is a drunkard who is "little better than a beast" when he is at his worst (84–89). This parade of national stereotypes is included purely for comedy. However, although it is not relevant to the workings of this scene, you may want to compare these ridiculous stereotypes with Shakespeare's later portrayal of Shylock. Shylock's characteristics are in many ways as crude a stereotype as those of the suitors, but a comparison illustrates that Shylock is a much more complex creation. The suitors inspire nothing but contempt from the audience, whereas Shylock can generate pity despite his apparently stereotypical qualities. Shylock has many more dimensions than the caricature that he is based on.

However, that is all to come later. Portia's mind is now turning to Bassanio. Although she pretends to be diffident about him (113–114), it is clear that Nerissa's description of Bassanio as "the best deserving a fair lady" is shared by Portia. This recalls Bassanio's belief that Portia favored him (I.1.163–164). The stage is clearly set for a romance. However, the scene also demonstrates Portia's precarious situation. Nerissa wonders what Portia would do if the drunken German chose the right casket. Portia deflects the question with a joke, but the dangers inherent in the instructions of Portia's father are apparent. The question also emphasises the obsta-

A casket.

cles that Bassanio and Portia will have to overcome if they are to be married. Shakespeare stresses these impending difficulties further at the end of the scene, as a servant announces the arrival of yet another suitor, the Duke of Morocco.

The function of this scene is to give the audience an outline of the casket-test, and to depict the dangerous position of Portia, who risks being married to a husband she despises.

However, despite the fairy-tale nature of the scene, Portia is not a fairy-tale princess. She is an intelligent woman with a sharp and satirical sense of humor. She is also full of youthful passion and is bored and frustrated by the rules that govern her life. Shakespeare gives Portia these qualities because they are essential in the later scene in which she saves the day by disguising herself as a lawyer (IV.1).

Act 1, Scene 3

Antonio and Bassanio visit Shylock to arrange a loan. There is a long-standing hatred between Antonio and Shylock. Shylock agrees to the loan, but with a pound of flesh as the forfeit.

ACT I, SCENE 3.
Venice, a public place.

[*Enter* BASSANIO *with* SHYLOCK *the Jew.*]

Shylock Three thousand ducats — well.

Bassanio Ay, sir, for three months.

Shylock For three months — well.

Bassanio For the which, as I told you, Antonio
shall be bound   5

Shylock Antonio shall become bound — well.

Bassanio May you stead me? Will you pleasure
me? Shall I know your answer?

Shylock Three thousand ducats for three months,
and Antonio bound.   10

Bassanio Your answer to that.

Shylock Antonio is a good man.

Bassanio Have you heard any imputation to the
contrary?

Shylock Ho no, no, no, no! My meaning in saying   15
he is a good man is to have you understand me that
he is sufficient. Yet his means are in supposition.
He hath an argosy bound to Tripolis, another to
the Indies; I understand, moreover, upon the Rialto,
he hath a third at Mexico, a fourth for England —   20
and other ventures he hath squand'red abroad. But
ships are but boards, sailors but men; there be land
rats and water rats, water thieves and land thieves —
I mean pirates; and then there is the peril of waters,
winds, and rocks. The man is, notwithstanding,   25
sufficient. Three thousand ducats — I think I may
take his bond.

NOTES

1.　　*ducats:* Italian gold coins.

5.　　*bound:* held responsible for repayment of the loan.

7.　　*stead:* accommodate.

17.　　*sufficient:* financially secure.

　　　in supposition: now engaged, in hazard, uncertain.

19.　　*the Rialto:* the exchange in Venice where business was transacted.

Bassanio Be assured you may.

Shylock I will be assurred I may; and that I may
be assured, I will bethink me. May I speak with   30
Antonio?

Bassanio If it please you to dine with us.

Shylock Yes, to smell pork, to eat of the habitation
which your prophet the Nazarite conjured the devil
into! I will buy with you, sell with you, talk with   35
you, walk with you, and so following; but I will not
eat with you, drink with you, nor pray with you.
What news on the Rialto? Who is he comes here?

[*Enter* ANTONIO.]

Bassanio This is Signior Antonio.

Shylock [*aside*] How like a fawning publican he   40
    looks.
I hate him for he is a Christian;
But more, for that in low simplicity
He lends out money gratis and brings down
The rate of usance here with us in Venice.
If I can catch him once upon the hip,   45
I will feed fat the ancient grudge I bear him.
He hates our sacred nation, and he rails,
Even there where merchants most do congregate,
On me, my bargains, and my well-won thrift,
Which he calls interest. Cursed be my tribe   50
If I forgive him.

Bassanio   Shylock, do you hear?

Shylock I am debating of my present store,
And by the near guess of my memory
I cannot instantly raise up the gross
Of full three thousand ducats. What of that?   55
Tubal, a wealthy Hebrew of my tribe,
Will furnish me. But soft, how many months
Do you desire? [*to* ANTONIO] Rest you fair, good
    signior!
Your worship was the last man in our mouths.

34.   *Nazarite . . . devil:* Shylock refers to Matthew 8: 30–32, in which Christ exorcises two devils and casts them into a herd of swine.

40.   *publican:* the word sometimes means innkeeper, but here the reference is to those Jews who collected taxes for the Roman governor. Shylock is saying that Antonio is behaving like a man come to ask for money.

42.   *low simplicity:* humble foolishness.

44.   *usance:* interest on a loan.

45.   *upon the hip:* at a disadvantage; the term is from wrestling.

59.   *last . . . mouths:* i.e.. we were just speaking of you; ironic flattery.

Antonio Shylock, albeit I neither lend nor borrow   60
  By taking nor by giving of excess,
  Yet to supply the ripe wants of my friend,
  I'll break a custom. [*to* BASSANIO] Is he yet pos-
    sessed
  How much ye would?

Shylock   Ay, ay, three thousand ducats.

Antonio And for three months.   65

Shylock I had forgot — three months, you told
  me so.
  Well then, your bond. And let me see — but hear
  you,
  Methoughts you said you neither lend nor borrow
  Upon advantage.

Antonio   I do never use it.

Shylock When Jacob grazed his uncle Laban's   70
    sheep —
  This Jacob from our holy Abram was,
  As his wise mother wrought in his behalf,
  The third possessor; ay, he was the third —

Antonio And what of him? Did he take interest?

Shylock No, not take interest — not as you would   75
    say
  Directly int'rest. Mark what Jacob did:
  When Laban and himself were compromised
  That all the eanlings which were streaked and pied
  Should fall as Jacob's hire, the ewes being rank
  In end of autumn turned to the rams;   80
  And when the work of generation was
  Between these wooly breeders in the act,
  The skillful shepherd peeled me certain wands,
  And in the doing of the deed of kind
  He stuck them up before the fulsome ewes,   85
  Who then conceiving, did in eaning time
  Fall parti-colored lambs, and those were Jacob's.
  This was a way to thrive, and he was blest;
  And thrift is blessing if men steal it not.

61. *excess:* interest.

70. *Jacob . . . sheep:* see Genesis 27, 30: 25–43.

77. *compromised:* agreed.

78. *eanlings:* lambs.

79. *rank:* in heat.

81. *work of generation:* i.e., the producing of future generations.

83. *peeled me:* peeled (the addition of *me* is a common Elizabethan form).

    wands: branches.

84. *in the doing of the deed of kind:* i.e. while the sheep were mating.

85. *fulsome:* fat.

86. *eaning:* lambing.

89. *And . . . not:* i.e., Jacob made a profit by his skill in sheep-breeding, and all such profit is blessed, so long as it does not involve theft.

Antonio This was a venture, sir, that Jacob served   90
     for,
A thing not in his power to bring to pass,
But swayed and fashioned by the hand of heaven.
Was this inserted to make interest good?
Or is your gold and silver ewes and rams?

Shylock I cannot tell; I make it breed as fast.   95
But note me, signior —

Antonio   Mark you this, Bassanio,
The devil can cite Scripture for his purpose.
An evil soul producing holy witness
Is like a villain with a smiling cheek,
A goodly apple rotten at the heart.   100
O what a goodly outside falsehood hath!

Shylock Three thousand ducats — 'tis a good
     round sum.
Three months from twelve — then let me see, the
rate —

Antonio Well, Shylock, shall we be beholding to
     you?

Shylock Signior Antonio, many a time and oft   105
In the Rialto you have rated me
About my moneys and my usances.
Still have I borne it with a patient shrug,
For suff'rance is the badge of all our tribe.
You call me misbeliever, cutthroat dog,   110
And spit upon my Jewish gaberdine,
And all for use of that which is mine own.
Well then, it now appears you need my help.
Go to then. You come to me and you say,
"Shylock, we would have moneys" — you say so,   115
You that did void your rheum upon my beard
And foot me as you spurn a stranger cur
Over your threshold! Moneys is your suit.
What should I say to you? Should I not say,
"Hath a dog money? is it possible   120
A cur can lend three thousand ducats?" Or
Shall I bend low, and in a bondman's key,
With bated breath and whisp'ring humbleness,
Say this:

93. *Was . . . good?:* Antonio rejects the analogy between sheep-breeding and the charging of interest.

104. *beholding:* indebted.

106. *rated:* berated, sharply criticized.

109. *suff'rance:* patient suffering.

111. *gaberdine:* long cloak, often associated with stage Jews.

116. *void your rheum:* spit.

122. *bondman's:* slave's.

"Fair sir, you spit on me on Wednesday last,   125
You spurned me such a day, another time
You called me dog; and for these courtesies
I'll lend you thus much moneys"?

Antonio I am as like to call thee so again,
To spit on thee again, to spurn thee too.   130
If thou wilt lend this money, lend it not
As to thy friends — for when did friendship take
A breed for barren metal of his friend? —
But lend it rather to thine enemy,
Who if he break, thou mayst with better face   135
Exact the penalty.

Shylock   Why look you, how you storm!
I would be friends with you and have your love,
Forget the shames that you have stained me with,
Supply your present wants, and take no doit
Of usance for my moneys; and you'll not hear me.   140
This is kind I offer.

Bassanio This were kindness.

Shylock   This kindness will I show:
Go with me to a notary; seal me there
Your single bond, and — in a merry sport —
If you repay me not on such a day,   145
In such a place, such sum or sums as are
Expressed in the condition, let the forfeit
Be nominated for an equal pound
Of your fair flesh, to be cut off and taken
In what part of your body pleaseth me.   150

Antonio Content, in faith. I'll seal to such a bond,
And say there is much kindness in the Jew.

Bassanio You shall not seal to such a bond for me!
I'll rather dwell in my necessity.

Antonio Why fear not, man; I will not forfeit it.   155
Within these two months — that's a month before
This bond expires — I do expect return
Of thrice three times the value of this bond.

Shylock O father Abram, what these Christians
        are,
Whose own hard dealings teaches them suspect   160

133. *breed:* interest, the product of metal or gold. Those opposed to usury often argued that interest was unnatural because it involves the "breeding" of metal, which is not alive and therefore should not reproduce itself.

135. *break:* i.e., this promise to pay, go bankrupt.

139. *doit:* cheap Dutch coin.

143. *seal:* set a seal on, agree to.
144. *single:* with no other security.

148. *nominated:* named.

The thoughts of others! Pray you tell me this:
If he should break his day, what should I gain
By the exaction of the forfeiture?
A pound of man's flesh taken from a man
Is not so estimable, profitable neither,   165
As flesh of muttons, beefs, or goats. I say
To buy his favor I extend this friendship.
If he will take it, so; if not, adieu.
And for my love I pray you wrong me not.

Antonio Yes, Shylock, I will seal unto this bond.   170

Shylock Then meet me forthwith at the notary's;
Give him direction for this merry bond,
And I will go and purse the ducats straight,
See to my house, left in the fearful guard
Of an unthrifty knave, and presently   175
I'll be with you. [*Exit.*]

Antonio   Hie thee, gentle Jew.
The Hebrew will turn Christian; he grows kind.

Bassanio I like not fair terms and a villain's mind.

Antonio Come on. In this there can be no dismay;
My ships come home a month before the day.   180
[*Exeunt.*]

162.   *break his day:* fail to pay on the prescribed day.

174.   *fearful:* untrustworthy.

176.   *gentle:* here and elsewhere in the play this word is used with a pun on gentile.

COMMENTARY

We now return to Venice. Bassanio is attempting to secure a loan for the money he needs, using Antonio's good reputation as credit. He has therefore come to see Shylock, the usurer. Usurers were the Renaissance equivalent of today's loan sharks. They lent money to people but demanded a high rate of interest on its repayment and extracted harsh forfeits if the payment was not received on time. Usurers were a despised but necessary feature of every Renaissance city.

In this scene, Shakespeare introduces Shylock, who invariably makes a strong impression on his first entrance. In the original staging, he probably wore the traditional costume of a stage Jew: a gaberdine (long cloak) and perhaps a red wig. In *The Jew of Malta*, a play whose Jewish villain was probably the inspiration for Shylock (see Introduction), the actor who played the Jew even wore a false nose, but there is no evidence that Shylock did.

Understandably, modern productions reject this stereotype, but that does not mean that Shylock's entrance is no longer powerful. An actor can still create a powerful stage presence when portraying Shylock, because of the language that Shakespeare gives to the character. In Shylock's first three lines (1, 3, 6), he is simply repeating Bassanio's words and adding a thoughtful "well" to the end of them. The effect is sinister. Shylock is making Bassanio uncomfortable, by pretending to be undecided about the loan. In the longer speech (15–26), Shylock deliberately unsettles Bassanio by reminding him that even wealthy men can be ruined by pirates and shipwrecks.

The Rialto, where Venetian merchants traded.

Why does Shylock do this? Quite simply, he is enjoying his position of power. Bassanio and Antonio are relying on him to provide them with money, and Shylock knows that no matter how rude he is, they will still need him. Bassanio generously offers to invite Shylock to dinner, but Shylock spurns the invitation rudely, saying that, as a Jew, he finds Christian mannerisms repugnant (31–36). Again, Shylock relishes the opportunity to make a Christian feel uncomfortable.

At this point, Antonio enters, and Shylock begins a long *aside* (a speech delivered directly to the audience). Asides were a common convention of the Elizabethan theatre. In this instance, the aside has the effect of making the audience feel that the villain is trusting them with his secrets. . This speech ("I hate him for he is a Christian. . . .") is often cut in modern productions that want to make Shylock immediately sympathetic. Some present-day directors find the blunt hatred in the speech too much like a stereotypical Jewish villain. But although Shylock is certainly a caricature at this point, he does not remain that way throughout the play. Indeed, a comparison of this speech with lines 104–112 illustrates that religious hatred is a characteristic of both Shylock and Antonio.

Even so, Shylock's speech is ominous and reveals him to be a dangerous man with an "ancient grudge" against Antonio. When Shylock breaks off his aside, he continues to gloat over his new customers. The hatred between Antonio and Shylock exists for two reasons. The first is that Antonio disapproves of usury on principle and often lends money to people without charging interest (41–42, 58–59). The second reason is the religious differences between Antonio and Shylock. But the two reasons are linked. Antonio disapproves of usury because the Christian faith forbade it, whereas the Jewish faith did not.

However, Antonio has now sacrificed his moral principles and has come to borrow money, which is why Shylock is enjoying the situation so much. He asks in mock-surprise, "Methought you said you neither lend nor borrow / Upon advantage?" (67–68). Antonio responds with curt sentences, trying not to show his annoyance. He is clearly embarrassed, but he needs the money to help Bassanio.

Shylock's long speech about Laban, Jacob, and the sheep is an attempt at using Biblical scripture to defend usury. The language is difficult, and reading Genesis 30:25–43 helps to clarify it. Shylock uses Jacob's cunning method of gaining Laban's sheep as an analogy of the way he can make money "breed" (94). But Antonio (like many playgoers) is baffled by the story's relevance to the matter at hand (89–93), and Shylock's sardonic reply suggests that he told the story merely in order to irritate Antonio by continuing to prevaricate.

So far, there has been little to make us disagree with Antonio's angry description of Shylock: "the devil can cite Scripture for his purpose" (96). But at this point, Shakespeare complicates the presentation of Shylock by telling us about his suffering.

Shylock describes the way he and all his "tribe" are treated by the Christians. He is abused, disdained, spat on, and even kicked (104–111, 115–117). Of course, the original London audience would not necessarily have been sympathetic. Some of them may well have behaved toward Jews in the same way that Antonio does. But this speech has the important effect of giving Shylock a *reason* for his hatred. He is no longer a caricatured comic villain who is evil just for the sake of being evil. He is now revealed to be a man whose evil has been generated by

A gaberdine, or long overcoat.

the continuous hatred that has been directed toward him. He is making Antonio and Bassanio suffer as revenge for the suffering inflicted on him in the past.

Because he has been abused in the past, Shylock is delighted that he has the opportunity to belittle Antonio. He now has the chance to accuse Antonio of being a hypocrite and does so in lines 113–127. Shylock performs an impersonation of the way that he thinks Antonio wants to see him, whispering and cringing like a humble slave (121–122). But the boot is now on the other foot, and Shylock revels in the situation.

Antonio's response is to cite the conventional Renaissance argument against usury: Making money "breed" is unnatural. Metal is a lifeless, "barren" material, and to make it procreate is a perversion of nature. Of course, Antonio is being hypocritical, because he has come to a usurer with the very purpose of borrowing money. But he has found a way to justify this. He tells Shylock that the real sin of usury is lending money to your friends, and then asking them to pay interest. Antonio finds this a despicable way to treat one's friends. But he argues further that to do the same thing to one's enemies is perfectly justifiable. If Shylock lends money to Antonio, he will not have to feel any guilt if he needs to extract the penalty, because Antonio is his enemy.

Antonio's complicated justification has the unexpected effect of forming an idea in Shylock's mind. Shylock decides that they will be "friends" after all, and that he'll lend them the money without any interest. But there is a catch. If Antonio fails to repay the loan on the correct day, Shylock will be permitted to cut a pound of flesh from his body.

Some people say it is ridiculous that Antonio agrees to the bond of a pound of flesh. But we must remember that Antonio does not think he will ever have to pay it. He explains to Bassanio that he is expecting a large amount of money to come in, long before the deadline for repayment (155–158). Antonio has been confident and sure of himself throughout this scene; when he fearlessly agrees to Shylock's terms, he is asserting himself and refusing to be intimidated.

Shylock also knows that Antonio is wealthy and cannot foresee the ensuing shipwrecks. He may *hope* that Antonio will fail to repay the debt, but he has no reason for expecting such a thing. Shylock describes the agreement as "this merry bond" and both he and Antonio clearly find it amusing (172, 176). The scene ends with Antonio's confident claim, "My ships come home a month before the day" (180). But this final line is ominous. Shakespeare continually reminds us of the sudden dangers that can befall shipping (I.1.22–40, I.3.21–6), and it is obvious to the audience that something similar will happen to Antonio.

In this scene, Shakespeare introduces the character of Shylock and sets in place a chain of events that will result in the trial scene (IV.1). Shylock is characterized as a man full of resentment at the Christians who have oppressed him, whereas Antonio is portrayed as an idealistic but arrogant and hypocritical merchant. It is difficult to say how the Elizabethan audience would have felt toward Shylock. One thing is certain, though: they would have *enjoyed* him. Shylock is an entertaining character, from the minute he walks onto the stage. His unusual speech patterns and cheerful malice make him fascinating to watch and listen to. He is a comic villain — but he has depth and complexity, much more so than the two Christians who share the stage with him.

Notes

THE MERCHANT OF VENICE

ACT II

Morocco *This first, of gold, who this inscription bears,*
"Who chooseth me shal gain what many men desire";
The second, silver, which this promise carries,
"Who chooseth me shall get as much as he deserves";
This third, dull lead, with earning all as blunt, "Who
chooseth me must give and hazard all he hath."
How shall I know if I do choose the right?

Act II, Scene 1

The Prince of Morocco arrives at Portia's house. He intends to try the test to win her hand in marriage.

ACT II, SCENE 1.
A room in Portia's house.

[*Flourish of cornets. Enter the* PRINCE OF MOROCCO, *a tawny Moor all in white, and three or four Followers accordingly, with* PORTIA, NERISSA, *and their Train.*]

Morocco Mislike me not for my complexion,
The shadowed livery of the burnished sun,
To whom I am a neighbor and near bred.
Bring me the fairest creature northward born,
Where Phoebus' fire scarce thaws the icicles,   5
And let us make incision for your love
To prove whose blood is reddest, his or mine.
I tell thee, lady, this aspect of mine
Hath feared the valiant. By my love I swear
The best-regarded virgins of our clime   10
Have loved it too. I would not change this hue,
Except to steal your thoughts, my gentle queen.

Portia In terms of choice I am not solely led
By nice direction of a maiden's eyes.
Besides, the lott'ry of my destiny   15
Bars me the right of voluntary choosing.
But if my father had not scanted me,
And hedged me by his wit to yield myself
His wife who wins me by that means I told you,
Yourself, renowned Prince, then stood as fair   20
As any comer I have looked on yet
For my affection.

Morocco   Even for that I thank you.
Therefore I pray you lead me to the caskets
To try my fortune. By this scimitar,

NOTES

2. *shadowed . . . sun:* the uniform of subjects of the sun, i.e., dark skin.

5. *Phoebus':* the sun's.

6. *make incision:* cut our flesh.

8. *aspect:* appearance.

9. *feared:* frightened.

12. *steal your thoughts:* i.e., take possession of your affection.

14. *nice direction:* fastidious guidance.

17. *scanted:* limited.

That slew the Sophy and a Persian prince   25
That won three fields of Sultan Solyman,
I would o'erstare the sternest eyes that look,
Outbrave the heart most daring on the earth,
Pluck the young sucking cubs from the she-bear,
Yea, mock the lion when 'a roars for prey,   30
To win thee, lady. But alas the while,
If Hercules and Lichas play at dice
Which is the better man, the greater throw
May turn by fortune from the weaker hand.
So is Alcides beaten by his rogue,   35
And so may I, blind Fortune leading me,
Miss that which one unworthier may attain,
And die with grieving.

Portia You must take your chance,
And either not attempt to choose at all
Or swear before you choose, if you choose wrong   40
Never to speak to lady afterward
In way of marriage. Therefore be advised.

Morocco Nor will not. Come, bring me unto my
chance.

Portia First, forward to the temple; after dinner
Your hazard shall be made.   45

Morocco   Good fortune then,
To make me blest or cursed'st among men!

[*Flourish of cornets. Exeunt.*]

25. *the Sophy:* the Shah of Persia.

26. *Solyman:* Suleiman the Magnificent, Sultan of Turkey, who was continuously at war with the Persians.

32. *Hercules and Lichas:* Hercules, the heroic strongman of classical legend, and Lichas, his servant.

35. *Alcides:* Greek name for Hercules

rogue: servant.

43. *Nor will not:* nor will I.

44. *to the temple:* i.e., to swear an oath to abide by the conditions of the choice.

COMMENTARY

The printed text rarely does justice to the visual effect of a play. Here, a sumptuous stage picture is created as the Prince of Morocco and his train enter, dressed in their exotic finery. Morocco is a "tawny Moor," which means that he is a North African Muslim. The Elizabethan attitude toward Muslims was very different from that toward Jews; they did not despise Muslims. The Moors were rulers of vast trading empires and were highly regarded for their nobility and power. Even so, the Elizabethans often made disparaging remarks about their skin color, and many would have found the notion of an interracial marriage shocking. Shakespeare dramatized these issues in his play *Othello*, which is also set in Venice and has a Moor as its hero.

A scimitar.

Morocco expects Portia to "mislike" him for his "complexion." But his opening speech introduces the notion that all men are alike under the skin (1–12). This idea becomes important later in the play, when Shylock makes his plea for humanity (III.1.58–73). Like Shylock, Morocco is proud of his background and considers himself to be as "red-blooded" (virile) as any other man—white or black.

In his second speech, Morocco begins to sound more pompous, as he makes grand claims about his bravery and his prowess in battle. Some actors play Morocco as a ridiculous figure who waves his scimitar about and roars his lines. But in fact, Shakespeare portrays Morocco quite sympathetically. He is nothing like the foolish suitors described by Portia earlier (I.2). For example, in lines 31–38 he demonstrates humility; he recognizes that his military prowess will be of no assistance in choosing the correct casket and that the test is a "leveling device." He uses the analogy of Hercules being beaten at dice by his servant in order to show that the casket test makes everybody equal.

Of course, we know that Morocco will not pass the test. This is a story with a fairy-tale plot, and it is obvious that Bassanio must be the winner. But that doesn't spoil the play. It simply means that when Morocco takes the test, the audience will be looking to see *why* he fails, rather than *whether* he fails.

Act II, Scene 2

Shylock's servant, Launcelot, feels guilty because he has decided to desert his master. He meets his father and plays a joke on him. Then he successfully begs Bassanio to employ him.

ACT II, SCENE 2.
Venice. A street.

[*Enter* LAUNCELOT GOBBO, *the Clown, alone.*]

Launcelot Certainly my conscience will serve me
to run from this Jew my master. The fiend is at
mine elbow and tempts me, saying to me, "Gobbo,
Launcelot Gobbo, good Launcelot," or "good Gobbo" or "good Launcelot Gobbo—use your legs, take   5
the start, run away." My conscience says, "No. Take
heed, honest Launcelot; take heed, honest Gobbo,"
or as aforesaid, "honest Launcelot Gobbo—do not
run; scorn running with thy heels." Well, the most
courageous fiend bids me pack. "Fia!" says the   10
fiend; "away!" says the fiend. "For the heavens,
rouse up a brave mind," says the fiend, "and run."
Well, my conscience hanging about the neck of my
heart says very wisely to me, "My honest friend
Launcelot, being an honest man's son"—or rather   15
"an honest woman's son," for indeed my father did
something smack, something grow to; he had a kind
of taste—Well, my conscience says, "Launcelot,
budge not." "Budge," says the fiend. "Budge not,"
says my conscience. "Conscience," say I, "You coun-   20
sel well." "Fiend," say I, "you counsel well." To be
ruled by my conscience, I should stay with the Jew
my master who, God bless the mark, is a kind of
devil; and to run away from the Jew, I should be
ruled by the fiend who, saving your reverence, is the   25
devil himself. Certainly the Jew is the very devil in-
carnation; and in my conscience, my conscience is
but a kind of hard conscience to offer to counsel me
to stay with the Jew. The fiend gives the more
friendly counsel. I will run, fiend; my heels are at   30
your commandment; I will run.

[*Enter* OLD GOBBO *with a basket.*]

NOTES

10. *Fia:* Forward! (from the Italian via.)

17. *smack . . . to:* have a taste for; here Launcelot implies that his father's tastes were not entirely honest.

23–25. *God . . . reverence:* conventional phrases of apology used when the devil was mentioned.

Gobbo Master young man, you, I pray you, which
is the way to Master Jew's?

Launcelot [*aside*] O heavens, this is my true-be-
gotten father who, being more than sand-blind,
high-gravel-blind, knows me not. I will try confusions with him.

Gobbo Master young gentleman, I pray you, which
is the way to Master Jew's?

Launcelot Turn up on your right hand at the next
turning, but at the next turning of all, on your left;
marry, at the very next turning turn of no hand, but
turn down indirectly to the Jew's house.

Gobbo Be God's sonties, 'twill be a hard way to
hit! Can you tell me whether one Launcelot that
dwells with him, dwell with him or no?

Launcelot Talk you of young Master Launcelot?
[*aside*] Mark me now; now will I raise the waters.—Talk you of young Master Launcelot?

Gobbo No master, sir, but a poor man's son. His
father, though I say't, is an honest exceeding poor
man and, God be thanked, well to live.

Launcelot Well, let his father be what 'a will, we
talk of young Master Launcelot.

Gobbo Your worship's friend, and Launcelot, sir.

Launcelot But I pray you, ergo old man, ergo I beseech you, talk you of young Master Launcelot?

Gobbo Of Launcelot, an't please your mastership.

Launcelot Ergo, Master Launcelot. Talk not of
Master Launcelot, father, for the young gentleman,
according to Fates and Destinies and such odd say-
ings, the Sisters Three and such branches of learning, is indeed deceased, or as you would say in
plain terms, gone to heaven.

Gobbo Marry, God forbid! The boy was the very
staff of my age, my very prop.

Launcelot Do I look like a cudgel or a hovel-post,
a staff or a prop? Do you know me, father?

35

40

45

50

55

60

65

35. *sand-blind:* nearly blind, and and therefore
high-gravel-blind is almost completely blind.

44. *sonties:* saints.

48. *raise the waters:* stir things up, or possibly raise fears.

52. *well to live:* well and alive.

56. *ergo:* Latin for "therefore."

62. *Sisters Three:* the three Fates.

Gobbo Alack the day, I know you not, young gentleman! but I pray you tell me, is my boy, God rest   70
his soul, alive or dead?

Launcelot Do you not know me, father?

Gobbo Alack, sir, I am sand-blind! I know you not.

Launcelot Nay, indeed if you had your eyes you
might fail of the knowing me; it is a wise father that   75
knows his own child. Well, old man, I will tell you
news of your son. [*Kneels.*] Give me your blessing.
Truth will come to light; murder cannot be hid
long — a man's son may, but in the end truth will
out.   80

Gobbo Pray you, sir, stand up. I am sure you
are not Launcelot my boy.

Launcelot Pray you let's have no more fooling
about it, but give me your blessing. I am Launcelot — your boy that was, your son that is, your   85
child that shall be.

Gobbo I cannot think you are my son.

Launcelot I know not what I shall think of that;
but I am Launcelot, the Jew's man, and I am sure
Margery your wife is my mother.   90

Gobbo Her name is Margery indeed! I'll be
sworn, if thou be Launcelot thou art mine own flesh
and blood. Lord worshiped might he be, what a
beard hast thou got! Thou hast got more hair on
thy chin than Dobbin my fill-horse has on his tail.   95

Launcelot [*rises*] It should seem then that Dobbin's tail grows backward. I am sure he had more
hair of his tail than I have of my face when I last
saw him.

Gobbo Lord, how art thou changed! How dost   100
thou and thy master agree? I have brought him a
present. How 'gree you now?

Launcelot Well, well; but for mine own part, as I
have set up my rest to run away, so I will not rest till
I have run some ground. My master's a very Jew.   105
Give him a present? Give him a halter! I am fam-

93–94. *what a beard:* in most productions the old man's
hand is on the top of Launcelot's head.

95. *fill-horse:* cart horse.

104. *set up my rest:* determined, prepared. The term is
from archery and is used here to make the word play
with rest and run.

ished in his service; you may tell every finger I have
with my ribs. Father, I am glad you are come.
Give me your present to one Master Bassanio, who
indeed gives rare new liveries. If I serve not him,   110
I will run as far as God has any ground. O rare fortune, here comes the man! To him, father, for I am
a Jew if I serve the Jew any longer.

[*Enter* BASSANIO, *with* LEONARDO *and a Follower or two.*]

Bassanio You may do so, but let it be so hasted
that supper be ready at the farthest by five of the   115
clock. See these letters delivered, put the liveries
to making, and desire Gratiano to come anon to my
lodging. [*Exit one of his Men.*]

Launcelot To him, father!

Gobbo God bless your worship!   120

Bassanio Gramercy. Wouldst thou aught with me?

Gobbo Here's my son, sir, a poor boy—

Launcelot Not a poor boy, sir, but the rich Jew's
man that would, sir, as my father shall specify—

Gobbo He hath a great infection, sir, as one would   125
say, to serve—

Launcelot Indeed, the short and the long is, I serve
the Jew, and have a desire, as my father shall
specify—

Gobbo His master and he, saving your worship's   130
reverence, are scarce cater-cousins.

Launcelot To be brief, the very truth is that the
Jew having done me wrong doth cause me, as my
father, being I hope an old man, shall frutify unto
you—   135

Gobbo I have here a dish of doves that I would be-
stow upon your worship, and my suit is—
Launcelot. In very brief, the suit is impertinent to
myself, as your worship shall know by this honest
old man, and though I say it, though old man, yet   140
poor man, my father.

Bassanio One speak for both. What would you?

---

110. *liveries:* servants' uniforms.

117. *anon:* at once.

121. *Gramercy:* many thanks.

125. *infection:* a mistake for affection; Shakespeare gives his clowns a great many of these verbal blunders.

131. *cater-cousins:* close friends.

134. *frutify:* a mistake. probably for notify.

138. *impertinent:* a mistake for pertinent.

Launcelot Serve you, sir.

Gobbo That is the very defect of the matter, sir.

Bassanio I know thee well; thou has obtained thy   145
   suit.
Shylock thy master spoke with me this day,
And bath preferred thee, if it be preferment
To leave a rich Jew's service to become
The follower of so poor a gentleman.

Launcelot The old proverb is very well parted be-   150
tween my master Shylock and you, sir. You have the
grace of God, sir, and he hath enough.

Bassanio Thou speak'st it well. Go, father, with
   thy son;
Take leave of thy old master and inquire
My lodging out. [*to a Servant*] Give him a livery   155
More guarded than his fellows'. See it done.

Launcelot Father, in. I cannot get a service; no!
I have ne'er a tongue in my head; well! [*Looks at
his palm.*] If any man in Italy have a fairer table
which doth offer to swear upon a book— I shall   160
have good fortune! Go to, here's a simple line of
life. Here's a small trifle of wives! Alas, fifteen
wives is nothing; eleven widows and nine
maids is a simple coming-in for one man. And
then to scape drowning thrice, and to be in peril   165
of my life with the edge of a feather-bed! Here are
simple scapes. Well, if Fortune be a woman, she's
a good wench for this gear. Father, come. I'll take
my leave of the Jew in the twinkling.

[*Exit* LAUNCELOT, *with* OLD GOBBO.]

Bassanio I pray thee, good Leonardo, think on   170
   this:
These things being bought and orderly bestowed,
Return in haste, for I do feast tonight
My best-esteemed acquaintance. Hie thee, go.

Leonardo My best endeavors shall be done herein.

[*Enter* GRATIANO.]

Gratiano Where's your master?   175

---

144. *defect:* a mistake for effect.

147. *preferred:* recommended.

150. *The old proverb:* i.e., He who has the grace of God hath enough.

    parted: shared.

156. *guarded:* braided.

159. *fable:* palm of the hand.

166. *feather-bed:* i.e.. marriage.

167. *scapes:* escapes.

Leonardo   Yonder, sir, he walks. [*Exit.*]

Gratiano Signior Bassanio!

Bassanio Gratiano!

Gratiano I have suit to you.

Bassiano   You have obtained it.

Gratiano You must not deny me. I must go with
    you to Belmont.

Bassanio Why then you must. But hear thee,   180
    Gratiano:
Thou art too wild, too rude, and bold of voice—
Parts that become thee happily enough
And in such eyes as ours appear not faults;
But where thou art not known, why there they show
Something too liberal. Pray thee take pain   185
To allay with some cold drops of modesty
Thy skipping spirit, lest through thy wild behavior
I be misconst'red in the place I go to,
And lose my hopes.

Gratiano   Signior Bassanio, hear me:
If I do not put on a sober habit,   190
Talk with respect, and swear but now and then,
Wear prayer books in my pocket, look demurely —
Nay more, while grace is saying hood mine eyes
Thus with my hat, and sigh and say amen,
Use all the observance of civility   195
Like one well studied in a sad ostent
To please his grandam—never trust me more.

Bassanio Well, we shall see your bearing.

Gratiano Nay, but I bar tonight. You shall not
    gauge me
By what we do tonight.   200

Bassanio   No, that were pity.
I would entreat you rather to put on
Your boldest suit of mirth, for we have friends
That purpose merriment. But fare you well;
I have some business.

Gratiano And I must to Lorenzo and the rest,   205
But we will visit you at supper time. [*Exeunt.*]

---

182. *parts:* qualities.

188. *misconst'red:* misconstrued.

196. *sad ostent:* grave appearance.

199. *gauge:* judge.

COMMENTARY

Here we encounter Launcelot Gobbo, the clown. Originally, this role would have been performed by Will Kemp, who was the clown of Shakespeare's acting company. Each Elizabethan acting company employed a professional clown, whose job it was to supply slapstick comedy and bawdy humour. The clowns were extremely popular with Elizabethan audiences, and the playwrights had a duty to write them into each of their plays. A talented clown such as Kemp, could be funny with even the most unpromising material. Indeed, it was said that the best clowns could make the audience laugh when they were only glimpsed through a curtain.

Modern productions of *The Merchant of Venice* often remove Launcelot because they feel that his raucous comedy can spoil the seriousness of the play. However, we must remember that Elizabethan drama was not afraid to combine beautiful, polished verse with crude and bawdy prose. To understand why, we need to look at the type of humor the clown uses.

In this play, the clown is Shylock's servant. However, he wants to run away from his master. He gives no reason, except that "my master's a very Jew" (100). Launcelot associates Jews with the Devil (22–24, 24–27), and has therefore decided to leave Shylock's service. But his conscience tells him that he shouldn't leave, because it would be unlawful for a servant to run away from his master. Launcelot, torn by indecision, imagines two allegorical figures, Fiend and Conscience, pulling him this way and that. Fiend is telling him to leave his master, but Conscience is telling him to do the lawful thing and stay. This speech is a great opportunity for a comic actor to strut his stuff. Launcelot imitates the voices of both figures and probably imitates their gestures as well; a saintly posture for Conscience and a scary, demonic posture for Fiend.

Launcelot knows that he should follow Conscience. But he doesn't want to, so he finds a flaw in Conscience's reasoning: If Jews are associated with the Devil, then Conscience is wrong to tell Launcelot to work for a devil. Launcelot concludes, "the Fiend gives the more friendly counsel" and prepares to run off.

Elizabethan clowns use a wicked form of humor, which often pokes fun at the rigidity of moral structures. Here, Launcelot succeeds in finding a loophole to avoid behaving in a moral way. His conscience has been pricking him because he knows that Shylock has certain rights. But, by redefining Shylock as a "devil," he can argue that the legal rules do not apply—in other words, that Fiend is in the right. Launcelot cheerfully rearranges the law to suit what he wants to do and goes on his way. This part of the scene may not seem relevant to the rest of the story, but consider Portia's legal tactic at IV.1.345–362. She redefines Shylock as an "alien," so that the state can legally claim half his property. In both instances, Christians use Shylock's status as a second-class citizen to defeat him.

The comedy continues as Launcelot teases Old Gobbo, his blind father. Note the asides to the audience (32–35, 46). In these asides, the clown tells the audience that he is about to play a trick on his father. The aside has two effects. First, it raises a sense of anticipation, as the audience looks forward to the laughs that the tricks will generate. Second, it makes the audience *like* Launcelot. The clown is drawing the audience into a conspiracy of laughter, in which actor and audience all laugh together at the foolish old man. This technique builds a feeling of togetherness between the actor and the audience because it blurs the distinction between the "real world" and the "stage world."

This effect can also be seen in I.3.38–49, in which Shylock describes his hatred of Antonio. Like Launcelot, Shylock shares his feelings with the audience, and the audience anticipates Antonio's downfall. Of course, the audience does not expect a humorous response from it; but it still looks forward to some thrilling entertainment. In that sense, Shylock's aside has the effect of making the audience *enjoy* him, even it they doesn't necessarily *like* him.

Old Gobbo is trying to find his son. But he is "sand-blind" (that is, he has very poor vision) and does not realize that Launcelot is the very man that he is talking to. This situation has plenty of comic potential, and Shakespeare exploits it fully. Much of it is physical humor and requires some explanation.

Will Kemp was a fat man. This is why Launcelot is comically baffled when Gobbo refers to him as "the very staff of my age" (staffs are long and thin). Launcelot asks the audience rhetorically, "Do I *look* like a cudgel or a hovel-post, a staff or a prop?" (65–66) All these objects are long and thin.

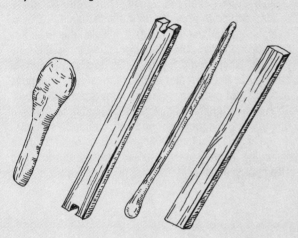

A cudgel, a hovel-post, a staff, and a prop.

When Launcelot admits that he has been fooling Gobbo and kneels to him, Gobbo places a hand on his head, but is astonished to find so much hair. He thinks he is feeling Launcelot's face and stroking a beard (89–91).

In lines 98–102 the clown tells us that he wants to leave Shylock because he is "famished in his service" (101–102). But Kemp was fat. The joke here seems to be that Launcelot places his spread fingers over his chest, and then brings Old Gobbo's hand up to feel them. They feel like a ribcage to the blind old man. But if Launcelot is lying about being starved, what does this tell us about Shylock? Launcelot must want to escape for some reason, but we never find out what it is. Launcelot simply complains that Shylock is "a very Jew" and that he is starving (which is very obviously untrue). One cannot help suspecting that Launcelot has annoyed Shylock by eating too much. Shakespeare seems to be leaving the truth of Shylock's devilishness open to question at this point, as Launcelot's opinions are vague and contradictory.

Launcelot has decided to leave Shylock's service and join instead the household of Bassanio. The reason seems to be that Bassanio is a Christian. Bassanio expresses surprise that Launcelot would leave a rich Jew to become the servant of a "poor gentleman" like himself. Launcelot's explanation refers to "the old proverb" (141): "He who has the grace of God has enough." As far as Launcelot is concerned, Shylock may have enough money, but only Bassanio has the "grace of God" (143). As in the vague hints earlier in the scene, it is clear that something has prompted Launcelot to seek out a Christian master. Again, Launcelot says that the Jew has done him wrong (125). But Shakespeare does not tell us exactly what caused Launcelot's desire to escape. The scene simply suggests something vaguely ominous about Shylock's household.

Much of the comedy in the next sequence comes from the double-act of Launcelot and Old Gobbo, as they interrupt each other and finish each other's sentences. Launcelot wants to appear as respectable and serious as possible, so that Bassanio will be impressed with him; but Old Gobbo continually hampers Launcelot's plans. Gobbo begins by describing Launcelot as a "poor boy," which embarrasses the clown. He interrupts Gobbo to explain that he is "Not a poor boy, sir, but the rich Jew's man;" but Gobbo interrupts him again and then bungles his words, mistakenly saying that Launcelot has an "infection" (118). And so the scene goes.

Rather surprisingly, Bassanio agrees to hire Launcelot, on the grounds that Shylock has recommended the clown to him. Again, this contradicts Launcelot's claim that the Jew has done him wrong. The implication continues that Launcelot's condemnation of Shylock is unjustified.

The uniform of a household fool.

Bassanio then offers Launcelot "a livery / More guarded than his fellows'" (146–147). "Guarded" means "ornamented with braiding" in this situation, which may mean that Launcelot is to be a senior servant. But worth remembering is the fact that the traditional costume of a fool was a coat with yellow braiding; perhaps Bassanio is employing Launcelot to be his household jester—a responsibility for which he is eminently suited.

The final part of this scene returns us to the main plot. Bassanio is preparing for his journey to Belmont, and Gratiano wants to come, too. But Bassanio is planning to woo Portia, and wants to make a good impression. He is concerned that Gratiano is "too wild, too rude and bold of voice" (172). He thinks that Gratiano's boisterous humor will be embarrassing. But Gratiano insists that he can behave in a "sober" manner and will behave seriously and solemnly the entire time he is in Belmont. This dialogue raises the audience's anticipation of the Belmont scenes, for they will enjoy seeing Gratiano's attempts at being "sober." The final lines of the scene hint to the audience that something else is going to happen, for Bassanio says "we have friends / That purpose merriment" (193–194). This ensuing plot development is not explained further. Again, the purpose is to intrigue the audience and keep them watching.

To a modern reader, II.2 may seem rather pointless. But in addition to providing some entertaining comedy (which is no bad thing in itself), it has also raised important questions. Why did Launcelot leave, and what is the "wrong" Shylock did to him? Is Shylock really a cruel master? Or is Launcelot simply motivated by religious hatred? And is it right to equate Jews with the devil? These questions are not answered, but they build an ominous atmosphere around the audience's mental image of Shylock's household, which is important for the following scene, in which Shylock's daughter also attempts to escape.

Act II, Scene 3

Launcelot says goodbye to Jessica, Shylock's daughter. She gives him a letter to take to her lover, Lorenzo.

ACT II, SCENE 3.
A room in Shylock's house.

[*Enter* JESSICA *and* LAUNCELOT.]

Jessica I am sorry thou wilt leave my father so;
Our house is hell, and thou a merry devil
Didst rob it of some taste of tediousness.
But fare thee well; there is a ducat for thee.
And, Launcelot, soon at supper shalt thou see   5
Lorenzo, who is thy new master's guest.
Give him this letter; do it secretly.
And so farewell; I would not have my father
See me in talk with thee.

Launcelot Adieu! Tears exhibit my tongue. Most   10
beautiful pagan, most sweet Jew! if a Christian did
not play the knave and get thee, I am much deceived.
But adieu! These foolish drops do something drown
my manly spirit. Adieu!

Jessica Farewell, good Launcelot.   15

[*Exit* LAUNCELOT.]
Alack, what heinous sin is it in me
To be ashamed to be my father's child.
But though I am a daughter to his blood,
I am not to his manners. O Lorenzo,
If thou keep promise, I shall end this strife,   20
Become a Christian and thy loving wife! [*Exit.*]

NOTES

10. *exhibit:* a mistake for inhibit.

12. *get:* beget.

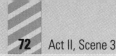

COMMENTARY

This scene begins another plotline: the elopement of Shylock's daughter, Jessica. Jessica wants to escape because "Our house is hell" (2), but again, as with Launcelot in II.2, she does not explain precisely *why* it is hell, except to say that it is tedious (3).

The clown sobs noisily because he will miss Jessica. However, Launcelot finds it necessary to apologize for the fact that he loves her. He finds it hard to admit that a Jew can be "beautiful" and "sweet," and can only offer the explanation that her mother must have cheated on Shylock with a Christian man (11–12). This little speech demonstrates the difficult task faced by an Elizabethan playwright who wants to create a genuinely admirable Jewish character. Shakespeare succeeded, but it is sad that he could only do so by making Jessica convert to Christianity. She ends this short scene by vowing to reject her father and his religion.

Act II, Scene 4

Launcelot gives the letter to Lorenzo. Jessica and Lorenzo are planning to elope in the evening, while Shylock is away.

ACT II, SCENE 4.
Venice. A street.

[*Enter* GRATIANO, LORENZO, SALERIO, *and*
    SOLANIO.]

Lorenzo Nay, we will slink away in supper time,
    Disguise us at my lodging, and return
    All in an hour.

Gratiano We have not made good preparation.

Salerio We have not spoke us yet of torchbearers.   5

Solanio 'Tis vile, unless it may be quaintly ordered,
    And better in my mind not undertook.

Lorenzo 'Tis now but four of clock. We have two
        hours
    To furnish us.

[*Enter* LAUNCELOT *with a letter.*]
                    Friend Launcelot, what's the news?

Launcelot An it shall please you to break up this, it   10
    shall seem to signify.

Lorenzo I know the hand. In faith, 'tis a fair hand,
    And whiter than the paper it writ on
    Is the fair hand that writ.

Gratiano   Love-news, in faith!

Launcelot By your leave, sir.   15

Lorenzo Whither goest thou?

Launcelot Marry, sir, to bid my old master the Jew
    to sup tonight with my new master the Christian.

NOTES

6. *quaintly ordered:* elaborately planned or arranged.

Lorenzo Hold here, take this. [*Gives money.*] Tell
    gentle Jessica
I will not fail her. Speak it privately.   20

[*Exit* LAUNCELOT.]
  Go, gentlemen;
  Will you prepare you for this masque tonight?
  I am provided of a torchbearer.

Salerio Ay marry, I'll be gone about it straight.

Solanio And so will I.   25

Lorenzo   Meet me and Gratiano
  At Gratiano's lodging some hour hence.

Salerio 'Tis good we do so.

[*Exeunt* SALERIO *and* SOLANIO.]

Gratiano Was not that letter from fair Jessica?

Lorenzo I must needs tell thee all. She hath
    directed
  How I shall take her from her father's house,   30
  What gold and jewels she is furnished with,
  What page's suit she hath in readiness.
  If e'er the Jew her father come to heaven,
  It will he for his gentle daughter's sake;
  And never dare misfortune cross her foot,   35
  Unless she do it under this excuse,
  That she is issue to a faithless Jew.
  Come, go with me; peruse this as thou goest.
  Fair Jessica shall be my torchbearer.
  [*Exeunt with* GRATIANO.]

23. See line 39.

36. *she:* i.e. misfortune
37. *she:* i.e. Jessica
     issue: offspring.

COMMENTARY

Lorenzo and the rest of the gallants are planning to surprise Bassanio by staging a farewell masque. Masques were a form of amateur theatre that were popular in aristocratic households as part of the entertainment at parties. Some members of the gathering would slip away and reenter in costumes, including masks. They would perform music, dance, and sometimes dramatic poetry.

Some readers are puzzled that we never get to see the masque in this play, but its true dramatic function is to provide Lorenzo and the others with disguises for their secret journey to Shylock's house.

This section begins the elopement subplot. The letter from Jessica tells Lorenzo that she will disguise herself as a page (a boyservant) so that she can escape.

Renaissance masquers.

As in II.3.10–12, there is evidence of the religious complexities that Shakespeare opened up when he created Jessica. Lorenzo says that if Shylock is admitted to heaven it will be because of his virtuous daughter. But then he says that if anything bad happens to her, it will be heaven's punishment for her Jewishness (33–37). Why do both Launcelot and Lorenzo say these contradictory things? Here is one explanation: By giving such speeches to his Christian characters, Shakespeare may be highlighting the difficulty that they have in accepting that a Jewish woman can be desirable and virtuous. The speeches raise the audience's awareness of the complex issues that religious discrimination creates when it conflicts with the emotions of the characters.

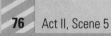

Act II, Scene 5

Shylock leaves his house to have dinner at Bassanio's. He orders Jessica to keep the house locked while he is out.

ACT II, SCENE 5.
Before Shylock's house.

[*Enter* SHYLOCK *and* LAUNCELOT.]

Shylock Well, thou shalt see, thy eyes shall be thy
    judge,
The difference of old Shylock and Bassanio—
What, Jessica!—Thou shalt not gormandize
As thou hast done with me—What, Jessica!—
And sleep, and snore, and rend apparel out—   5
Why, Jessica, I say!

Launcelot   Why, Jessica!

Shylock Who bids thee call? I do not bid thee call.

Launcelot Your worship was wont to tell me I could
  do nothing without bidding.

[*Enter* JESSICA.]

Jessica Call you? What is your will?   10

Shylock I am bid forth to supper, Jessica.
  There are my keys. But wherefore should I go?
  I am not bid for love—they flatter me—
  But I'll go in hate to feed upon
  The prodigal Christian. Jessica my girl,   15
  Look to my house. I am right loath to go.
  There is some ill a-brewing towards my rest,
  For I did dream of money bags tonight.

Launcelot I beseech you, sir, go. My young master
  doth expect your reproach.   20

Shylock So do I his.

Launcelot And they have conspired together. I will
  not say you shall see a masque, but if you do, then it
  was not for nothing that my nose fell a-bleeding on
  Black Monday last at six o'clock i' th' morning, fall-   25

NOTES

5.   *rend apparel out:* wear or tear clothes.

9.   *bidding:* here in the two senses of (1) being told, (2) calling out.

17.   *towards my rest:* against my peace of mind.

20.   *reproach:* a mistake for "approach."

ing out that year on Ash Wednesday was four year
in th' afternoon.

Shylock What, are there masques? Hear you me,
    Jessica:
Lock up my doors; and when you hear the drum
And the vile squealing of the wry-necked fife,   30
Clamber not you up to the casements then,
Nor thrust your head into the public street
To gaze on Christian fools with varnished faces;
But stop my house's ears—I mean my casements;
Let not the sound of shallow fopp'ry enter   35
My sober house. By Jacob's staff I swear
I have no mind of feasting forth tonight;
But I will go. Go you before me, sirrah.
Say I will come.

Launcelot   I will go before, sir.
Mistress, look out at window for all this: 40
    There will come a Christian by
    Will be worth a Jewess' eye. [*Exit.*]

Shylock What says that fool of Hagar's off-
    spring? ha?

Jessica His words were "Farewell, mistress"—
nothing else.

Shylock The patch is kind enough, but a huge   45
    feeder,
Snail-slow in profit, and he sleeps by day
More than the wildcat. Drones hive not with me;
Therefore I part with him, and part with him
To one that I would have him help to waste
His borrowed purse. Well, Jessica, go in.   50
Perhaps I will return immediately.
Do as I bid you; shut doors after you.
Fast bind, fast find —
A proverb never stale in thrifty mind. [*Exit.*]

Jessica Farewell; and if my fortune be not crossed,   55
I have a father, you a daughter, lost. [*Exit.*]

25-27. Launcelot's nonsense is a parody of all superstitious prediction, and a response to Shylock's talk of his "dream."

30. *wry-necked fife:* so called because the player turned his face away from the instrument.

33. *varnished faces:* i.e., wearing painted masks.

43. *Hagar's offspring:* the outcast Ishmael, Abraham's son by an Egyptian slave, Hagar.

45. *patch:* clown or fool.

46. *profit:* work which produces a profit.

53. *fast:* secure.

COMMENTARY

Now we finally see Shylock's household, about which so many questions were raised in the preceding scenes. Shylock is revealed to be a humorless old miser. As he walks onto the stage, he is grumbling about Launcelot's behaviour and shouting for Jessica.

The humor in this scene comes from the fact that Shylock won't leave. He is supposed to be going to dinner at Bassanio's house, but he keeps hesitating. He gives Jessica the keys (13), but then wonders why he should bother going, since his hosts are only flattering him (13–14). Obviously, this makes Jessica anxious—but Shylock then decides that he will "go in hate" and exploit Bassanio's generosity (15–16). Just before Shylock leaves, he warns Jessica "Perhaps I will return immediately" (53). All of this makes the scene very tense—and leaves the audience wondering whether Jessica's escape will be successful.

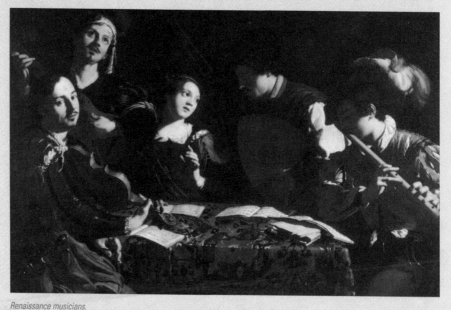

Renaissance musicians.
The Cummer Museum of Art and Gardens, Jacksonville/SuperStock.

Shylock says that he runs a "sober house" (37), which means that he will not allow anything frivolous within its walls. When he hears that there will be masquers running about in the streets, he is determined to exclude their noises from his house. He tells Jessica to close all the windows to prevent the music from being heard. In addition, he behaves like a miser when he trots out the proverb "Fast bind, fast find" (55), which means "if you keep things secure, you won't lose them." This is a useful proverb for a "thrifty mind," according to Shylock. However, there is an irony here, because Shylock is about to lose his daughter.

Shylock is a man for whom fun is incomprehensible. This explains Jessica's earlier comment that her house was tedious (II.3.3). Her father's insistence on sobriety and thrift has frustrated Jessica so much that she has decided to escape from him. Shylock is contrasted unfavorably with Bassanio, whom Shylock calls a "prodigal," or money-waster (16). Bassanio does waste his money, but his generous invitation to Shylock is more attractive than Shylock's silent and tedious home. We can understand why Jessica wants to leave—and Launcelot too, for that matter.

At this point, the audience is unlikely to feel much sympathy for Shylock. His grouchy behavior marks him as one of the traditional misers of English comedy. The deepening of his emotional responses will come later.

Act II, Scene 6

Lorenzo and his friends gather outside Shylock's house. Jessica comes out, and they all escape, taking some of Shylock's treasure with them.

ACT II, SCENE 6.
Before Shylock's house.

[*Enter the Masquers,* GRATIANO, *and* SALERIO.]

Gratiano This is the penthouse under which Lorenzo
Desired us to make stand.

Salerio   His hour is almost past.

Gratiano And it is marvel he outdwells his hour,
For lovers ever run before the clock.

Salerio O ten times faster Venus' pigeons fly   5
To seal love's bonds new-made than they are wont
To keep obliged faith unforfeited!

Gratiano That ever holds. Who riseth from a feast
With that keen appetite that he sits down?
Where is the horse that doth untread again   10
His tedious measures with the unbated fire
That he did pace them first? All things that are
Are with more spirit chased than enjoyed.
How like a younker or a prodigal
The scarfed bark puts from her native bay,   15
Hugged and embraced by the strumpet wind!
How like the prodigal doth she return,
With over-weathered ribs and ragged sails,
Lean, rent, and beggared by the strumpet wind!

[*Enter* LORENZO.]

Salerio Here comes Lorenzo; more of this here-   20
after.

Lorenzo Sweet friends, your patience for my long
abode.
Not I but my affairs have made you wait.
When you shall please to play the thieves for wives,
I'll watch as long for you then. Approach;

NOTES

1. *Penthouse:* porch or overhanging roof.

5. *Venus' pigeons:* doves, always represented as drawing Venus' chariot.

7. *obliged faith:* faith bound by contract. Salerio means that Venus' doves fly faster to consummate a new love than to continue with marital faithfulness.

11. *tedious measures:* intricate exercise movements.

14. *younker:* youngster.

    prodigal: the younger son of the parable.

15. *scarfed:* with flags flying.

21. *abode:* delay.

23. *play the thieves:* steal.

24. *watch:* wait.

Here dwells my father Jew. Ho! who's within? 25

[*Enter* JESSICA *above, in boy's clothes.*]

Jessica Who are you? Tell me for more certainty,
Albeit I'll swear that I do know your tongue.

Lorenzo Lorenzo, and thy love.

Jessica Lorenzo certain, and my love indeed,
For who love I so much And now who knows 30
But you, Lorenzo, whether I am yours?

Lorenzo Heaven and thy thoughts are witness that
thou art.

Jessica Here, catch this casket; it is worth the
pains.
I am glad 'tis night—you do not look on me—
For I am much ashamed of my exchange. 35
But love is blind, and lovers cannot see
The pretty follies that themselves commit;
For if they could, Cupid himself would blush
To see me thus transformed to a boy.

Lorenzo Descend, for you must be my torchbearer. 40

Jessica What, must I hold a candle to my shames?
They in themselves, good sooth, are too too light.
Why, 'tis an office of discovery, love —
And I should be obscured.

Lorenzo   So are you, sweet,
Even in the lovely garnish of a boy. 45
But come at once,
For the close night doth play the runaway,
And we are stayed for at Bassanio's feast.

Jessica I will make fast the doors, and gild myself
With some moe ducats, and be with you straight. 50

[*Exit above.*]

Gratiano Now by my hood, a gentle and no Jew!

Lorenzo Beshrow me but I love her heartily!
For she is wise, if I can judge of her,

35. *exchange:* i.e., of her woman's clothes for those of a boy.

42. *light:* shameful, with a pun on the illumination of the candle.

43. *office of discovery:* i.e., carrying a torch brings me into the light.

45. *garnish:* dress.

47. *close:* secret.

play the runaway: i.e., like Jessica. the night is stealing away.

48. *stayed for:* waited for.

51. *gentle:* the gentle-gentile pun.

And fair she is, if that mine eyes be true,
And true she is, as she hath proved herself;   55
And therefore, like herself, wise, fair, and true,
Shall she be placed in my constant soul.

[*Enter* JESSICA *below.*]
What, art thou come? On, gentlemen, away!
Our masquing mates by this time for us stay.

[*Exit with* JESSICA *and* SALERIO.]

[*Enter* ANTONIO.]

Antonio Who's there?   60

Gratiano Signior Antonio?

Antonio Fie, fie, Gratiano! where are all the rest?
'Tis nine o'clock; our friends all stay for you.
No masque tonight. The wind is come about;
Bassanio presently will go aboard.   65
I have sent twenty out to seek for you.

Gratiano I am glad on't. I desire no more delight
Than to be under sail and gone tonight. [*Exeunt.*]

COMMENTARY

In this scene, we are now *outside* Shylock's house, not inside. Above the stage doors of an Elizabethan theatre was a balcony-like structure. Shakespeare's most famous use of this structure is the balcony scene of *Romeo and Juliet*. Here, he uses it to represent the window of Shylock's house, while the stage, where Gratiano and Salerio stand, represents the street below.

The two gallants, Gratiano and Salerio, engage in some cynical talk about marriage, as they laugh at Lorenzo. Salerio jokes that people are much more keen to begin a new love affair ("love's bonds new-made") than they are to remain faithfully married in "obliged faith" (6–8). Gratiano develops this idea with reference to other things, such as food, horse riding and sailing. In each example, the activity is enjoyable to begin with, but becomes tedious and exhausting when repeated too often. So it is with courtship, according to Gratiano; men put more energy into chasing things than enjoying them when they've got them.

These are ominous sentiments, and they undermine our feelings about Lorenzo and Jessica. Is Lorenzo too hasty? Will he become bored with her? It is difficult to believe this could happen when Lorenzo does arrive, because he is clearly dizzy with love (53–58). But we can imagine Gratiano winking at Salerio as if to say that their point is proven. Similar questions are raised about the love between Lorenzo and Jessica in Act V, Scene 1. Shakespeare seems to want us to observe their elopement without any romantic illusions.

However, Jessica's plan goes very smoothly. The theatre audience is treated to an exciting visual spectacle as Jessica, on the balcony, throws down a casket (34) and Lorenzo catches it. The casket contains some of Shylock's treasure, and Jessica is wearing more treasure on her body (50–51). Some people feel that it is cruel of Jessica to steal Shylock's money. But seen from Jessica's point of view, it is poetic justice. She hates the tedious thrift of her father's house, and so she runs away with an exciting gallant and steals Shylock's money. As a method of revenge, it is entirely appropriate, because Shylock will lose both of his loves: his daughter and his ducats.

The scene ends with a rather obvious plotting device: The wind has suddenly changed, and Bassanio must leave at once. Shakespeare has now set up all of the plotlines: Bassanio has the money to embark for Belmont; Antonio has signed Shylock's bond; and when Shylock returns to his house after dinner, he will discover something that will make him want to seek revenge.

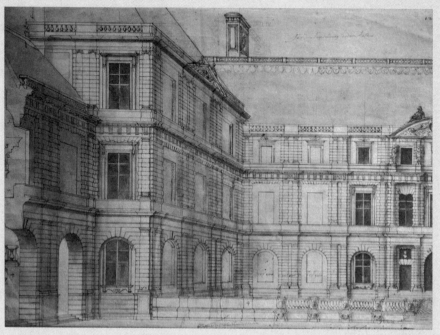

A Renaissance house.
Musee de Louvre, Paris/Giraudon, Paris/SuperStock.

Act II, Scene 7

The Prince of Morocco attempts the casket test. He chooses the gold casket, but it is the wrong decision.

ACT II, SCENE 7
Belmont. A room in Portia's house.

[*Flourish of cornets. Enter* PORTIA *with* MOROCCO *and both their Trains.*]

Portia Go, draw aside the curtains and discover
The several caskets to this noble Prince.
Now make your choice.

Morocco This first, of gold, who this inscription
    bears,
"Who chooseth me shall gain what many men   5
    desire";
The second, silver, which this promise carries,
"Who chooseth me shall get as much as he de-
    serves";
This third, dull lead, with warning all as blunt,
"Who chooseth me must give and hazard all he
    hath."
How shall I know if I do choose the right?   10

Portia The one of them contains my picture,
    Prince,
If you choose that, then I am yours withal.

Morocco Some god direct my judgment! Let me
    see—
I will survey th' inscriptions back again.
What says this leaden casket?   15
"Who chooseth me must give and hazard all he hath."
Must give—for what? for lead! hazard for lead?
This casket threatens; men that hazard all
Do it in hope of fair advantages.
A golden mind stoops not to shows of dross;   20
I'll then nor give nor hazard aught for lead.
What says the silver with her virgin hue?
"Who chooseth me shall get as much as he deserves."

NOTES

1.   *discover:* reveal. The curtain of the stage's "discovery space" would here be drawn aside to reveal the caskets.

9.   *hazard:* risk, gamble.

22.   *virgin hue:* whiteness; the Elizabethans usually spoke of silver as being white.

As much as he deserves? Pause there, Morocco,
And weigh thy value with an even hand: 25
If thou be'st rated by thy estimation,
Thou dost deserve enough; and yet enough
May not extend so far as to the lady;
And yet to be afeard of my deserving
Were but a weak disabling of myself.   30
As much as I deserve? Why that's the lady!
I do in birth deserve her, and in fortunes,
In graces, and in qualities of breeding;
But more than these, in love I do deserve.
What if I strayed no farther, but chose here?   35
Let's see once more this saying graved in gold:
"Who chooseth me shall gain what many men
    desire."
Why that's the lady! All the world desires her;
From the four corners of the earth they come
To kiss this shrine, this mortal breathing saint.   40
The Hyrcanian deserts and the vasty wilds
Of wide Arabia are as throughfares now
For princes to come view fair Portia.
The watery kingdom, whose ambitious head
Spits in the face of heaven, is no bar   45
To stop the foreign spirits, but they come
As o'er a brook to see fair Portia.
One of these three contains her heavenly picture.
Is't like that lead contains her? 'Twere damnation   50
To think so base a thought; it were too gross
To rib her cerecloth in the obscure grave.
Or shall I think in silver she's immured,
Being ten times undervalued to tried gold?
O sinful thought! Never so rich a gem
Was set in worse than gold. They have in England   55
A coin that bears the figure of an angel
Stamped in gold—but that's insculped upon;
But here an angel in a golden bed
Lies all within. Deliver me the key.
Here do I choose, and thrive I as I may!   60

26. *estimation:* reputation.

29–30. Yet to doubt that I deserve her would be a timid failure to believe in myself.

41. *Hyrcanian deserts:* these lay south of the Caspian Sea and were notorious for their wildness.

51. *rib:* enclose.

cerecloth: shroud.

57. *insculped upon:* engraved upon.

Portia There, take it, Prince; and if my form lie there,
Then I am yours. [*He opens the golden casket.*]

Morocco   O hell! what have we here?
A carrion Death, within whose empty eye
There is a written scroll! I'll read the writing.
    "All that glisters is not gold;   65
    Often have you heard that told.
    Many a man his life hath sold
    But my outside to behold.
    Gilded tombs do worms infold.
    Had you been as wise as bold,   70
    Young in limbs, in judgment old,
    Your answer had not been inscrolled.
    Fare you well, your suit is cold."
Cold indeed, and labor lost.
Then farewell heat, and welcome frost!   75
Portia, adieu. I have too grieved a heart
To take a tedious leave. Thus losers part.

[*Exit with his Train. Flourish of cornets.*]

Portia A gentle riddance. Draw the curtains, go.
Let all of his complexion choose me so. [*Exeunt.*]

63. *carrion Death:* a skull.

65. *glisters:* glitters.

68. *outside:* i.e. gold.

72. *inscrolled:* here inscribed.

77. *tedious:* lengthy.

COMMENTARY

The action now returns to Belmont. In this scene, Shakespeare finally shows us the details of the test that Bassanio (and Portia's other suitors) must undertake. The suitors must choose one of three caskets: gold, silver, or lead. One of the caskets contains a portrait of Portia; the others do not. If the suitor chooses the casket containing Portia's picture, he has won the right to marry her. But none has succeeded so far.

Attached to the caskets are inscriptions. The inscription on the leaden casket does not sound as enticing as the others, because it requires the chooser to risk everything he has. The inscriptions on the gold and silver caskets are different; they tell the chooser that he will gain something by choosing them. But the inscriptions have double meanings.

The audience can probably assume that Portia does not know which is the correct casket. The scene is all the more dramatic because Portia is fearful that Morocco will choose correctly. Shakespeare incorporates moments of tension for Portia, such as when Morocco pauses to think carefully about his decision (25). However, in a fairytale story like this, the audience

can be sure that Morocco will fail, and that Bassanio will succeed. For the audience, the interest lies in seeing *why* Morroco fails.

Morocco immediately rejects the leaden casket. He is not opposed to the idea of risking everything he has; but he cannot imagine risking it for something as worthless as lead. He reveals excessive pride when he says pompously "A golden mind stoops not to shows of dross" (20).

Morocco hesitates at the silver casket, for this one promises him all that he deserves. As far as Morocco is concerned, he deserves Portia; his breeding, wealth, and manners make him

A Moorish nobleman.

extremely worthy of her; and he even says that he loves her as well. What more could a woman want? This part of the speech also reveals Morocco's pride, which makes him an unsuitable match for Portia.

Morocco is about to choose the silver casket, when he decides to check the inscription on the golden one. And here he finds something even more appealing. Morocco decides that only the golden casket could contain Portia's portrait. He cannot imagine that it would belong in a leaden or a silver casket—indeed, such thoughts are damnable and sinful to him (49, 54). As far as Morocco is concerned, a beautiful thing could only belong inside another beautiful thing.

In other words, what you see on the surface reflects what is on the inside. Shakespeare suggests that Morocco is not only proud but also superficial, and unable to see that worthiness can also appear in humble places.

The moments when the suitors open the caskets can be exciting for the audience because, although they are sure that it will not contain Portia's portrait, they do not know exactly what *is* inside it. In this case, Morocco has a nasty shock when the golden casket turns out to contain a skull. His startled exclamation, "O hell!" is an amusing contrast to his previously ornate speeches. His pride and self-belief has been punctured instantly.

The scroll inside the casket tells the chooser why he chose wrongly. Morocco is reminded that just because something is beautiful on the outside, it is not necessarily good ("All that glisters is not gold"). And he is further reminded that no matter how wealthy you are, you cannot be saved from death ("Gilded tombs do worms enfold"). The golden casket was clearly designed by Portia's father to "weed out" those suitors who have a superficial love of riches without an understanding of the world beyond it.

An angel coin.

Act II, Scene 8

Salerio and Solanio discuss the events of the night. Bassanio has set sail for Belmont; Lorenzo and Jessica have escaped; and Shylock is furious.

ACT II, SCENE 8
Venice. A street.

[*Enter* SALERIO *and* SOLANIO.]

Salerio Why, man, I saw Bassanio under sail;
  With him is Gratiano gone along,
  And in their ship I am sure Lorenzo is not.

Solanio The villain Jew with outcries raised the
      Duke,
  Who went with him to search Bassanio's ship.   5

Salerio He came too late—the ship was under sail,
  But there the Duke was given to understand
  That in a gondola were seen together
  Lorenzo and his amorous Jessica.
  Besides, Antonio certified the Duke   10
  They were not with Bassanio in his ship.

Solanio I never heard a passion so confused,
  So strange, outrageous, and so variable
  As the dog Jew did utter in the streets:
  "My daughter! O my ducats! O my daughter!   15
  Fled with a Christian! O my Christian ducats!
  Justice! the law! my ducats and my daughter!
  A sealed bag, two sealed bags of ducats,
  Of double ducats, stol'n from me by my daughter!
  And jewels—two stones, two rich and precious   20
      stones,
  Stol'n by my daughter! Justice! Find the girl!
  She hath the stones upon her, and the ducats!"

Salerio Why, all the boys in Venice follow him,
  Crying his stones, his daughter, and his ducats.

Solanio Let good Antonio look he keep his day,   25
  Or he shall pay for this.

25. *keep his day:* repay his debt on the appointed day.

Salerio   Marry, well rememb'red.
I reasoned with a Frenchman yesterday,
Who told me, in the narrow seas that part
The French and English there miscarried
A vessel of our country richly fraught.   30
I thought upon Antonio when he told me,
And wished in silence that it were not his.

Solanio You were best to tell Antonio what you
    hear.
Yet do not suddenly, for it may grieve him.

Salerio A kinder gentleman treads not the earth.   35
I saw Bassanio and Antonio part:
Bassanio told him he would make some speed
Of his return; he answered, "Do not so.
Slubber not business for my sake, Bassanio,
But stay the very riping of the time;   40
And for the Jew's bond which he hath of me,
Let it not enter in your mind of love.
Be merry, and employ your chiefest thoughts
To courtship and such fair ostents of love
As shall conveniently become you there."   45
And even there, his eye being big with tears,
Turning his face, he put his hand behind him,
And with affection wondrous sensible
He wrung Bassanio's hand; and so they parted.

Solanio I think he only loves the world for him.   50
I pray thee let us go and find him out,
And quicken his embraced heaviness
With some delight or other.

Salerio   Do we so. [*Exeunt.*]

30. *fraught:* laden.

39. *Slubber:* make a mess of.

40. *stay the very riping:* wait until the business can be best completed.

44. *ostents:* expressions.

48. *wondrous sensible:* very deeply felt.

52. *embraced heaviness:* grief kept to himself.

COMMENTARY

In this scene, Shakespeare uses Salerio and Solanio to describe events that have happened offstage. Perhaps Shakespeare thought that the previous events of the night—the Duke searching Bassanio's ship for the errant Jessica, Lorenzo and Jessica escaping in a gondola, and Shylock being followed through the streets by laughing boys—were too long-winded or complicated to depict onstage.

In lines 12–22, Salerio repeats Shylock's words. Here, the actor must imitate Shylock's gestures and voice. He should probably do this in an exaggerated fashion, because he is making fun of Shylock. The point of his impersonation is to suggest that Shylock does not distinguish between his daughter and his money. Shylock cries, "My daughter! O, my ducats!", which makes it sound as though his daughter is no more important than his money. Compare this with Salerio's imitation of Antonio (38–45), which is not satirical at all.

Shakespeare seems to have put Shylock's words into Salerio's mouth in order to prevent the audience from sympathizing with the usurer. Rather than make Shylock's distress real, he ridicules it and satirizes Shylock's acquisitiveness. However, the description of Shylock being tormented by the Venetian boys (23–24) may convey some of the sadness of Shylock's position. Shakespeare may have wanted the audience to wonder whether there is a difference between Salerio's description of Shylock's grief and what Shylock really feels.

In line 25, Salerio and Solanio suddenly realize the seriousness of the situation. News has been heard of a sunken Venetian vessel (27–32). This news concerns Salerio and Solanio, because Antonio is now in a very vulnerable position. His enemy, Shylock, has become an angry, vengeful man, who rightly suspects Antonio and Bassanio of harboring his daughter. Therefore, if Antonio fails to repay the loan, Shylock will not only claim his pound of flesh, he will *enjoy* claiming it. Jessica's elopement is clearly the cause of Shylock's vengeful anger. His desire for revenge is a refinement of the original story that Shakespeare based the play on, in which the Jew was cruel for no reason (see the Introduction). Giving Shylock a reason for his actions enriches the dramatic experience by preventing the play from being a simple case of good versus evil.

A gondola, with covered sides for privacy.

The description of Antonio's farewell to Bassanio stresses once more his intense love for the young man. Renaissance men were much more ready to express their emotions than modern men. We must also remember that many books on aristocratic conduct regarded friendship between men as more noble than love between men and women. Antonio's love for Bassanio is very real, and Shakespeare makes much of this in Acts IV and V.

Act II, Scene 9

Portia faces another suitor, the Prince of Arragon. He attempts the test, and chooses the silver casket, but it is the wrong decision.

ACT II, SCENE 9.
Belmont. A room in Portia's house.

[*Enter* NERISSA *and a Servant.*]

Nerissa Quick, quick I pray thee! draw the curtain
straight.
The Prince of Arragon hath ta'en his oath,
And comes to his election presently.

[*Flourish of cornets. Enter* ARRAGON, *his Train, and*
PORTIA.]

Portia Behold, there stand the caskets, noble
Prince.
If you choose that wherein I am contained,   5
Straight shall our nuptial rites be solemnized;
But if you fail, without more speech, my lord,
You must be gone from hence immediately.

Arragon I am enjoined by oath to observe three
things:
First, never to unfold to any one   10
Which casket 'twas I chose; next, if I fail
Of the right casket, never in my life
To woo a maid in way of marriage;
Lastly, if I do fail in fortune of my choice,
Immediately to leave you and be gone.   15

Portia To these injunctions every one doth swear
That comes to hazard for my worthless self.

Arragon And so have I addressed me. Fortune now
To my heart's hope! Gold, silver, and base lead.
"Who chooseth me must give and hazard all he   20
hath."
You shall look fairer ere I give or hazard.
What says the golden chest? Ha, let me see!

NOTES

3. *presently:* immediately.

21. This line is addressed to the leaden casket.

"Who chooseth me shall gain what many men desire."
What many men desire—that "many" may be meant
By the fool multitude that choose by show,   25
Not learning more than the fond eye doth teach,
Which pries not to th' interior, but like the martlet
Builds in the weather on the outward wall,
Even in the force and road of casualty.
I will not choose what many men desire,   30
Because I will not jump with common spirits
And rank me with the barbarous multitudes.
Why then, to thee, thou silver treasure house!
Tell me once more what title thou dost bear.
"Who chooseth me shall get as much as he deserves."   35
And well said too, for who shall go about
To cozen fortune, and be honorable
Without the stamp of merit? Let none presume
To wear an undeserved dignity.
O that estates, degrees, and offices   40
Were not derived corruptly, and that clear honor
Were purchased by the merit of the wearer!
How many then should cover that stand bare,
How many be commanded that command;
How much low peasantry would then be gleaned   45
From the true seed of honor, and how much honor
Picked from the chaff and ruin of the times
To be new varnished. Well, but to my choice.
"Who chooseth me shall get as much as he deserves."
I will assume desert. Give me a key for this,   50
And instantly unlock my fortunes here.

[*He opens the silver casket.*]

Portia Too long a pause for that which you find
      there.

Arragon What's here? The portrait of a blinking
      idiot
Presenting me a schedule! I will read it.
How much unlike art thou to Portia!   55
How much unlike my hopes and my deservings!
"Who chooseth me shall have as much as he
      deserves."

26. *fond:* foolish.

27. *martlet:* the house-martin, a bird that builds its nests on the outside walls of buildings.

29. *force and road:* power and path.

31. *jump:* agree.

37. *cozen:* cheat.

43. *should . . . bare;* i.e., wear hats who now must remove them, to keep one's hat on was a mark of social standing.

45. *gleaned:* culled.

48. *new varnished:* newly polished.

54. *schedule:* scroll.

Did I deserve no more than a fool's head?
Is that my prize? Are my deserts no better?

Portia To offend and judge are distinct offices,　　　60
And of opposed natures.

Arragon　　　　　　　What is here?
　　"The fire seven times tried this;
　　Seven times tried that judgment is
　　That did never choose amiss.
　　Some there be that shadows kiss;　　　65
　　Such have but a shadow's bliss.
　　There be fools alive iwis,
　　Silvered o'er, and so was this.
　　Take what wife you will to bed,
　　I will ever be your head.　　　70
　　So be gone; you are sped."
Still more fool I shall appear
By the time I linger here.
With one fool's head I came to woo,
But I go away with two.　　　75
Sweet, adieu. I'll keep my oath,
Patiently to bear my wroath. [*Exit with his Train.*]

Portia Thus hath the candle singed the moth.
O these deliberate fools! When they do choose,
They have the wisdom by their wit to lose.　　　80

Nerissa The ancient saying is no heresy:
Hanging and wiving goes by destiny.

Portia Come draw the curtain, Nerissa.

[*Enter* MESSENGER.]

Messenger Where is my lady?

Portia　　　　　　　　Here. What would my lord?

Messenger Madam, there is alighted at your gate　　　85
A young Venetian, one that comes before
To signify th' approaching of his lord,
From whom he bringeth sensible regreets,
To wit, besides commends and courteous breath,
Gifts of rich value. Yet I have not seen　　　90

60–61. *To . . . natures:* i.e., to commit an offense and then sit in judgment on it are two different things.

62. *tried:* tested.

67. *iwis:* I wis, I know, certainly.

70. *I:* i.e., the fool's head.

71. *sped:* literally shot off, like an arrow; done for, finished.

77. *wroath:* wrath or disappointment.

79. *deliberate:* i.e., who spends too much time deliberating.

84. *my lord:* a playful reply, teasing the messenger.

88. *sensible regreets:* tangible greetings, gifts.

So likely an ambassador of love.
A day in April never came so sweet
To show how costly summer was at hand,
As this fore-spurrer comes before his lord,

Portia No more, I pray thee. I am half afeard   95
Thou wilt say anon he is some kin to thee,
Thou spend'st such high-day wit in praising him.
Come, come, Nerissa for I long to see
Quick Cupid's post that comes so mannerly.

Nerissa Bassanio, Lord Love, if thy will it be!   100

[*Exeunt.*]

93. *costly:* lavish.

97. *high-day:* holiday, high-flown.

99. *post:* messenger.

COMMENTARY

The Prince of Arragon is a Spanish nobleman. He appears in only one scene, but the role is a good opportunity for a comic actor to steal the show. Arragon is excessively proud, but the ways in which this pride manifests itself are entirely up to the actor. Many productions portray Arragon as an ancient, doddering old man (the Jonathan Miller TV adaptation is one example), but the text does not specify this, and he could equally be portrayed as a foolish young aristocrat. The original productions probably emphasized Arragon's nationality. Only seven years before Shakespeare wrote the play, the Spanish Armada had attempted to invade England. In consequence, English audiences hated the Spanish and would have enjoyed watching a Spaniard being made to look foolish.

Morocco failed the test because he could not see that appearances can be deceptive. He chose the golden casket because he could not imagine that any "lesser" metal would contain the goal that he was hoping for. Arragon does not fall into this trap. He says that ordinary people choose "by show." In other words, they know only what their eyes tell them and do not search for deeper meanings. Arragon compares these people to birds that build nests on the outsides of houses, not knowing that there is warmth and shelter on the inside.

Arragon is on the right track. However, he makes two mistakes. First, he does not follow his own rules, because he only spurns the leaden casket on the grounds that it doesn't look nice (20–21). Second, Arragon refuses the golden casket because he does not want "what many men desire." He regards himself as being higher in status than everyone else and, therefore, turns down the gold, for fear of having the same desires as the "barbarous multitudes" (33).

The "martlet" (house-martin), nesting on a building's outer wall.

Arragon may think he has seen through the inscription's ploys, but when he sees the inscription on the silver casket, he is immediately seduced. "Who chooseth me shall get as much as he deserves" (36). As far as Arragon is concerned, few people are as deserving as he is. Indeed, he embarks on a diatribe about the lack of true "merit" among the leaders of the world. He says that the positions of importance are filled by people who have risen by corrupt means. Arragon believes that people in such positions should earn those positions by their merits, not by bribery (41–43). He imagines all these undeserving officers being forced to doff their caps, and those who had commanded others being forced to be commanded themselves (44–45). All of this seems perfectly sensible, of course; but Arragon's speech is not the idealistic egalitarianism that it seems. He goes on to speak of "low peasantry" being ousted from the ranks of the honorable, which makes it clear that he believes true merit is a result of breeding, not of actual worth (46–49). Arragon's beliefs in the connection between breeding and merit are demonstrated further when he reads once more the inscription and then says "I will assume desert" (51). By his own standards, Arragon should *earn* desert, not *assume* it. Arragon is revealed to have an overconfident belief in his own merit.

For this reason, Arragon's opening of the silver casket can be one of the funniest moments in the play. The more pompous the actor has been, the more crushing is his defeat when he finds only "the portrait of a blinking idiot" in the casket (54), probably wearing the traditional cap and bells of the fool.

The scroll inside the casket reminds Arragon that even though he thought he was wise enough to avoid being fooled by appearances, there are plenty of fools "silvered o'er" (69). Arragon exits in great embarrassment, but his final speech hints that he has recognized his folly, and may be a changed man in the future.

A fool's cap: "the portrait of a blinking idiot."

This scene (and the scene in which Morocco failed the test) makes it clear to the audience why Portia's father designed the casket test in this way. The test is designed to remove from consideration those suitors who are either pompous or superficial. In order to pass the test, Bassanio will have to prove to be neither.

Bassanio's entrance is described in language that is a welcome break from the bombast that has filled the previous three Belmont scenes. "A day in April never came so sweet" makes us think of April showers and the coming of spring, suggesting that the previous suitors are now washed away. But note that it is Nerissa that does the eulogizing. Shakespeare reminds us of Portia's characteristic coolness as she pretends to be only mildly interested in Bassanio (96–98).

Notes

Notes

CLIFFSCOMPLETE

THE MERCHANT OF VENICE

ACT III

Shylock *Hath not a Jew eyes?*
Hath not a Jew hands, organs, dimensions,
senses, affections, passions? — fed with the same
food, hurt with the same weapons, subject to the
same diseases, healed by the same means, warmed
and cooled by the same winter and summer as a
Christian is? If you prick us, do we not bleed? If
you tickle us, do we not laugh? If you poison us, do
we not die? And if you wrong us, shall we not revenge?

Act III, Scene 1

Salerio and Solanio meet Shylock and tease him about his misfortunes. Then Shylock meets his friend Tubal, who has been looking for Jessica and Lorenzo. Tubal delights Shylock by revealing that one of Antonio's ships has sunk.

ACT III, SCENE 1
Venice. A street.

[*Enter* SOLANIO *and* SALERIO.]

Solanio Now what news on the Rialto?

Salerio Why, yet it lives there unchecked that Antonio hath a ship of rich lading wracked on the narrow seas — the Goodwins I think they call the place, a very dangerous flat, and fatal, where the carcasses   5
of many a tall ship lie buried as they say, if my gossip Report be an honest woman of her word.

Salerio I would she were as lying a gossip in that as ever knapped ginger or made her neighbors believe she wept for the death of a third husband. But   10
it is true, without any slips of prolixity or crossing the plain highway of talk, that the good Antonio, the honest Antonio — O that I had a title good enough to keep his name company!

Salerio Come, the full stop!   15

Solanio Ha, what sayest thou? Why the end is, he hath lost a ship.

Salerio I would it might prove the end of his losses.

Solanio Let me say amen betimes lest the devil cross my prayer, for here he comes in the likeness of   20
a Jew.
[*Enter* SHYLOCK.]
How now, Shylock? What news among the merchants?

Shylock You knew, none so well, none so well as you, of my daughter's flight.   25

NOTES

2.   *lives there unchecked:* continues without contradiction.

4.   *the Goodwins:* Goodwin Sands, off the English coast, are particularly dangerous to navigation.

6.   *gossip:* a female companion.

7.   *Report:* rumor.

9.   *knapped:* nibbled.

11.   *slips of prolixity:* lapses info wordiness; Shakespeare now makes Solanio himself lapse in just this way.

15.   *full stop:* the period, end of the statement.

20.   *cross:* thwart.

Salerio That's certain. I for my part knew the
tailor that made the wings she flew withal.

Solanio And Shylock for his own part knew the
bird was fledge, and then it is the complexion of
them all to leave the dam. 30

Shylock She is damned for it.

Salerio That's certain, if the devil may be her judge.

Shylock My own flesh and blood to rebel!

Solanio Out upon it, old carrion! Rebels it at these years? 35

Shylock I say my daughter is my flesh and my
blood.

Salerio There is more difference between thy flesh
and hers than between jet and ivory, more between 40
your bloods than there is between red wine and
Rhenish. But tell us, do you hear whether Antonio
have had any loss at sea or no?

Shylock There I have another bad match! A bankrout, a prodigal, who dare scarce show his head on 45
the Rialto, a beggar that was used to come so smug
upon the mart! Let him look to his bond. He was
wont to call me usurer. Let him look to his bond. 50
He was wont to lend money for a Christian cursy.
Let him look to his bond.

Salerio Why, I am sure if he forfeit thou wilt not
take his flesh. What's that good for?

Shylock To bait fish withal. If it will feed nothing
else, it will feed my revenge. He hath disgraced me
and hind'red me half a million, laughed at my losses, 55
mocked at my gains, scorned my nation, thwarted my
bargains, cooled my friends, heated mine enemies —
and what's his reason? I am a Jew. Hath not a Jew
eyes? Hath not a Jew hands, organs, dimensions,
senses, affections, passions? — fed with the same 60
food, hurt with the same weapons, subject to the
same diseases, healed by the same means, warmed
and cooled by the same winter and summer as a

29.   *fledge:* able to fly.

      complexion: nature.

30.   *dam:* mother, i.e., parent.

42.   *Rhenish:* German white wine.

44.   *bankrout:* bankrupt.

49.   *Christian cursy:* Christian charity.

Famous of Speeches of all of Shakespeare

59.   *dimensions:* bodily frame.

Christian is? If you prick us, do we not bleed? If
you tickle us, do we not laugh? If you poison us, do   65
we not die? And if you wrong us, shall we not re-
venge? If we are like you in the rest, we will re-
semble you in that. If a Jew wrong a Christian, what   70
is his humility? Revenge. If a Christian wrong a
Jew, what should his sufferance be by Christian example? Why revenge! The villainy you teach me I
will execute, and it shall go hard but I will better
the instruction.

[*Enter a Servant.*]

Servant Gentlemen, my master Antonio is at his
house and desires to speak with you both.   75

Salerio We have been up and down to seek him.

[*Enter* TUBAL.]

Solanio Here comes another of the tribe. A third
cannot be matched, unless the devil himself turn Jew.

[*Exeunt* SOLANIO, SALERIO, *and Servant.*]

Shylock How now, Tubal! What news from
Genoa? Hast thou found my daughter?   80

Tubal I often came where I did hear of her, but
cannot find her.

Shylock Why there, there, there, there! A diamond
gone cost me two thousand ducats in Frankford!
The curse never fell upon our nation till now; I never   85
felt it till now. Two thousand ducats in that, and
other precious, precious jewels. I would my daughter were dead at my foot, and the jewels in her ear!
Would she were hearsed at my foot, and the ducats
in her coffin! No news of them, why so? — and I   90
know not what's spent in the search. Why thou loss
upon loss! the thief gone with so much, and so much
to find the thief! — and no satisfaction, no revenge!
nor no ill luck stirring but what lights o' my shoul-
ders, no sighs but o' my breathing, no tears but o' my   95
shedding.

69. *humility:* Christian kindness (sarcastic)

     his: i.e., the Christian's.

70. *his:* i.e., the Jew's.

78. *cannot be matched:* i.e., cannot be found to match them.

84. *Frankford:* Frankfort fair.

Tubal Yes, other men have ill luck too. Antonio,
as I heard in Genoa —

Shylock What, what, what? Ill luck, ill luck?

Tubal Hath an argosy cast away coming from   100
Tripolis.

Shylock I thank God, I thank God! Is it true? is
it true?

Tubal I spoke with some of the sailors that escaped
the wrack.   105

Shylock I thank thee, good Tubal. Good news,
good news! Ha, ha! Heard in Genoa?

Tubal Your daughter spent in Genoa, as I heard,
one night fourscore ducats.

Shylock Thou stick'st a dagger in me. I shall never   110
see my gold again. Fourscore ducats at a sitting,
fourscore ducats!

Tubal There came divers of Antonio's creditors
in my company to Venice that swear he cannot
choose but break.   115

Shylock I am very glad of it. I'll plague him; I'll
torture him. I am glad of it.

Tubal One of them showed me a ring that he had
of your daughter for a monkey.

Shylock Out upon her! Thou torturest me, Tubal.   120
It was my turquoise; I had it of Leah when I was a
bachelor. I would not have given it for a wilderness of monkeys.

Tubal But Antonio is certainly undone.

Shylock Nay, that's true, that's very true. Go,   125
Tubal, fee me an officer; bespeak him a fortnight before. I will have the heart of him if he forfeit, for
were he out of Venice I can make what merchandise
will. Go, Tubal, and meet me at our synagogue;
go, good Tubal; at our synagogue, Tubal. [*Exeunt.*]   130

113.   *divers:* several.

121.   *Leah:* Shylock's wife.

122.   *a wilderness:* a whole jungle.

126.   *fee:* engage.

　　　　bespeak: notify.

128–129.   *I can . . . will:* drive any sort of bargains I want to.

COMMENTARY

The inevitable has happened: one of Antonio's ships has sunk. The "Goodwins" were a dangerous region of sandbanks in Kent, just up the river from London. Shakespeare is making the image of the shipwreck more vivid for his audience by referring to a place they may have seen with their own eyes.

This scene is the culmination of the constant references to the dangers of merchant shipping that have been made throughout the play. The sinking of Antonio's ship is not, therefore, a surprise revelation; Shakespeare has made the audience well aware that it will happen—and that Shylock will claim his bond. The intriguing question is, "What will happen next?"

Mere words on a page cannot convey the dramatic power of Shylock's entrance in this scene. He has not appeared since the scene before Jessica's escape (II.5). Although we have been told about Shylock's anger, we have not seen it ourselves. Shylock enters and points at Salerio and Solanio, accusing them furiously: "You knew, none so well, none so well as you, of my daughter's flight" (23–24). Shylock's anger contrasts sharply with the carefree way in which the gallants laugh off his accusations. Salerio and Solanio treat Shylock's anger as a joke and torment him by freely admitting that they were instrumental in helping Jessica escape.

In II.8, Solanio caricatured Shylock's grief, stressing the fact that Shylock was just as worried about his ducats as he was about his daughter. At the time, we may have wondered how accurate Shakespeare's portrayal of Shylock was. But in *this* scene, Shakespeare begins to generate audience sympathy for Shylock. Perhaps this, coupled with the taunts of the gallants, makes Shylock more sympathetic as Shakespeare prepares for the next speeches.

Salerio now mentions the loss of Antonio's ship to Shylock. He may do this because he thinks Shylock is not serious about the bond. But Shylock's response demonstrates the danger that Antonio is in.

The speech in lines 41–47 is essentially a reprisal of Shylock's gloating over Antonio in I.3. But now there is no humor in it; Shylock's mood has become serious. Infuriated by what he sees as Antonio's complicity in Jessica's elopement, he is now contemplating revenge on Antonio. Shakespeare creates a sinister effect with Shylock's repetitive speech patterns, as he insistently repeats, "Let him look to his bond" (44, 45, 46–47). The bond is no longer "merry," as it was in Act I, Scene 3. Shylock has been so tormented that he is now prepared to take it seriously.

Shylock's famous speech in lines 50–69 is the moment in the play that vindicates it for modern audiences, whose sensitivity toward anti-Semitism is greater than audiences in Elizabethan times. Shylock's speech is immensely powerful, especially when spoken to a couple of nonentities such as Salerio and Solanio. The speech articulates strongly and fully the underlying questions that have been expressed more subtly elsewhere in the play.

Shylock protests that he is a human being, just like the Christians are, and that he should not be disgraced, hindered, mocked, and thwarted (51–53) simply because of his religion. However, as many have pointed out, the ultimate point of Shylock's argument comes when he says "And if you wrong us, shall we not revenge?" (62–63). He is using his plea for tolerance to justify something appalling—the mutilation of another man. Yet, this is not the end of the story.

Shylock points out the hypocrisy of Christians like Antonio, who show no humility toward him. He, therefore, justifies his revenge by showing no humility to them in return. The key line is, "The villainy you teach me I will execute. . . " (67–68). With this line, Shakespeare lifts Shylock out of the stereotype of the wicked Jew. Not only does Shylock have a reason for his anger (the loss of his daughter), but he makes us aware that his desire for revenge is fueled by the intolerance that

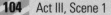

he has suffered for years at the hands of Christians. Shylock is evil because people have done evil to him. This sequence reverses the emphasis of the previous scenes, but not for long.

Shylock's plea for humanity is allowed to detonate in the audience's minds, but then Shakespeare plunges us back into enjoying the villain's wickedness. Shylock falls back into moaning about his ducats, and even wishes, "I would my daughter were dead at my foot, and the jewels in her ear!" (83–84).

Shylock now learns that another of Antonio's ships has been lost. He is delighted, and laughs with joy. Again, this recalls his cheerful gloating in I.3, but now that the bond has become serious, it has a sinister edge. An actor can play this scene in one of many different ways, but Shylock's joy in Antonio's misfortune is very evident regardless. Shylock can be an entertaining character, no matter how seriously the actor plays the part. This scene provides an opportunity to portray a "comic villain" who entertains the audience by laughing about his crimes. The difficulty for an actor lies in incorporating this humor into a more tragic reading of the role.

However, Shakespeare does provide a transition-point for the actor to switch from comedy to tragedy. Shylock suddenly loses his stereotypical wickedness when he talks about the ring that Jessica stole: "It was my turquoise; I had it of Leah when I was a bachelor"

(113–115). This line humanizes Shylock by suggesting that he had a wife and that she is no longer with him. An actor can very easily swing the audience's sympathies back to Shylock with this line, as Shylock recalls a happier past that he has lost. The turquoise is a type of jewel that is especially suited to such an emotional moment: Renaissance people believed that a turquoise could fade or brighten according to its owner's health.

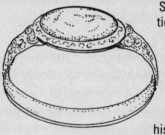

A turquoise set in a ring.

Shylock's characterization is not consistent in this scene. But Shakespeare is doing two things: He is presenting the traditional comically villainous Jew, who laughs over his crimes and wails about his ducats; and he is also humanizing Shylock, showing where his evil comes from. In other words, the issues are being complicated. The audience's reactions lurch violently between sympathy and hatred for Shylock, and this effect seems to be deliberate. Shakespeare is ensuring that the forthcoming trial scene will *not* be a simple battle between good and evil, but will acknowledge some of the complexity of the situation, as Shylock's undoubted evil is set against his reasons for doing it.

Act III, Scene 2

Bassanio arrives in Belmont and attempts the casket test. To Portia's delight, he chooses the right casket. But their joy is interrupted when they learn that Antonio cannot repay his loan to Shylock, and must pay the forfeit of a pound of flesh.

ACT III, SCENE 2
Belmont. A room in Portia's house.

[*Enter* BASSANIO, PORTIA, GRATIANO, NERISSA, *and all their Trains.*]

Portia I pray you tarry; pause a day or two
Before you hazard, for in choosing wrong
I lose your company. Therefore forbear awhile.
There's something tells me, but it is not love,
I would not lose you; and you know yourself   5
Hate counsels not in such a quality.
But lest you should not understand me well —
And yet a maiden hath no tongue but thought —
I would detain you here some month or two
Before you venture for me. I could teach you   10
How to choose right, but then I am forsworn.
So will I never be. So may you miss me.
But if you do, you'll make me wish a sin —
That I had been forsworn. Beshrow your eyes!
They have o'erlooked me and divided me;   15
One half of me is yours, the other half yours —
Mine own I would say; but if mine then yours,
And so all yours! O these naughty times
Puts bars between the owners and their rights!
And so, though yours, not yours. Prove it so,   20
Let fortune go to hell for it, not I.
I speak too long, but 'tis to peize the time,
To eke it and to draw it out in length,
To stay you from election.

Bassanio   Let me choose,
For as I am, I live upon the rack.   25

Portia Upon the rack, Bassanio? Then confess
What treason there is mingled with your love.

NOTES

6.   *Hate . . . quality:* it is not hate that gives such advice.

20.   *Prove it so:* if it prove so.

22.   *peize:* piece out, delay.

26–27.   *confess/ What treason:* i.e., if you are being tortured, you must have done something treasonable.

Bassanio None but that ugly treason of mistrust
　Which makes me fear th' enjoying of my love.
　There may as well be amity and life　　　　　　　30
　'Tween snow and fire, as treason and my love.

Portia Ay, but I fear you speak upon the rack,
　Where men enforced do speak anything.

Bassanio Promise me life and I'll confess the truth.

Portia Well then, confess and live.　　　　　　　35

Bassanio　　　　　　　　　　　　Confess and love
　Had been the very sum of my confession!
　O happy torment, when my torturer
　Doth teach me answers for deliverance.
　But let me to my fortune and the caskets.

Portia Away then! I am locked in one of them;　40
　If you do love me, you will find me out.
　Nerissa and the rest, stand all aloof.
　Let music sound while he doth make his choice;
　Then if he lose he makes a swanlike end,
　Fading in music. That the comparison　　　　45
　May stand more proper, my eye shall be the stream
　And wat'ry deathbed for him. He may win;
　Arid what is music then? Then music is
　Even as the flourish when true subjects bow
　To a new-crowned monarch. Such it is　　　50
　As are those dulcet sounds in break of day
　That creep into the dreaming bridegroom's ear
　And summon him to marriage. Now he goes,
　With no less presence but with much more love
　Than young Alcides when he did redeem　　55
　The virgin tribute paid by howling Troy
　To the sea monster. I stand for sacrifice;
　The rest aloof are the Dardanian wives,
　With bleared visages come forth to view
　The issue of th' exploit. Go, Hercules!　　　60
　Live thou, I live. With much, much more dismay
　I view the fight than thou that mak'st the fray.

[*A song the whilst* BASSANIO *comments on the caskets to
　himself.*]

44. *swanlike:* the swan, normally mute, was thought to sing just before its death.

49. *flourish:* notes sounded on trumpets.

55. *Alcides:* according to Ovid, Hercules (Alcides) rescued the daughter of the King of Troy from a sea monster.

57. *stand for sacrifice:* represent a sacrificial victim.

58. *Dardanian:* Trojan.

59. *bleared:* tearstained.

61. *Live thou:* if you live; Portia imagines herself as the maiden to be rescued by Hercules.

Tell me where is fancy bred,
Or in the heart, or in the head?
How begot, how nourished?   65
   Reply, reply.
It is engend'red in the eyes,
With gazing fed, and fancy dies
In the cradle where it lies.
   Let us all ring fancy's knell.   70
   I'll begin it — Ding, dong, bell.

All   Ding, dong, bell.

Bassanio So may the outward shows be least
   themselves;
The world is still deceived with ornament.
In law, what plea so tainted and corrupt,   75
But being seasoned with a gracious voice,
Obscures the show of evil? In religion,
What damned error but some sober brow
Will bless it and approve it with a text,
Hiding the grossness with fair ornament?   80
There is no vice so simple but assumes
Some mark of virtue on his outward parts.
How many cowards whose hearts are all as false
As stairs of sand, wear yet upon their chins
The beards of Hercules and frowning Mars,   85
Who inward searched, have livers white as milk!
And these assume but valor's excrement
To render them redoubted. Look on beauty,
And you shall see 'tis purchased by the weight,
Which therein works a miracle in nature,   90
Making them lightest that wear most of it:
So are those crisped snaky golden locks,
Which maketh such wanton gambols with the wind
Upon supposed fairness, often known
To be the dowry of a second head,   95
The skull that bred them in the sepulcher.
Thus ornament is but the guiled shore
To a most dangerous sea, the beauteous scarf
Veiling an Indian beauty; in a word,
The seeming truth which cunning times put on   100
To entrap the wisest. Therefore then, thou gaudy
   gold,

63. *fancy:* lighthearted love, infatuation.

74. *still:* always.

76. *seasoned:* spiced.

87. *excrement:* outgrowth, usually of hair, as the beards of Hercules.

88. *redoubted:* feared.

89. *purchased by the weight:* i.e., cosmetics are sold by weight; this leads to the play on the word *light* (meaning both lacking weight and frivolous) in line 91.

92. *crisped:* curly.

94. *Upon supposed fairness:* on a head artificially made beautiful.

95. *dowry:* inheritance, i.e., from the skull of line 96.

97. *guiled:* beguiling.

99. *Indian:* dark, swarthy.

Hard food for Midas, I will none of thee;
Nor none of thee, thou pale and common drudge
'Tween man and man. But thou, thou meager lead
Which rather threaten'st than dost promise aught,   105
Thy paleness moves me more than eloquence;
And here choose I. Joy be the consequence!

Portia [*aside*] How all the other passions fleet to
        air:
As doubtful thoughts, and rash-embraced despair,
And shudd'ring fear, and green-eyed jealousy.   110
O love, be moderate, allay thy ecstacy,
In measure rain thy joy, scant this excess!
I feel too much thy blessing. Make it less
For fear I surfeit.

Bassanio [*opening the leaden casket*] What find I
        here?
Fair Portia's counterfeit! What demigod   115
Hath come so near creation? Move these eyes?
Or whether, riding on the balls of mine,
Seem they in motion? Here are severed lips
Parted with sugar breath; so sweet a bar
Should sunder such sweet friends. Here in her hairs   120
The painter plays the spider, and hath woven
A golden mesh t' entrap the hearts of men
Faster than gnats in cobwebs. But her eyes —
How could he see to do them? Having made one,
Methinks it should have power to steal both his   125
And leave itself unfurnished. Yet look, how far
The substance of my praise doth wrong this shadow
In underprizing it, so far this shadow
Doth limp behind the substance. Here's the scroll,
The continent and summary of my fortune.   130
        "You that choose not by the view
        Chance as fair, and choose as true.
        Since this fortune falls to you,
        Be content and seek no new.
        If you be well pleased with this   135
        And hold your fortune for your bliss,
        Turn you where your lady is,
        And claim her with a loving kiss."
A gentle scroll. Fair lady, by your leave. [*Kisses her.*]

102. *Hard food:* all Midas touched turned to gold, and he was therefore unable to eat.

103. *pale . . . drudge:* silver.

115–116. *What . . . creation?:* i.e., what artist, almost divine in his work, has so nearly reproduced the living subject?

120. *sweet friends:* i.e., the two lips.

124–126. *Having . . . unfurnished:* i.e., having painted one eye, and blinded by its beauty, the painter would be unable to complete the other.

127. *shadow:* the painting.

130. *continent:* container.

132. *Chance as fair:* guess as fortunately.

I come by note, to give and to receive.   140
Like one of two contending in a prize,
That thinks he hath done well in people's eyes,
Hearing applause and universal shout,
Giddy in spirit, still gazing in a doubt
Whether those peals of praise be his or no —   145
So, thrice-fair lady, stand I even so,
As doubtful whether what I see be true,
Until confirmed, signed, ratified by you.

Portia You see me, Lord Bassanio, where I stand,
Such as I am. Though for myself alone   150
I would not be ambitious in my wish
To wish myself much better, yet for you
I would be trebled twenty times myself,
A thousand times more fair, ten thousand times more
        rich,
That only to stand high in your account,   155
I might in virtues, beauties, livings, friends,
Exceed account. But the full sum of me
Is sum of something — which, to term in gross,
Is an unlessoned girl, unschooled, unpracticed;
Happy in this, she is not yet so old   160
But she may learn; happier than this,
She is not bred so dull but she can learn;
Happiest of all, is that her gentle spirit
Commits itself to yours to be directed,
As from her lord, her governor, her king.   165
Myself and what is mine to you and yours
Is now converted. But now I was the lord
Of this fair mansion, master of my servants,
Queen o'er myself; and even now, but now,
This house, these servants, and this same myself   170
Are yours, my lord's. I give them with this ring,
Which when you part from, lose, or give away,
Let it presage the ruin of your love
And be my vantage to exclaim on you.

Bassanio Madam, you have bereft me of all words.   175
Only my blood speaks to you in my veins,
And there is such confusion in my powers
As, after some oration fairly spoke

---

140. *by note:* according to written directions.

156. *livings:* possessions.

158. *term in gross:* give in full.

Ring Story

174. *vantage to exclaim on you:* opportunity to reproach.

177. *powers:* faculties.

By a beloved prince, there doth appear
Among the buzzing pleased multitude,   180
Where every something being blent together
Turns to a wild of nothing, save of joy
Expressed and not expressed. But when this ring
Parts from this finger, then parts life from hence;
O then be bold to say Bassanio's dead!   185

Nerissa My lord and lady, it is now our time,
That have stood by and seen our wishes prosper,
To cry "good joy." Good joy, my lord and lady!

Gratiano My Lord Bassanio, and my gentle lady,
I wish you all the joy that you can wish —   190
For I am sure you can wish none from me;
And when your honors mean to solemnize
The bargain of your faith, I do beseech you
Even at that time I may be married too.

Bassanio With all my heart, so thou canst get a wife.   195

Gratiano I thank your lordship; you have got
    me one.
My eyes, my lord, can look as swift as yours:
You saw the mistress, I beheld the maid.
You loved, I loved; for intermission
No more pertains to me, my lord, than you.   200
Your fortune stood upon the caskets there,
And so did mine too, as the matter falls;
For wooing here until I sweat again,
And swearing till my very roof was dry
With oaths of love, at last — if promise last —   205
got a promise of this fair one here
To have her love, provided that your fortune
Achieved her mistress.

Portia   Is this true, Nerissa?

Nerissa Madam, it is, so you stand pleased withal.

Bassanio And do you, Gratiano, mean good faith?   210

Gratiano Yes, faith, my lord.

Bassanio Our feast shall be much honored in your
    marriage.

191. *none from me:* i.e., wish no more (for yourselves) than I wish you.

199. *intermission:* delay.

204. *roof:* of the mouth.

Gratiano We'll play with them the first boy, for a
thousand ducats.   215

Nerissa What, and stake down?

Gratiano No, we shall near win at that sport, and
stake down.
But who comes here? Lorenzo and his infidel!
What, and my old Venetian friend Salerio!   220

[*Enter* LORENZO, JESSICA, *and* SALERIO, *a Messenger
from Venice.*]

Bassanio Lorenzo and Salerio, welcome hither,
If that the youth of my new int'rest here
Have power to bid you welcome. By your leave,
I bid my very friends and countrymen,
Sweet Portia, welcome.   225

Portia   So do I, my lord.
They are entirely welcome.

Lorenzo I thank your honor. For my part, my lord,
My purpose was not to have seen you here,
But meeting with Salerio by the way,
He did entreat me past all saying nay   230
To come with him along.

Salerio   I did, my lord.
And I have reason for it. Signior Antonio
Commends him to you. [*Gives* BASSANIO *a letter.*]

Bassanio   Ere I ope his letter,
I pray you tell me how my good friend doth.

Salerio Not sick, my lord, unless it be in mind,   235
Nor well unless in mind. His letter there
Will show you his estate. [BASSANIO *opens the letter.*]

Gratiano Nerissa, cheer yond stranger; bid her
welcome.
Your hand, Salerio. What's the news from Venice?
How doth that royal merchant, good Antonio?   240
I know he will be glad of our success;
We are the Jasons, we have won the Fleece.

Salerio I would you had won the fleece that he
hath lost!

214–215. *We'll . . . ducats:* we'll wager a thousand ducats we produce a boy before they do.

216. *stake down?:* i.e., cash down, a gambler's term deliberately misunderstood by Gratiano in order to produce the ribald jest of 217–218.

219. *infidel:* Jessica.

222–223. *If . . . welcome:* if my new position in the household gives me the right to greet you.

242. *Jasons:* the reference is again to the search for the Golden Fleece; see I.1.171.

Portia There are some shrewd contents in yond
    same paper
That steals the color from Bassanio's cheek: 245
Some dear friend dead, else nothing in the world
Could turn so much the constitution
Of any constant man. What, worse and worse?
With leave, Bassanio — I am half yourself,
And I must freely have the half of anything   250
That this same paper brings you.

Bassanio   O sweet Portia,
Here are a few of the unpleasant'st words
That ever blotted paper! Gentle lady,
When I did first impart my love to you,
I freely told you all the wealth I had   255
Ran in my veins — I was a gentleman —
And then I told you true; and yet, dear lady,
Rating myself at nothing, you shall see
How much I was a braggart. When I told you
My state was nothing, I should then have told you   260
That I was worse than nothing; for indeed
I have engaged myself to a dear friend,
Engaged my friend to his mere enemy
To feed my means. Here is a letter, lady,
The paper as the body of my friend,   265
And every word in it a gaping wound
Issuing lifeblood. But is it true, Salerio?
Hath all his ventures failed? What, not one hit?
From Tripolis, from Mexico and England,
From Lisbon, Barbary, and India   270
And not one vessel scape the dreadful touch
Of merchant-marring rocks?

Salerio   Not one, my lord.
Besides, it should appear that if he had
The present money to discharge the Jew,
He would not take it. Never did I know   275
A creature that did bear the shape of man
So keen and greedy to confound a man.
He plies the Duke at morning and at night,

244. *shrewd:* sharp, bitter.

262. *engaged:* pledged, bound.

263. *mere:* absolute, unqualified.

272. *merchant:* merchant ship.

275. *He:* Shylock.

And doth impeach the freedom of the state
If they deny him justice. Twenty merchants,   280
The Duke himself, and the magnificoes
Of greatest port have all persuaded with him,
But none can drive him from the envious plea
Of forfeiture, of justice, and his bond.

Jessica When I was with him, I have heard him   285
swear
To Tubal and to Chus, his countrymen,
That he would rather have Antonio's flesh
Than twenty times the value of the sum
That he did owe him; and I know, my lord,
If law, authority, and power deny not,   290
It will go hard with poor Antonio.

Portia Is it your dear friend that is thus in
trouble?

Bassanio The dearest friend to me, the kindest
man,
The best-conditioned and unwearied spirit
In doing courtesies, and one in whom   295
The ancient Roman honor more appears
Than any that draws breath in Italy.

Portia What sum owes he the Jew?

Bassanio For me, three thousand ducats.

Portia   What, no more?
Pay him six thousand, and deface the bond.   300
Double six thousand and then treble that,
Before a friend of this description
Shall lose a hair through Bassanio's fault.
First go with me to church and call me wife,
And then away to Venice to your friend!   305
For never shall you lie by Portia's side
With an unquiet soul. You shall have gold
To pay the petty debt twenty times over;
When it is paid, bring your true friend along.
My maid Nerissa and myself meantime   310
Will live as maids and widows. Come away!

279–280. *impeach . . . justice:* i.e., if he is denied justice he will charge the city for not upholding the rules of its own charter of freedom; Venice, as a great trading center, had to abide by certain rules, and these included overseeing and disciplining its own traders.

281. *magnificoes:* magnates, great men.

282. *port:* standing, dignity.

283. *envious:* malicious.

300. *deface:* cancel.

For you shall hence upon your wedding day.
Bid your friends welcome, show a merry cheer;
Since you are dear bought, I will love you dear.
But let me hear the letter of your friend.   315

Bassanio [*reads*] "Sweet Bassanio, my ships have
all miscarried, my creditors grow cruel, my estate is
very low, my bond to the Jew is forfeit. And since in
paying it, it is impossible I should live, all debts are
cleared between you and I if I might but see you at   320
my death. Notwithstanding, use your pleasure. If
your love do not persuade you to come, let not my
letter."

Portia O love, dispatch all business and be gone!

Bassanio Since I have your good leave to go away,
I will make haste, but till I come again   325
No bed shall e'er be guilty of my stay,
Nor rest be interposer 'twixt us twain. [*Exeunt.*]

312.   *hence:* go hence,

COMMENTARY

Portia and Bassanio have said very little since Shakespeare introduces them to us in Act I, Scene 1, and Act II, Scene 2. They have been onstage several times, but Bassanio has been overshadowed by the plot involving Shylock and Jessica, while Portia simply made polite remarks to her overbearing suitors. Shakespeare begins this scene by reminding us of Portia's love for Bassanio, and also of her fear that he will fail the casket test. She begs Bassanio to wait a while, because she is fearful of losing his company. But Shakespeare also reminds us of her proud wit as she insists that "it is not love" that makes her say this (4).

Bassanio's primary reason for sailing to Belmont was to gain Portia's wealth in order to pay off his debts. Bassanio says as much himself (I.1.132–134). This raises the question, "Will Bassanio prove to be anything other than a fortune-hunter?"

The answer is probably "yes." Although this scene *could* be played in a cynical way, with Bassanio impatient to solve the riddle and gain the money, such an interpretation would seem to be playing *against* the text. Bassanio stresses that he is in love with Portia, and there is no mention of Portia's wealth. Why has this change occurred? Why has the cash-starved prodigal now become an archetypal romantic hero?

The Merchant of Venice continually shifts between idealism and realism. The play expresses many lofty ideals. One of these ideals is expressed in Portia's famous speech on mercy (IV.1.182–203); other examples are the sentiments expressed by the casket test, such as the notion that one should not judge by appearances. These noble ideals are always associated with Portia and Belmont.

Readers and theatergoers have never failed to notice that Venice is a more realistic setting than Belmont. In the opening scene, Shakespeare associates Venice with money, emphasising its trading power. Venice is a place where running out of money results in hardship and danger, as Antonio and Bassanio discover. Of course, Antonio has certain ideals. He believes that usury is wicked and that money should be lent without interest. But in Venice, such idealism cannot operate. In Venice, usurers flourish because poverty never vanishes, and even Antonio finds himself forced to borrow money from a usurer.

In Belmont, it is much easier to be idealistic. It is a fairy-tale land of riddles and beautiful heiresses, which makes it a haven, secluded from the danger and suffering of the real world. In Belmont, Bassanio can be a noble romantic hero, who will solve the riddle thanks to his own good nature. It is only when Portia and Bassanio travel to Venice that their situation becomes complicated.

Thus, when Portia makes her beautiful speech about music (43–53), it is impossible not to take it seriously. Portia and Bassanio's earlier conversation, in which the torment of their position made them feel like torture victims (24–39) stresses the intensity of their emotions. So when Portia compares Bassanio to Alcides (or Hercules) rescuing a princess from a sea-monster, it fits, no matter how wimpy the actor.

The song is a warning against "fancy." To an Elizabethan, the word "fancy" meant a superficial desire for a trivial object. The song tells us that fancy is the kind of desire that comes not from the head or the heart, but from the eyes. In other words it is the desire for something simply because it is beautiful, not because it has any worth in and of itself.

The subject of the song is obviously important when played alongside Bassanio's decision-making. Indeed, some people think that Portia deliberately stages this song in order to give a hint to Bassanio that he should

Hercules (Alcides).
Christie's Images/SuperStock

not choose the gold or silver caskets (after all, she didn't present the song to her other suitors). Although this could be amusing in performance, a humorous portrayal could spoil the scene's romantic tone. For the scene to work as a idealistic romance, Bassanio must figure out the answer to the riddle himself.

Bassanio comes to the correct conclusion straight away. He knows already that the gold and silver caskets cannot be the right answer because "outward shows" (73) often have the least substance within. Shakespeare now uses this idea to satirize the world in general. Bassanio notices that a good lawyer can persuade a court that something is true even when it isn't; the Bible can be cited to justify evil; and cowards can put on a show of bravery. Throughout the world, beauty can be used to disguise corruption and danger (73–101).

Bassanio is aware of the dangers of gold and silver, and he is reminded of the story of King Midas, whose love of gold brought him to his death. This must inevitably remind us of the far-off world of Venice, where gold caused all of the characters' problems. Despite the attractions of gold and the intense desire for it, which has motivated all the characters, gold has brought them nothing but danger and suffering. Bassanio has seen all this, and perhaps that is why he instinctively knows to choose the leaden casket, which is not beautiful or valuable, but contains treasure that is not dangerous.

Portia's joy is expressed as an intense passion. She casts from her mind all the bad things about love: doubt, despair, fear, and jealousy (109–110). They have no place in the life that she imagines with Bassanio. Just as in

I.2.17–22, Shakespeare is portraying Portia as a passionate woman who tries to keep her passions restrained by common sense.

The message on the scroll congratulates Bassanio for not being seduced by the "view," or appearance of the casket. Bassanio is being congratulated for his lack of superficiality—but he has arrived in Belmont on a borrowed ship, wearing clothes bought with borrowed money. Beneath Bassanio's finery is a bankrupt spendthrift. One could argue that Bassanio's stage image is the precise opposite of what the scroll is saying.

Although this is an element of the scene, recall the inscription on the leaden casket that had repelled the other suitors. "Who chooseth me must give and hazard all he hath." Bassanio's journey to Belmont has been a risk and a hazard. He has risked everything to win Portia's love. More importantly, the inscription hints that to love somebody inevitably requires the risking of everything. Shakespeare reminds us of the dangers that come with love. First, there is the jealousy and fear that Portia rejects (108–110). Second, when Bassanio sees Portia's portrait, he describes its attractiveness in frightening terms. Her hair is a "golden web" where men are caught by her beauty, like gnats caught by a spider (120–123). And her face is so beautiful that the portrait painter must have been almost blinded by her beauty (123–126). These images of fear and danger remind us of the dangerous side of love—but they also show the bravery of Bassanio in "hazarding" so much to gain Portia's hand.

Portia must also "give and hazard" all she has. In Elizabethan England, women lost all their power when they married. Portia must now hand over to Bassanio her vast fortune, her household, and even her right to make her own decisions. Bassanio will become "her lord, her governor, her king" (165). Portia emphasizes that in marrying Bassanio, she will be giving up a great deal. Again, this scene stresses that "giving and hazarding" are an essential part of what Portia and Bassanio are undertaking.

At this time, Portia seems happy to follow traditional values and give up her power. She says that she is lacking in knowledge and maturity, and is content to be

"directed" by Bassanio's "spirit" (157–167). Of course, this statement raises some questions, because we know that Bassanio's problems began with his wild spending habits (see I.1.122–134). We might, therefore, feel that Bassanio will not be a success at governing the estate. In addition, Shakespeare's portrayal of Portia thus far has not given the impression that she is particularly "gentle" or "unschooled"; indeed, she has come across as an intelligent and assertive woman. The scenes that follow will confirm these thoughts. But for now, Shakespeare is stressing the power that Portia must legally give up, and therefore the sacrifice that both lovers have made to arrive at this point.

Shakespeare strongly emphasizes the exchanging of the rings (171–174, 183–185), as Bassanio and Portia vow that to lose the rings would be equivalent to death. With this, Shakespeare sets up the complications of Act V.

The announcement that Gratiano and Nerissa are also engaged begins a gradual descent from the heights of romantic idealism to the more physical side of love. But a strong strain of idealism still exists here. Recall that in II.6.9–20, Gratiano was the man who poured scorn on Lorenzo's engagement to Jessica, and refused to believe that love could remain after marriage without going stale. Now, in the peaceful environs of Belmont, Gratiano has changed into an idealistic romantic hero, just like Bassanio.

However, Gratiano's description of his courtship with Nerissa introduces humor to the scene. He describes his attempts to woo Nerissa as an arduous task that brought him out in a sweat (203) and made his mouth dry with repeated protestations of love (204). The humor recalls the characters as they appeared in previous scenes. Gratiano was the blunt, arrogant joker who refused to take anything seriously. Nerissa was the bossy, motherly, and sensible maid. The idea of these two attempting to court each other is funny, and also rather touching, because we cannot imagine how either of them could have managed to utter the serious words of love that are required.

In Elizabethan drama, noble, serious scenes are commonly mixed with earthy humor. When Gratiano turns to the real reason for marriage—the begetting of children—Shakespeare illustrates this mix of seriousness and humor. Gratiano jokingly suggests a race to see who can conceive the first boy-child (213–217). The effect of this apparent clashing of "high" and "low" drama is implicitly to laugh at the stylized romantic dialogue of Portia and Bassanio, reminding everyone that love has both a romantic side and a physical side. Shakespeare uses this technique to stage an idealized romance, without sentimentalizing it.

At this point, the heroes and heroines are returned abruptly to Venetian reality. The Venetians enter, bringing with them the bad news about Antonio. The tranquillity and apparent safety of Belmont has been broken and the characters are reminded that beyond its walls is the dark and dangerous world of Venice.

Note that Bassanio has now begun to act as the "lord of the manor." It is now his responsibility to greet the new arrivals. He is hesitant at first, being uncertain whether he has the "power" to do this since his "new int'rest" (his mastership of the household) has only just begun (220–222).

The letter from Antonio informs Bassanio that the bond has been broken. Antonio's ships have all been lost, and he has no money to repay Shylock. Bassanio had defeated one obstacle in his quest for Portia; now he is faced with another. Bassanio must help Antonio out of the situation that Bassanio has placed him in.

With the entrance of the Venetians, the plot turns away from the idealistic world of love and back toward Venice, where money is the dominating force. A striking stage effect emphasizes this: Gratiano proudly tells his friends that "we have won the fleece" (241), but his joking remarks fall flat. He realizes that no one else is laughing, because Bassanio's face reveals his horror at what he is reading (244–247).

Bassanio must now confess to the state of his finances. He has already told Portia that he is penniless, and that the only "wealth" he had was the aristocratic blood in his veins (253–256). Now, he must confess to a further deception. He feels that his mind is just as worthless as his finances, because he has placed his friend in danger in order to get the money that he needed for himself (256–263).

Shakespeare stresses the completeness of Antonio's losses. The list of ships that Bassanio gives, "From Tripolis, from Mexico and England, / From Lisbon, Barbary, and India" (268–269) stresses that despite Antonio's numerous investments in all manner of different trades and ports, every single one of them has sunk. This is "fairy-tale" plotting, and it suggests to Bassanio that he is being punished for burdening Antonio in this way. Bassanio feels that he is responsible and acknowledges himself to be "worse than nothing" (260).

If Bassanio is being punished, as he seems to believe, how can he right his wrong? He must save Antonio from his enemy. But Salerio's speech emphasizes that this will be a difficult task. Salerio describes Shylock not as a man, but as an animal. He is a "creature" that only bears "the shape of man" (275). Shylock is desperate to extract his bond from Antonio; he is "keen and greedy" for it (276). Shylock's response recalls his gloating behavior in Act I, Scene 3; but now his jovial attitude has been transformed into a frightening desire for revenge.

Jessica's short speech adds further proof that Antonio is in terrible danger. Shylock has been longing to extract the bond from his enemy and would prefer to take the pound of flesh rather than receive twenty times the sum that he is owed.

However, Portia doesn't seem to hear this. She is convinced that Shylock will be satisfied if she simply repays the debt with treble the amount. Shylock is often thought to be a symbol of the desire for money above everything else, but as this scene illustrates, some things do come before money for Shylock, primarily revenge. Shylock is not interested in money at this point; he is interested in revenge. No money can draw Shylock away from his chance to inflict pain on the man who spurned him and treated him like a dog.

Portia nobly offers to give Antonio a huge amount of money. This demonstrates her Christian charity; the same kind of act that Antonio apparently did that caused Shylock to resent him (see I.3.41–42). In the real world

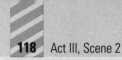

of Venice, however, things are not so simple. Shakespeare makes it clear in this scene that the Christians do not understand Shylock. They do not realize that his anger stems from something deeper than his desire for money. Jessica understands this. But no one listens to her. Could this be because she is only a Jew? Some directors depict the Christians as ignoring Jessica, or treating her with disdain (note that Gratiano jokingly calls her an "infidel" in line 218).

Finally, we should notice that despite her promise to relinquish her authority to Bassanio, Portia is making all the decisions here. She is impatient with Bassanio's moping (323) and makes sure everyone is firmly married before they rush off to Venice. This sets the stage for Act 4, Scene 1, in which Portia's intelligence saves the day in the courtroom scene.

Act III, Scene 3

Antonio is in prison. Shylock torments him because he knows that Venetian law is on his side.

ACT III, SCENE 3
Venice. A street.

[*Enter* SHYLOCK, SOLANIO, ANTONIO, *and the Jailer.*]

Shylock Jailer, look to him. Tell not me of mercy.
This is the fool that lent out money gratis.
Jailer, look to him.

Antonio   Hear me yet, good Shylock.

Shylock I'll have my bond! Speak not against my
   bond!
I have sworn an oath that I will have my bond.   5
Thou call'dst me dog before thou hadst a cause,
But since I am a dog, beware my fangs.
The Duke shall grant me justice. I do wonder,
Thou naughty jailer, that thou art so fond
To come abroad with him at his request.   10

Antonio I pray thee hear me speak.

Shylock I'll have my bond. I will not hear thee
   speak.
I'll have my bond, and therefore speak no more.
I'll not be made a soft and dull-eyed fool,
To shake the head, relent, and sigh, and yield   15
To Christian intercessors. Follow not.
I'll have no speaking; I will have my bond. [*Exit.*]

Solanio It is the most impenetrable cur
That ever kept with men.

Antonio   Let him alone;
I'll follow him no more with bootless prayers.   20
He seeks my life. His reason well I know:
I oft delivered from his forfeitures
Many that have at times made moan to me.
Therefore he hates me.

NOTES

9.   *naughty:* wicked; the word was much stronger for the Elizabethans than for us. *fond:* foolish.

19.   *kept:* dwelt.

22.   *I . . . forfeitures:* i.e., I often saved his debtors by paying their debts.

Solanio   I am sure the Duke
Will never grant this forfeiture to hold.   25

Antonio The Duke cannot deny the course of law;
For the commodity that strangers have
With us in Venice, if it be denied,
Will much impeach the justice of the state,
Since that the trade and profit of the city   30
Consisteth of all nations. Therefore go.
These griefs and losses have so bated me
That I shall hardly spare a pound of flesh
Tomorrow to my bloody creditor.
Well, jailer, on. Pray God Bassanio come   35
To see me pay his debt, and then I care not!

[*Exeunt.*]

27.   *commodity:* right to trade.

29.   *impeach:* cast doubt upon.

32.   *bated:* reduced.

COMMENTARY

The guards are taking Antonio to prison, and Shylock is once more gloating over his enemy. Shakespeare stresses again the fact that Shylock is punishing Antonio for the way Shylock has been treated by him. The man who was once called a dog is now playing up to the insult, and behaving like one (6–7).

Antonio's danger is compounded by the laws of Venice, which cannot help him. One of the Elizabethan myths about Venice was its reputation for scrupulous justice. Although its Christian citizens may have spurned the Jewish inhabitants, the law was applied equally to all races and faiths. This rule was not applied for high-minded moral reasons, however; it was applied so as not to harm Venice's trading relations with foreigners.

The hatred between Antonio and Shylock goes back many years, and it is impossible for the audience to know which of them is telling the truth. Shylock insists that their argument was begun by Antonio, who called him "dog" before there was any reason to (6). But Antonio believes that the hatred arose when he generously paid the debts of people whom Shylock had lent money to. Which of these versions is true? Shakespeare doesn't make this clear.

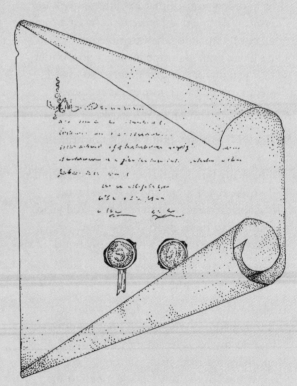

Shylock's bond.

Antonio clearly believes that nothing can save him. Neither prayers nor the law can help (19–31). Yet the scene ends with a strange sentence: Antonio will be happy so long as Bassanio is there to see his trial (35–36). The lines demonstrate Antonio's love for Bassanio, but there is a selfish side to his feelings as well.

Antonio wants Bassanio to *see* the suffering that he is undergoing for Bassanio's sake. Some critics argue that Antonio is jealous of Portia and wants to demonstrate that his love for Bassanio is greater than hers. These lines are the best evidence for that theory.

Act III, Scene 4

Portia and Nerissa plan to disguise themselves as lawyers and travel to Venice in order to save Antonio.

ACT III, SCENE 4
Belmont. A room in Portia's house.

[*Enter* PORTIA, NERISSA, LORENZO, JESSICA, *and*
    BALTHASAR.]

Lorenzo Madam, although I speak it in your
        presence,
    You have a noble and a true conceit
    Of godlike amity, which appears most strongly
    In bearing thus the absence of your lord.
    But if you knew to whom you show this honor,   5
    How true a gentleman you send relief,
    How dear a lover of my lord your husband,
    I know you would be prouder of the work
    Than customary bounty can enforce you.

Portia I never did repent for doing good,   10
    Nor shall not now; for in companions
    That do converse and waste the time together,
    Whose souls do bear an equal yoke of love,
    There must be needs a like proportion
    Of lineaments, of manners, and of spirit;   15
    Which makes me think that this Antonio,
    Being the bosom lover of my lord,
    Must needs be like my lord. If it be so,
    How little is the cost I have bestowed
    In purchasing the semblance of my soul   20
    From out the state of hellish cruelty!
    This comes too near the praising of myself;
    Therefore no more of it. Hear other things:
    Lorenzo, I commit into your hands
    The husbandry and manage of my house   25
    Until my lord's return. For mine own part,

NOTES

2. *conceit:* understanding, conception.

3. *godlike amity:* divine friendship.

9. *Than . . . you:* than ordinary acts of kindness
    might make you.

12. *waste:* pass.

20. *semblance of my soul:* i.e., Antonio, who resem-
    bles her soul mate Bassanio.

25. *husbandry:* management.

I have toward heaven breathed a secret vow
To live in prayer and contemplation,
Only attended by Nerissa here,
Until her husband and my lord's return.   30
There is a monastery two miles off,
And there we will abide. I do desire you
Not to deny this imposition,
The which my love and some necessity
Now lays upon you.   35

Lorenzo   Madam, with all my heart;
I shall obey you in all fair commands.

Portia My people do already know my mind
And will acknowledge you and Jessica
In place of Lord Bassanio and myself.
So fare you well till we shall meet again.   40

Lorenzo Fair thoughts and happy hours attend on
     you!

Jessica I wish your ladyship all heart's content.

Portia I thank you for your wish, and am well
     pleased
To wish it back on you. Fare you well, Jessica.

[*Exeunt* JESSICA *and* LORENZO.]
Now, Balthasar,   45
As I have ever found thee honest-true,
So let me find thee still. Take this same letter,
And use thou all th' endeavor of a man
In speed to Padua. See thou render this
Into my cousin's hands, Doctor Bellario;   50
And look, what notes and garments he doth give
     thee
Bring them, I pray thee, with imagined speed
Unto the traject, to the common ferry
Which trades to Venice. Waste no time in words
But get thee gone. I shall be there before thee.   55

Balthasar Madam, I go with all convenient speed.

[*Exit.*]

33. *this imposition:* this duty laid.

53. *traject:* ferry (from the Italian *traghetto*).

Portia Come on, Nerissa; I have work in hand
That you yet know not of. We'll see our husbands
Before they think of us.

Nerissa   Shall they see us?

Portia They shall, Nerissa, but in such a habit   60
That they shall think we are accomplished
With that we lack. I'll hold thee any wager,
When we are both accoutered like young men,
I'll prove the prettier fellow of the two,
And wear my dagger with the braver grace,   65
And speak between the change of man and boy
With a reed voice, and turn two mincing steps
Into a manly stride, and speak of frays
Like a fine bragging youth, and tell quaint lies,
How honorable ladies sought my love,   70
Which I denying, they fell sick and died—
I could not do withal! Then I'll repent,
And wish, for all that, that I had not killed them.
And twenty of these puny lies I'll tell,
That men shall swear I have discontinued school   75
Above a twelvemonth. I have within my mind
A thousand raw tricks of these bragging Jacks,
Which I will practice.

Nerissa   Why, shall we turn to men?

Portia Fie, what a question 's that,
If thou wert near a lewd interpreter!   80
But come, I'll tell thee all my whole device
When I am in my coach, which stays for us
At the park gate; and therefore haste away,
For we must measure twenty miles today. [*Exeunt.*]

61.   *accomplished:* equipped.

69.   *quaint:* ingenious, clever.

72.   *I . . . withal:* I could not help it.

77.   *Jacks:* fellows (contemptuous).

78.   *turn to:* a pun meaning (1) turn into, (2) embrace (see I.3.81); the second meaning produces Portia's reply.

COMMENTARY

The beginning of this scene continues the theme of the previous scene's last two lines. Lorenzo and Portia are discussing Bassanio's friendship with Antonio. Lorenzo is impressed with Portia's ability to remain free from jealousy while Bassanio leaves her to join Antonio (2–4). When Lorenzo talks of Portia's "conceit" of "godlike amity," (2–3) he is referring to *platonic* (non-sexual) love, which Plato believed to be the highest form of love. Lorenzo is admiring the fact that Portia does not feel threatened, and that she has offered money to help to rescue Antonio, whom she has never met.

The potential for conflict between platonic friendship and sexual love was an important feature of Elizabethan drama, including some of Shakespeare's plays such as *The Two Gentlemen of Verona* and *The Two Noble Kinsmen*. In this scene, Portia does not see any conflict at all. She reasons that if two friends can be so close, they must be very much alike. Therefore, Antonio must be similar to Bassanio, and Portia has no problem with saving someone who resembles the man she loves (10–21). As noted in the previous scene, however, Antonio may regard Portia as a rival.

After Lorenzo has gone, Portia and Nerissa discuss their secret plan to disguise themselves as boys and follow Bassanio to Venice. This plot device is a very silly one, and no one would pretend otherwise. But of course, the entire play is silly if it is viewed as a realistic depiction of life. The stories of the casket test and the pound of flesh are equally unrealistic. Elizabethan drama does not try to recreate life in a believable, realistic way. Instead, it shows us vivid stage images that symbolize the issues in people's lives. What is important is not the realism of the play's events but what those events represent.

Portia's plan to follow Bassanio tells us that she is an active woman, rather than a passive one. Shakespeare illustrates this by contrasting the story Portia tells Lorenzo with her real plans. She tells Lorenzo that she will spend the time during Bassanio's absence "in prayer and contemplation" at a monastery (28). This behavior is the ideal for a Renaissance wife, who was expected to accept passively everything that happened to her.

But Portia is not that kind of person. She wants to see her husband again (57–59), and has invented a daring plan to do so. Again, we can see that Portia is a more intelligent and capable person than Bassanio. Elizabethan playwrights often depicted women disguising themselves as men, and this example helps us to understand why. The position of women at the time was such that it was unfeasible for them to do "active" things, such as helping their husbands to save a friend. Dressing up as boys, however, gives the female characters temporary masculinity, and this allows them to do all the active things that social codes would normally have prevented women from doing. The technique makes the play more dramatically interesting. Had Portia behaved like a conventional wife, she would be much less exciting to watch. In addition, we must remember that in the Elizabethan theatre, the female roles were played by boys. When Portia and Nerissa change into male clothes, the audience would therefore have the strange effect of seeing the boy actors looking more like they would have looked in real life, even though they are supposed to be in disguise. One of the side effects of this type of staging is a blurring of the difference between men and women, because gender became a matter of clothing, rather than biology.

Act III, Scene 5

Launcelot jokes with Jessica and Lorenzo; then they admire the qualities of Portia and Bassanio.

ACT III, SCENE 5
Belmont. A garden.

[*Enter* LAUNCELOT *the* Clown *and* JESSICA.]

Launcelot Yes truly; for look you, the sins of the
father are to be laid upon the children. Therefore,
I promise you I fear you. I was always plain with
you, and so now I speak my agitation of the matter.
Therefore be o' good cheer, for truly I think you   5
are damned. There is but one hope in it that can do
you any good, and that is but a kind of bastard
hope neither.

Jessica And what hope is that, I pray thee?

Launcelot Marry, you may partly hope that your   10
father got you not — that you are not the Jew's
daughter.

Jessica That were a kind of bastard hope indeed!
So the sins of my mother should be visited upon me.

Launcelot Truly then, I fear you are damned   15
both by father and mother. Thus when I shun Scylla
your father, I fall into Charybdis your mother. Well,
you are gone both ways.

Jessica I shall be saved by my husband. He hath
made me a Christian.   20

Launcelot Truly, the more to blame he! We were
Christians enow before, e'en as many as could well
live one by another. This making of Christians will
raise the price of hogs; if we grow all to be pork-
eaters, we shall not shortly have a rasher on the   25
coals for money.

[*Enter* LORENZO.]

NOTES

3.   *fear you:* fear for you.

4.   *agitation:* a mistake for cogitation.

8.   *neither:* the meaning is, "nor is that anything but a bastard hope."

16–17.   *Scylla . . . Charybdis:* In Homer's Odyssey, Ulysses must sail between the twin dangers of the monster Scylla and the whirlpool Charybdis.

19–20.   *He . . . Christian:* see I Corinthians 7:14; the unbelieving wife is sanctified by the husband.

22.   *enow:* enough

25.   *rasher:* of bacon.

Jessica I'll tell my husband, Launcelot, what you
say. Here he comes.

Lorenzo I shall grow jealous of you shortly,
Launcelot, if you thus get my wife into corners.   30

Jessica Nay, you need not fear us, Lorenzo. Launcelot and I are out. He tells me flatly there's no mercy
for me in heaven because I am a Jew's daughter;
and he says you are no good member of the commonwealth, for in converting Jews to Christians   35
you raise the price of pork.

Lorenzo [*to* LAUNCELOT] I shall answer that better to the commonwealth than you can the getting
up of the Negro's belly. The Moor is with child by
you, Launcelot.   40

Launcelot It is much that the Moor should be more
than reason; but if she be less than an honest
woman, she is indeed more than I took her for.

Lorenzo How every fool can play upon the word!
I think the best grace of wit will shortly turn into   45
silence, and discourse grow commendable in none
only but parrots. Go in, sirrah; bid them prepare
for dinner.

Launcelot That is done, sir. They have all
stomachs.   50

Lorenzo Goodly Lord, what a wit-snapper are you!
Then bid them prepare dinner.

Launcelot That is done too, sir. Only "cover" is
the word.

Lorenzo Will you cover then, sir?   55

Launcelot Not so, sir, neither! I know my duty.

Lorenzo Yet more quarreling with occasion! Wilt
thou show the whole wealth of thy wit in an instant?
I pray thee understand a plain man in his plain
meaning: go to thy fellows, bid them cover the table,   60
serve in the meat, and we will come in to dinner.

32.	*are out:* have quarreled.
37.	*answer:* justify.
41–42.	*more than reason:* larger than is reasonable.
42.	*honest:* chaste.
44.	*play upon the word:* Launcelot has been doing this with *Moor* and *more* in the preceding speech.
53.	*cover:* to lay the table; i.e., all that is left to do is to lay the table.
56.	*my duty:* Launcelot now takes the word *cover* to mean "put on a cap," which he will not do in the presence of Lorenzo.
57.	*quarreling with occasion:* quarreling at every opportunity.

Launcelot For the table, sir, it shall be served in;
for the meat, sir, it shall be covered; for your
coming in to dinner, sir, why let it be as humors and
conceits shall govern. [*Exit* LAUNCELOT.]   65

Lorenzo O dear discretion, how his words are
    suited!
The fool hath planted in his memory
An army of good words; and I do know
A many fools that stand in better place,
Garnished like him, that for a tricksy word   70
Defy the matter. How cheer'st thou Jessica?
And now, good sweet, say thy opinion —
How dost thou like the Lord Bassanio's wife?

Jessica Past all expressing. It is very meet
The Lord Bassanio live an upright life   75
For having such a blessing in his lady;
He finds the joys of heaven here on earth,
And if on earth he do not merit it,
In reason he should never come to heaven.
Why, if two gods should play some heavenly match   80
And on the wager lay two earthly women,
And Portia one, there must be something else
Pawned with the other, for the poor rude world
Hath not her fellow.

Lorenzo   Even such a husband
Hast thou of me as she is for a wife.   85

Jessica Nay, but ask my opinion too of that!

Lorenzo I will anon. First let us go to dinner.

Jessica Nay, let me praise you while I have a
    stomach.

Lorenzo No, pray thee, let it serve for table-talk;
Then howsome'er thou speak'st, 'mong other things   90
I shall digest it.

Jessica   Well, I'll set you forth.

[*Exeunt.*]

---

62.   *table:* Launcelot now uses the word to mean the food itself.

63.   *covered:* served in a covered dish.

64–65.   *humors and conceits:* moods and fancy.

66.   *dear discretion:* fine discrimination (ironic).
    suited: made to match one another.

69.   *better place:* i.e., socially.

70.   *Garnished like him:* equipped like him (with a taste for punning).

71.   *Defy the matter:* ignore the real subject.
    How cheer'st thou?: what do you feel?

81.   *lay:* stake.

83.   *Pawned:* wagered.

84.   *fellow:* equal.

88.   *stomach:* appetite.

91.   *set you forth:* (1) prepare as for a feast, (2) praise you.

COMMENTARY

Launcelot Gobbo is still trying to reconcile his affection for Jessica with his belief that all Jews are devils. This theme continually recurs in the clown scenes, and it seems as though Shakespeare is deliberately making fun of the Christians' attitudes toward the Jews. Launcelot keeps discovering contradictions in his understanding of theology. For example, he is worried that even if Jessica has converted to Christianity, she will still be "damned," because she is the daughter of a Jew. Launcelot recalls the Biblical teaching that the sins of the father are laid on the children (Exodus 20:5, 34:7; Deuteronomy 5:9).

Scylla and Charybdis: a symbol of an impossible decision.

Launcelot can think of only one possible way in which Jessica might escape divine punishment: the possibility that Shylock is not really her father because her mother could have committed adultery with a Christian man. But this gets Launcelot into worse confusions, because if that were the case, Jessica is now damned by the sins of her mother (6–18). Launcelot gives up trying to think of a way to "save" Jessica.

Jessica clears up the confusion by insisting that marrying Lorenzo has "saved" her because he has made her a Christian (1 Corinthians 7:14). But Launcelot cannot let it rest at that. Now he cheekily

suggests that this is a bad thing, because the more Christians there are, the more expensive pork will be (because Christians eat pork and Jews do not).

The function of a clown is to misunderstand people and to undermine their assumptions by asking simple, obvious questions. By highlighting the confusion of biblical texts, and raising pragmatic questions about the conversion of Jews, Launcelot, in his clownish way, demonstrates the absurdities and complications that arise from the automatic damnation of a religious faith. Ultimately, he prevents the play from simplifying life too much.

The play's depiction of the relations between its different cultures are complicated even further when Lorenzo reveals that Launcelot has had an affair with a black woman (35–37). Even the severest racial bigot in this play has turned out to be a hypocrite. Beneath the

Servants setting a dinner table.
Stock Montage/SuperStock

apparently clear-cut divisions in the play is an awareness of the complexities of real life. Launcelot continues to "misunderstand" even as he leaves the room; he manages to make a simple job like laying the table, into a bewildering mass of complexities (46–61).

Launcelot's joking may seem pointless in this scene, but his techniques will later become useful to the more serious characters. Lorenzo sees that Launcelot's misbehavior is not restricted to clowns. This sort of "fool"—a person in a much higher social position who is able to slip around common sense with the use of "tricksy" words (66)—is found throughout the play. Indeed, it is worth remembering that one person who will behave in this way in the next scene is Portia, who will outwit Shylock by playing with the precise definition of the word "flesh."

Jessica's description of Portia's virtues (70–80) stresses them above those of Bassanio. Indeed, there is a brief suggestion that Bassanio may not enter the kingdom of heaven (74–75); Jessica may be referring to Bassanio's spendthrift behavior. Again, we have the contrast between Portia and her idyllic world of Belmont, compared with the "rude world" (79). "Rude" in this sense means "vulgar," and Jessica is implicitly comparing Portia with the real world of Venice to which she is traveling. Portia's entrance into Venice will serve as a symbol of virtue entering a seedy, realistic city.

Lorenzo immediately deflates Jessica's gushing tribute, by pompously announcing that he is the male equivalent of Portia. Jessica's sarcastic reply shows us that their relationship is built on teasing. The nature of their relationship will become more apparent in Act V, Scene 1. Some productions depict Jessica and Lorenzo as a bickering couple, but it is difficult to see such an interpretation in this scene, where the teasing seems to be affectionate rather than angry. Jessica and Lorenzo seem to have a healthy sense of irony and humor, which may indicate that, despite Gratiano's prediction in Act II, Scene 6, their relationship could be a success.

Notes

Notes

THE MERCHANT OF VENICE

ACT IV

Portia *The quality of mercy is not strained;*
It droppeth as the gentle rain from heaven
Upon the place beneath. It is twice blest;
It blesseth him that gives and him that takes.
'Tis mightiest in the mightiest; it becomes
The throned monarch better than his crown.
His scepter shows the force of temporal power,
The attribute to awe and majesty,
Wherein doth sit the dread and fear of kings;
But mercy is above this sceptered sway;
It is enthroned in the hearts of kings;
It is an attribute to God himself,
And earthly power doth then show likest God's
When mercy seasons justice.

Act IV, Scene 1

Antonio appears in court to find out whether Shylock is legally entitled to claim the pound of flesh from his body. Portia arrives in disguise, and tries to persuade Shylock to forgive Antonio. When he refuses, she finds a legal loophole that saves Antonio's life. She then uses her disguise to test Bassanio's faithfulness by asking for his wedding ring as payment.

ACT IV, SCENE 1

Venice. A court of justice.

[*Enter the* DUKE, *the Magnificoes*, ANTONIO, BASSANIO, SALERIO, *and* GRATIANO *with Others*.]

Duke What, is Antonio here?

Antonio Ready, so please your Grace.

Duke I am sorry for thee. Thou art come to answer
A stony adversary, an inhuman wretch,
Uncapable of pity, void and empty
From any dram of mercy.   5

Antonio   I have heard
Your Grace hath ta'en great pains to qualify
His rigorous course; but since he stands obdurate,
And that no lawful means can carry me
Out of his envy's reach, I do oppose   10
My patience to his fury, and am armed
To suffer with a quietness of spirit
The very tyranny and rage of his.

Duke Go one, and call the Jew into the court.

Salerio He is ready at the door; he comes, my lord.   15

[*Enter* SHYLOCK.]

Duke Make room, and let him stand before our
      face.
Shylock, the world thinks, and I think so too,
That thou but leadest this fashion of thy malice
To the last hour of act; and then 'tis thought
Thou'lt show thy mercy and remorse more strange   20
Than is thy strange apparent cruelty;
And where thou now exacts the penalty,
Which is a pound of this poor merchant's flesh,
Thou wilt not only loose the forfeiture,
But touched with human gentleness and love,   25

NOTES

6.   *From:* of.

7.   *qualify:* soften, limit.

16. *our:* the Duke uses the royal plural.

18. *That malice:* you only prolong this show of hatred.

21. *strange apparent:* strange-seeming.

24. *loose:* release.

Forgive a moiety of the principal,

Glancing an eye of pity on his losses,

That have of late so huddled on his back —

Enow to press a royal merchant down

And pluck commiseration of his state   30

From brassy bosoms and rough hearts of flint,

From stubborn Turks and Tartars never trained

To offices of tender courtesy.

We all expect a gentle answer, Jew.

Shylock I have possessed your Grace of what I   35
     purpose,

And by our holy Sabbath have I sworn

To have the due and forfeit of my bond.

If you deny it, let the danger light

Upon your charter and your city's freedom!

You'll ask me why I rather choose to have   40

A weight of carrion flesh than to receive

Three thousand ducats. I'll not answer that,

But say it is my humor. Is it answered?

What if my house be troubled with a rat,

And I be pleased to give ten thousand ducats   45

To have it baned? What, are you answered yet?

Some men there are love not a gaping pig,

Some that are mad if they behold a cat,

And others, when the bagpipe sings i' th' nose,

Cannot contain their urine; for affection,   50

Master of passion, sways it to the mood

Of what it likes or loathes. Now for your answer:

As there is no firm reason to be rend'red

Why he cannot abide a gaping pig,

Why he a harmless necessary cat,   55

Why he a woollen bagpipe, but of force

Must yield to such inevitable shame

As to offend, himself being offended;

So can I give no reason, nor I will not,

More than a lodged hate and a certain loathing   60

I bear Antonio, that I follow thus

A losing suit against him. Are you answered?

Bassanio This is no answer, thou unfeeling man,

To excuse the current of thy cruelty!

26. *moiety:* portion.

28. *huddled:* piled up, accumulated.

32. *Turks and Tartars:* notorious for inhumanity.

35. *possessed:* informed.

39. *your city's freedom:* see note at III.2.278.

46. *baned:* poisoned.

47. *gaping pig:* i.e., served at the table with the mouth propped open by an orange or apple.

49. *sings i'th' nose:* makes a nasal sound

50. *affection:* natural feeling.

56. *woollen:* covered with woolen cloth.

of force: perforce.

58. *himself being offended:* i.e., since he himself has been offended, he offends others.

60. *lodged:* fixed.

62. *losing suit:* an unprofitable case; Shylock loses three thousand ducats if he wins his case.

Shylock I am not bound to please thee with my   65
   answers.

Bassanio Do all men kill the things they do not love?

Shylock Hates any man the thing he would not kill?

Bassanio Every offense is not a hate at first.

Shylock What, wouldst thou have a serpent sting
   thee twice?

Antonio I pray you think you question with the   70
   Jew.
  You may as well go stand upon the beach
  And bid the main flood bate his usual height;
  You may as well use question with the wolf,
  Why he hath made the ewe bleat for the lamb;
  You may as well forbid the mountain pines   75
  To wag their high tops and to make no noise
  When they are fretten with the gusts of heaven;
  You may as well do anything most hard
  As seek to soften that — than which what's harder? —
  His Jewish heart. Therefore I do beseech you   80
  Make no moe offers, use no farther means,
  But with all brief and plain conveniency
  Let me have judgment, and the Jew his will.

Bassanio For thy three thousand ducats here is six.

Shylock If every ducat in six thousand ducats   85
  Were in six parts, and every part a ducat,
  I would not draw them. I would have my bond.

Duke How shalt thou hope for mercy, rend'ring
   none?

Shylock What judgment shall I dread, doing no
   wrong?
  You have among you many a purchased slave,   90
  Which like your asses and your dogs and mules
  You use in abject and in slavish parts,
  Because you bought them. Shall I say to you,
  "Let them be free! marry them to your heirs!
  Why sweat they under burdens? Let their beds   95
  Be made as soft as yours, and let their palates
  Be seasoned with such viands"? You will answer,
  "The slaves are ours." So do I answer you.

70. *think:* bear in mind.

question: argue, debate.

72. *main flood:* high tide.

bate: lower, abate.

74. *lamb:* i.e., which he has killed.

77. *fretten:* disturbed, moved.

81. *moe:* more.

87. *draw:* take.

The pound of flesh which I demand of him
Is dearly bought, is mine, and I will have it.   100
If you deny me, fie upon your law!
There is no force in the decrees of Venice.
I stand for judgment. Answer; shall I have it?

Duke Upon my power I may dismiss this court
Unless Bellario, a learned doctor   105
Whom I have sent for to determine this,
Come here today.

Salerio   My lord, here stays without
A messenger with letters from the doctor,
New come from Padua.

Duke Bring us the letters. Call the messenger.   110

Bassanio Good cheer, Antonio! What, man, cour-
    age yet!
The Jew shall have my flesh, blood, bones, and all,
Ere thou shalt lose for me one drop of blood.

Antonio I am a tainted wether of the flock,
Meetest for death. The weakest kind of fruit   115
Drops earliest to the ground, and so let me.
You cannot better be employed, Bassanio,
Than to live still, and write mine epitaph.

[*Enter* NERISSA *dressed like a Lawyer's Clerk.*]

Duke Came you from Padua, from Bellario?

Nerissa From both, my lord. Bellario greets your   120
    Grace. [*Presents a letter.*]

Bassanio Why dost thou whet thy knife so ear-
    nestly?

Shylock To cut the forfeiture from that bankrout
    there.

Gratiano Not on thy sole, but on thy soul, harsh
    Jew,
Thou mak'st thy knife keen; but no metal can —
No, not the hangman's axe — bear half the keen-   125
    ness
Of thy sharp envy. Can no prayers pierce thee?

Shylock No, none that thou hast wit enough to
    make.

104.   *Upon:* by, in accordance with.

114.   *tainted:* sinful, sick.

        wether: castrated ram. Antonio thinks of himself
        as a sacrificial victim, like Isaac (Genesis 22: 13).

115.   *Meetest:* fittest.

123.   *on thy sole:* Shylock sharpens his knife on his
        shoe.

125.   *hangman's:* executioner's.

Gratiano O be thou damned, inexecrable dog,
And for thy life let justice be accused!
Thou almost mak'st me waver in my faith — 130
To hold opinion with Pythagoras
That souls of animals infuse themselves
Into the trunks of men. Thy currish spirit
Governed a wolf who, hanged for human slaughter,
Even from the gallows did his fell soul fleet, 135
And whilst thou layest in thy unhallowed dam,
Infused itself in thee; for thy desires
Are wolvish, bloody, starved, and ravenous.

Shylock Till thou canst rail the seal from off my
  bond,
Thou but offend'st thy lungs to speak so loud. 140
Repair thy wit, good youth, or it will fall
To cureless ruin. I stand here for law.

Duke This letter from Bellario doth commend
A young and learned doctor to our court.
Where is he? 145

Nerissa He attendeth here hard by
To know your answer whether you'll admit him.

Duke With all my heart. Some three or four of
  you
Go give him courteous conduct to this place.
Meantime the court shall hear Bellario's letter.

Clerk [*reads*] "Your Grace shall understand that 150
at the receipt of your letter I am very sick; but in
the instant that your messenger came, in loving visi-
tation was with me a young doctor of Rome. His
name is Balthasar. I acquainted him with the cause
in controversy between the Jew and Antonio the 155
merchant. We turned o'er many books together. He
is furnished with my opinion which, bettered with
his own learning, the greatness whereof I cannot
enough commend, comes with him at my importunity
to fill up your Grace's request in my stead. I be- 160
seech you let his lack of years be no impediment
to let him lack a reverend estimation, for I never
knew so young a body with so old a head. I leave
him to your gracious acceptance, whose trial shall

129. *for thy life:* i.e., since you are allowed to live.

131. *Pythagoras:* a Greek philosopher who held that after death the souls of animals entered the bodies of certain men.

134. *hanged:* animals who had committed crimes were executed in this way.

135. *fell:* cruel.

144. *doctor:* of law.

159. *comes with him:* i.e., he brings my opinion with him.

160. *to . . . stead:* answers your Grace's request in my place.

162. *to let him lack:* to prevent his having.

better publish his commendation." 165

[*Enter* PORTIA, *dressed like a Doctor of Laws.*]

Duke You hear the learn'd Bellario, what he
writes;
And here, I take it, is the doctor come.
Give me your hand. Come you from old Bellario?

Portia I did, my lord.

Duke You are welcome; take your place.
Are you acquainted with the difference 170
That holds this present question in the court?

Portia I am informed throughly of the cause.
Which is the merchant here? and which the Jew?

Duke Antonio and old Shylock, both stand forth.

Portia Is your name Shylock? 175

Shylock Shylock is my name.

Portia Of a strange nature is the suit you follow,
Yet in such rule that the Venetian law
Cannot impugn you as you do proceed.
[*To* ANTONIO] You stand within his danger, do you
not?

Antonio Ay, so he says. 180

Portia Do you confess the bond?

Antonio I do.

Portia Then must the Jew be merciful.

Shylock On what compulsion must I? Tell me that.

Portia The quality of mercy is not strained;
It droppeth as the gentle rain from heaven
Upon the place beneath. It is twice blest; 185
It blesseth him that gives and him that takes.
'Tis mightiest in the mightiest; it becomes
The throned monarch better than his crown.
His scepter shows the force of temporal power,
The attribute to awe and majesty, 190
Wherein doth sit the dread and fear of kings;
But mercy is above this sceptered sway;
It is enthroned in the hearts of kings;

164. *trial:* test by performance.

170–171. *the . . . court:* i.e., do you know the dispute before the court?

172. *throughly:* thoroughly.

176. *suit you follow:* law suit you are engaged in.

178. *Cannot . . . proceed:* i.e., cannot object to your argument.

179. *danger:* power.

183. *is not strained:* cannot be constrained or compelled.

187. *becomes:* befits, suits.

190. *attribute:* symbol of.

It is an attribute to God himself,
And earthly power doth then show likest God's   195
When mercy seasons justice. Therefore, Jew,
Though justice be thy plea, consider this:
That in the course of justice none of us
Should see salvation. We do pray for mercy,
And that same prayer doth teach us all to render   200
The deeds of mercy. I have spoke thus much
To mitigate the justice of thy plea,
Which if thou follow, this strict court of Venice
Must needs give sentence 'gainst the merchant there.

Shylock My deeds upon my head! I crave the law,   205
The penalty and forfeit of my bond.

Portia Is he not able to discharge the money?

Bassanio Yes, here I tender it for him in the court,
Yea, thrice the sum. If that will not suffice,
I will be bound to pay it ten times o'er   210
On forfeit of my hands, my head, my heart.
If this will not suffice, it must appear
That malice bears down truth. And I beseech you,
Wrest once the law to your authority.
To do a great right, do a little wrong,   215
And curb this cruel devil of his will.

Portia It must not be. There is no power in Venice
Can alter a decree established.
'Twill be recorded for a precedent,
And many an error by the same example   220
Will rush into the state. It cannot be.

Shylock A Daniel come to judgment! yea, a
            Daniel!
O wise young judge, how I do honor thee!

Portia I pray you let me look upon the bond.

Shylock Here 'tis, most reverend Doctor, here it is.   225

Portia Shylock, there's thrice thy money off'red
            thee.

Shylock An oath, an oath! I have an oath in
            heaven;
Shall I lay perjury upon my soul?
No, not for Venice!

192. *sway:* power.

198–199. *That . . . salvation:* i.e., given justice alone and without mercy none of us would be saved.

202. *mitigate:* temper with mercy.

207. *discharge:* pay.

213. *bears down:* suppresses.

214. *Wrest . . . authority:* i.e., for once use your authority to qualify the law.

222. *Daniel:* the wise youth who proved in cross-examination, the guilt of the corrupt elders. The story occurs in the History of Susannah in the Apocrypha.

Portia   Why, this bond is forfeit;
And lawfully by this the Jew may claim   230
A pound of flesh, to be by him cut off
Nearest the merchant's heart. Be merciful.
Take thrice thy money; bid me tear the bond.

Shylock When it is paid, according to the tenor.
It doth appear you are a worthy judge;   235
You know the law, your exposition
Hath been most sound. I charge you by the law,
Whereof you are a well-deserving pillar,
Proceed to judgment. By my soul I swear
There is no power in the tongue of man   240
To alter me. I stay here on my bond.

Antonio Most heartily I do beseech the court
To give the judgment.

Portia   Why then, thus it is:
You must prepare your bosom for his knife

Shylock O noble judge! O excellent young man!   245

Portia For the intent and purpose of the law
Hath full relation to the penalty,
Which here appeareth due upon the bond.

Shylock 'Tis very true. O wise and upright judge!
How much more elder art thou than thy looks!   250

Portia Therefore lay bare your bosom.

Shylock   Ay, his breast —
So says the bond, doth it not, noble judge?
"Nearest his heart"; those are the very words.

Portia It is so. Art there balance here to weigh
The flesh?   255

Shylock   I have them ready.

Portia Have by some surgeon, Shylock, on your
charge.
To stop his wounds, lest he do bleed to death.

Shylock Is it so nominated in the bond?

Portia It is not so expressed, but what of that?
'Twere good you do so much for charity.   260

Shylock I cannot find it; 'tis not in the bond.

234.   *tenor:* terms of the bond.

241.   *stay:* stand.

247.   *Hath full relation to:* fully allows

254.   *balance:* balances, scales.

256.   *charge:* at your expense.

Portia You, merchant, have you anything to say?

Antonio But little. I am armed and well prepared.
Give me your hand, Bassanio; fare you well.
Grieve not that I am fall'n to this for you,   265
For herein Fortune shows herself more kind
Than is her custom: it is still her use
To let the wretched man outlive his wealth
To view with hollow eye and wrinkled brow
An age of poverty; from which ling'ring penance   270
Of such misery doth she cut me off.
Commend me to your honorable wife.
Tell her the process of Antonio's end,
Say how I loved you, speak me fair in death;
And when the tale is told, bid her be judge   275
Whether Bassanio had not once a love.
Repent but you that you shall lose your friend,
And he repents not that he pays your debt;
For if the Jew do cut but deep enough,
I'll pay it instantly with all my heart.   280

Bassanio Antonio, I am married to a wife
Which is as dear to me as life itself;
But life itself, my wife, and all the world
Are not with me esteemed above thy life.
I would lose all, ay sacrifice them all   285
Here to this devil, to deliver you.

Portia Your wife would give you little thanks for
that
If she were by to hear you make the offer.

Gratiano I have a wife who I protest I love.
I would she were in heaven, so she could   290
Entreat some power to change this currish Jew.

Nerissa 'Tis well you offer it behind her back;
The wish would make else an unquiet house.

Shylock These be the Christian husbands! I have
a daughter;
Would any of the stock of Barabbas   295
Had been her husband, rather than a Christian!
We trifle time. I pray thee pursue sentence.

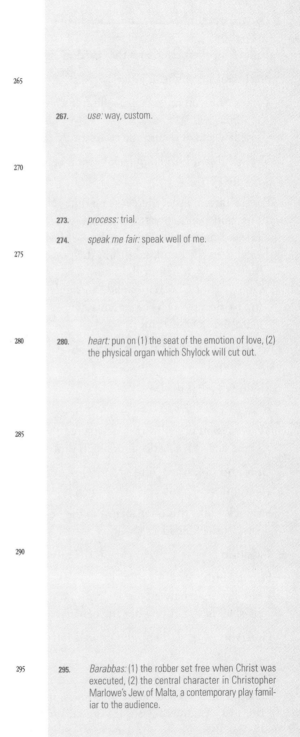

267.   *use:* way, custom.

273.   *process:* trial.

274.   *speak me fair:* speak well of me.

280.   *heart:* pun on (1) the seat of the emotion of love, (2) the physical organ which Shylock will cut out.

295.   *Barabbas:* (1) the robber set free when Christ was executed, (2) the central character in Christopher Marlowe's *Jew of Malta,* a contemporary play familiar to the audience.

Portia A pound of that same merchant's flesh is
      thine.
The court awards it, and the law doth give it —

Shylock Most rightful judge!   300

Portia And you must cut this flesh from off his
      breast.
The law allows it, and the court awards it.

Shylock Most learned judge! A sentence! Come,
      prepare!

Portia Tarry a little; there is something else.
This bond doth give thee here no jot of blood;   305
The words expressly are "a pound of flesh."
Take then thy bond, take thou thy pound of flesh;
But in the cutting it if thou dost shed
One drop of Christian blood, thy lands and goods
Are by the laws of Venice confiscate   310
Unto the state of Venice.

Loophole

Gratiano O upright judge! Mark, Jew. O learned
      judge!

Shylock Is that the law?

Portia   Thyself shalt see the act;
For, as thou urgest justice, be assured
Thou shalt have justice more than thou desir'st.   315

Gratiano O learned judge! Mark, Jew. A learned
      judge!

Shylock I take this offer then. Pay the bond thrice
And let the Christian go.

Bassanio   Here is the money.

Portia Soft!
The Jew shall have all justice. Soft, no haste;   320
He shall have nothing but the penalty.

Gratiano O Jew! an upright judge, a learned
      judge!

Portia Therefore prepare thee to cut off the flesh.
Shed thou no blood, nor cut thou less nor more
But just a pound of flesh. If thou tak'st more   325
Or less than a just pound, be it but so much

319.   *Soft:* not so fast.

320.   *all:* nothing but.

As makes it light or heavy in the substance
Or the division of the twentieth part
Of one poor scruple — nay, if the scale do turn
But in the estimation of a hair —   330
Thou diest, and all thy goods are confiscate.

Gratiano A second Daniel! a Daniel, Jew!
Now, infidel, I have you on the hip!

Portia Why doth the Jew pause? Take thy
    forfeiture.

Shylock Give me my principal, and let me go.   335

Bassanio I have it ready for thee; here it is.

Portia He hath refused it in the open court.
He shall have merely justice and his bond.

Gratiano A Daniel still say I, a second Daniel!
I thank thee, Jew for teaching me that word.   340

Shylock Shall I not have barely my principal?

Portia Thou shalt have nothing but the forfeiture,
To be so taken at thy peril, Jew.

Shylock Why, then the devil give him good of it!
I'll stay no longer question.   345

Portia   Tarry, Jew!
The law hath yet another hold on you.
It is enacted in the laws of Venice,
If it be proved against an alien
That by direct or indirect attempts
He seek the life of any citizen,   350
The party 'gainst the which he doth contrive
Shall seize one half his goods; the other half
Comes to the privy coffer of the state;
And the offender's life lies in the mercy
Of the Duke only, 'gainst all other voice.   355
In which predicament I say thou stand'st,
For it appears by manifest proceeding
That indirectly, and directly too,
Thou hast contrived against the very life
Of the defendant, and thou hast incurred   360
The danger formerly by me rehearsed.
Down therefore, and beg mercy of the Duke.

328–329. *the division . . . scruple:* by the twentieth part of a scruple, or any division of that twentieth.

329. *scruple:* a minute division of weight.

330. *estimation of a hair:* within a hair's breadth on the indicator of the scales.

333. *on the hip:* at a disadvantage in wrestling; the phrase echoes Shylock's wish at I.3.45.

341. *barely:* even.

343. *so taken:* i.e., as Portia has commanded.

345. *stay no longer question:* hear no further legal argument.

351. *contrive:* plot.

353. *privy coffer:* special fund.

355. *'gainst all other voice:* despite any contrary opinion.

361. *rehearsed:* described, outlined.

362. *Down:* kneel down.

Gratiano Beg that thou mayst have leave to hang
    thyself!
And yet, thy wealth being forfeit to the state,
Thou hast not left the value of a cord;   365
Therefore thou must be hanged at the state's charge.

Duke That thou shalt see the difference of our
    spirit,
I pardon thee thy life before thou ask it.
For half thy wealth, it is Antonio's;
The other half comes to the general state,   370
Which humbleness may drive unto a fine.

Portia Ay, for the state, not for Antonio.

Shylock Nay, take my life and all! Pardon not
    that!
You take my house when you do take the prop
That doth sustain my house. You take my life   375
When you do take the means whereby I live.

Portia What mercy can you render him, Antonio?

Gratiano A halter gratis! Nothing else, for God's
    sake!

Antonio So please my lord the Duke and all the
    court
To quit the fine for one half of his goods,   380
I am content; so he will let me have
The other half in use, to render it
Upon his death unto the gentleman
That lately stole his daughter.
Two things provided more: that for this favor   385
He presently become a Christian;
The other, that he do record a gift
Here in the court of all he dies possessed
Unto his son Lorenzo and his daughter.

Duke He shall do this, or else I do recant   390
The pardon that I late pronounced here.

Portia Art thou contented, Jew? What dost thou
    say?

Shylock I am content.

Portia   Clerk, draw a deed of gift.

---

367. *the difference of our spirit:* i.e., our mercy as opposed to your vindictiveness.

371. *Which . . . fine:* which your humility may reduce to a fine.

372. *for the . . . Antonio:* i.e., the state may reduce its penalty, but Antonio's will not be so reduced.

373. *Pardon not that!:* i.e., why pardon that?

380–384. *To . . . daughter:* i.e.. Shylock may keep half his wealth, and not pay his fine; Antonio will keep the other half in trust for Lorenzo and Jessica.

387. *record a gift:* sign a promise to give.

390. *recant:* withdraw.

Shylock I pray you give me leave to go from hence.
I am not well. Send the deed after me,   395
And I will sign it.

Duke   Get thee gone, but do it.

Gratiano In christ'ning shalt thou have two
      godfathers.
Had I been judge, thou shouldst have had ten more —
To bring thee to the gallows, not to the font.

[*Exit* SHYLOCK.]

Duke Sir, I entreat you home with me to dinner.   400

Portia I humbly do desire your Grace of pardon.
I must away this night toward Padua,
And it is meet I presently set forth.

Duke I am sorry that your leisure serves you not.
Antonio, gratify this gentleman,   405
For in my mind you are much bound to him.

[*Exit* DUKE *and his Train.*]

Bassanio Most worthy gentleman, I and my friend
Have by your wisdom been this day acquitted
Of grievous penalties, in lieu whereof,
Three thousand ducats due unto the Jew   410
We freely cope your courteous pains withal.

Antonio And stand indebted, over and above,
In love and service to you evermore.

Portia He is well paid that is well satisfied,
And I delivering you am satisfied,   415
And therein do account myself well paid;
My mind was never yet more mercenary.
I pray you know me when we meet again.
I wish you well, and so I take my leave.

Bassanio Dear sir, of force I must attempt you   420
      further.
Take some remembrance of us as a tribute,
Not as fee. Grant me two things, I pray you —
Not to deny me, and to pardon me.

Portia You press me far, and therefore I will yield.
Give me your gloves; I'll wear them for your sake.   425

---

398. *ten more:* i.e., to make up a jury of twelve.

404. *your . . . not:* i.e., you do not have the leisure.

405. *gratify:* reward, put yourself at the service of.

409. *in lieu whereof:* in return for which.

411. *cope:* offer as an equivalent for.

418. *know me:* recognize me.

420. *of . . . further:* i.e., I am compelled to try to persuade you.

423. *to pardon me:* i.e., for his insistence.

[BASSANIO *takes off his gloves.*]
And for your love I'll take this ring from you.
Do not draw back your hand; I'll take no more,
And you in love shall not deny me this.

Bassanio This ring, good sir, alas, it is a trifle!
I will not shame myself to give you this.   430

Portia I will have nothing else but only this,
And now methinks I have a mind to it.

Bassanio There's more depends on this than on the
    value.
The dearest ring in Venice will I give you,
And find it out by proclamation.   435
Only for this, I pray you pardon me.

Portia I see, sir, you are liberal in offers.
You taught me first to beg, and now methinks
You teach me how a beggar should be answered.

Bassanio Good sir, this ring was given me by my   440
    wife,
And when she put it on she made me vow
That I should neither sell nor give nor lose it.

Portia That 'scuse serves many men to save their
    gifts.
And if your wife be not a madwoman,
And know how well I have deserved this ring,   445
She would not hold out enemy for ever
For giving it to me. Well, peace be with you!

[*Exeunt* PORTIA *and* NERISSA.]

Antonio My Lord Bassanio, let him have the ring.
Let his deservings, and my love withal,
Be valued 'gainst your wife's commandement.   450

Bassanio Go, Gratiano, run and overtake him;
Give him the ring and bring him if thou canst
Unto Antonio's house. Away, make haste!

[*Exit* GRATIANO.]
Come, you and I will thither presently,
And in the morning early will we both   455
Fly toward Belmont. Come, Antonio. [*Exeunt.*]

428. *and you in love:* and since you love me.

433. *There's . . . value:* i.e., other values besides that
of the ring are involved.

436. *pardon me:* release me from this obligation.

439. *how . . . answered:* a reference to the proverbial
"beggars can't be choosers."

COMMENTARY

The scene begins with a grand entrance, as the Duke of Venice and his *Magnificoes* (Venetian lords) enter majestically and take their places for the trial. In the original productions, the Duke and the Magnificoes would have sat on thrones and worn magnificent costumes, demonstrating the power of the Duke and his court.

The Doge (or Duke) of Venice.

However, the Duke does not behave as we might expect an unbiased judge to behave. He tells Antonio that he is sorry for him, and calls Shylock "an inhuman wretch" (3–6). This trial will not be an impartial one. The judge, jury, and witnesses are all completely sympathetic to Antonio. However, the law has trapped them. The trial is not about whether Shylock has the *right* to cut his pound of flesh from Antonio; it is about whether there is any way to stop him. The court has assembled in the hope of persuading Shylock to relent, or to find a loophole by which Antonio can be saved.

Antonio's behavior throughout this scene is passive and even fatalistic. He does not believe that he will be saved. His speech in lines 6–13 contrasts the Christian ideals of peace and nonviolence with Shylock's desire for revenge. Shakespeare begins the scene by placing everyone on the moral high ground against Shylock—but Shylock still has the power of the law on his side.

Shylock's entrance in line 16 is, therefore, very powerful. The entire courtroom looks on him with loathing. But Shylock is accustomed to this response. We have seen beforehand that it was partly the hatred of the Venetian citizens toward their Jewish neighbors that turned Shylock into a revenge-seeker. Shylock knows that the law is on his side, and he is enjoying his feeling of power, as he did in Act I, Scene 3. When the Duke says "Make room," (16), the reader must imagine Shylock pressing his way through a crowd of hostile Christians. Shylock is visibly isolated.

The Duke's tactic is to treat Shylock as though he were only *pretending* to go ahead with his case (17–21). He suggests to Shylock that he take pity on the ruined Antonio and forgive him (22–34). But Shylock flatly refuses (35–62). The reaction of the crowd throughout this scene is important. Murmurs of anger and horror can be heard when Shylock refuses to back down.

Shylock's attempt at justifying himself is extremely cursory. He says that he will torment Antonio simply because he feels like it. His speech describes the curious fact that some people have inexplicable allergic reactions to pigs, cats, and bagpipes. He suggests that his own hatred of Antonio and his desire to harm him are equally inexplicable (47–62). Human beings have "affection(s)" (50) and find themselves drawn whichever way their uncontrollable instincts guide them.

Bassanio protests that, "This is no answer," (63) but of course Shylock is perfectly aware that his justification is ridiculous. His reason for making this speech is to demonstrate that he does not need to give an answer. The letter of the law has given him the right to cut Antonio's flesh, and his reason for pursuing it is irrelevant. As Shylock says (perhaps after studying the words of the bond carefully), "I am not bound to please thee with my answers" (65).

Antonio's fatalistic attitude deepens in his speech in lines 70–83. As far as he is concerned, all Jews have hard hearts, a fact as natural as the hunger of a wolf or the sounds of trees in the wind. But Shylock's response is to undermine the confidence of the Christians in their own moral superiority. Shylock reminds the Christians that they employ slave labor. In other words, the buying of human flesh is a common feature of Venetian life. Just as the Christians would never dream of freeing their slaves and permitting them to live as human beings, so they should not be surprised if Shylock "buys" the flesh of another man.

However, this is *not* an antislavery speech. The antislavery movement did not begin until the 1700s, and Shakespeare is not criticizing the idea of slavery. What he is doing is confusing the morality of the scene. Shylock has highlighted the fact that the Christians do exactly the same sort of things that he does. This complication makes the morality of the trial scene less simple and, therefore, more dramatically interesting. Although he will soon emphasize the horror that Antonio faces, Shakespeare begins by making us aware that the Christians in the scene are not as different from Shylock as they seem. This bears out Shylock's earlier claim that he learned his wickedness from them (III.1.67–69).

Antonio's reaction to the proceedings is one of increasing fatalism. In his first speech (6–13), he seemed to be contrasting Christian pacifism with Shylock's revengeful malice. But in his second, he seems to have completely given up the fight; he asks the court to get on with it and allow Shylock to take his forfeit (80–83). In his third speech, he goes further, and describes himself as a "tainted wether" (114), that is, a scapegoat or a sacrifice victim. This phrase has never been fully explained, but perhaps more important is the phrase "meetest for death" (115). Antonio compares himself to a "weak fruit" ready to fall to the ground; he is regarding himself as worthless and ready to be removed from life. Those critics who find Antonio's love for Bassanio important in the play argue that Antonio is ready to die because he has lost the undivided love of Bassanio. The lines are certainly moving, as both men are prepared to die for each other (111–113, 114–118).

Shakespeare provides a brilliant theatrical image when Shylock begins to whet (sharpen) his knife upon the sole of his shoe (121–122). Actors can create a sinister effect with Shylock's slow, methodical movements of the knife. They stress the implacability of his desire for blood.

Gratiano is the character who most energetically opposes Shylock. In most productions, he physically assaults Shylock as he shouts at him, before another member of the cast restrains him. The important element here is that Gratiano's anger and energy are unable to prevent Shylock from carrying out his mission. Shylock challenges Gratiano to "rail the seal from off my bond"—that is, to remove Antonio's agreement from the bond by shouting. Shylock knows that no matter how much Gratiano protests, Shylock is legally in the right, and Shylock positions himself as the upholder of the law: "I stand here for law" (142).

A wax seal, used to "sign" a document.

The trial is at a deadlock, and something is needed to break it. That something is Portia, who enters now.

Portia's mission is to find a way to break the apparent deadlock that has arisen. She must save Antonio by persuading Shylock not to carry out his bond. In this scene, Portia behaves as a kind of angel of mercy. She treats the matter in a completely different way from the other characters, avoiding the fatalism of Antonio or the violence of Gratiano. She works through the logic of the case in a step-by-step manner but does not neglect to consider human feelings. Some people think that Portia has already decided on her plan of action when she enters, but the scene is more interesting if Portia is continually thinking on her feet and coming up with new ideas. Portia begins by assuming that Antonio would never have agreed to the bond's conditions. She asks him "Do you confess the bond?" but he replies "I do" (179–180). Antonio's honest response closes off one avenue of approach. Antonio has admitted that he agreed to the bond and signed it. Therefore, Portia reasons, there is no other alternative: "Then must the Jew be merciful" (180). But the whole point of Shylock's argument is that he has no need to be merciful. As far as he is concerned, the legal justice of his case means that he has no "compulsion" to be merciful at all (181).

The brilliance of Portia is her ability to think of a response immediately, in an effort to break Shylock's deadlock. In her long speech in lines 182–203, Portia explains that justice is not the most important thing in life. Humans cannot survive with justice alone. It must be combined with mercy. Portia uses the example of a powerful king holding a scepter—in fact, she probably gestures at the Duke on his throne to illustrate her point. A scepter is the symbol of kingly power, justice, and the law.

Portia insists that mercy is located inside the king's *heart* (192). The king who is most like a God, is the king who combines justice with mercy (194–195). And because everybody expects mercy from others, they should give it to others in return (198–200). Portia argues that Shylock, having made his point about justice, should now exercise the power of mercy and forgive Antonio.

Shylock's response to Portia's speech about mercy is to reject it utterly, and insist once more on the need for "law" (206). "My deeds upon my head!" (205) means

"Let God judge my deeds." The precise tone of Shylock's response depends on the individual actor. Actors who want to portray Shylock as a symbol of evil tend to speak the line angrily. Actors who portray Shylock as sympathetic tend to agonize over the decision before they eventually decide to go on ahead with the deed. Either choice is dramatic, but the way these lines are spoken affects the way the audience perceives Shylock throughout the rest of the trial.

Bassanio tries to pay Shylock off with three times the sum owed him by Antonio, but Shylock will not accept it (207–213, 226–233). Many people say that Shylock is a symbol of the insatiable love of money, but his refusal of Bassanio's money argues against this interpretation. Shylock does not want money in this scene. He wants to exact his revenge on Antonio, and he wants to feel that the law of Venice is on his side when he does it. It is the Christians who are baffled by Shylock's refusal to accept the money as a payment.

Portia's appeal to mercy has failed, and the case is at deadlock again. Now Bassanio suggests another way out of the situation: The law could be changed. He begs "Balthasar" (Portia dressed as a man) to exercise his authority to change The law so that Shylock cannot extract the bond. But Portia knows that the laws of Venice cannot

A balance, or set of scales.

be changed. The laws of precedent bind them: what was decided once must always be done. If they change the law, it will cause problems for other people later on.

Once more the court is at a deadlock, and only Shylock is happy. Portia's lack of success is emphasized by Shylock's praise of her as a "wise young judge." He now challenges her to stop trying to find loopholes, and to "Proceed to judgement" (239). Antonio also begs the court to stop prolonging his misery (242–243).

Again, some critics have suggested that Portia knows exactly what to do and is simply building up tension. But why she should want to do this is

unknown. It makes the scene more intense if even the intelligent and sophisticated Portia, who burst into the courtroom like a savior, is now apparently defeated by Shylock's simple refusal to listen to her. There is a much greater sense of horror when Portia can think of nothing but to ask Antonio to open his shirt and prepare himself for the knife.

At this point, the full horror of Shylock's intention is made visually apparent on stage. Shylock has brought with him a knife and a pair of scales (in some productions he is carrying the scales as he walks in; in others he produces them from a box at line 255). The scales will weigh the flesh, to ensure that Shylock has cut a whole pound from Antonio's body. When the audience sees these, the tools of the trade, they invariably feel queasy. The scales and the knife bring home the gruesome nature of what Shylock is about to do.

Antonio's speech once more describes his fatalism and his love for Bassanio. He says that he is glad to die because it will save him from a life of poverty (263–271). He also asks Bassanio to tell Portia about his love (272–276). Again, it is possible to see in these lines a man determined to make Bassanio understand the depths of his love. The speech has the desired effect, as Bassanio is moved to say that he would rather Portia and himself were killed by Shylock than see Antonio suffer. This is another one of those speeches, like Shylock's "Hath not a Jew eyes. . . ." speech, that jolts the audience into a new perspective. Despite their admiration for the deep love between Antonio and Bassanio, the presence of Portia on the stage makes the existence of a "conflict" between platonic and sexual love visibly apparent, especially because Portia is comically offended by Bassanio's remark (287). Shakespeare is setting up this conflict in order to prepare the audience for the themes of Act V.

The next sequence can be incredibly tense in performance. Portia is still stymied by the legal difficulty of the case. Antonio's shirt is open, and Shylock advances with the knife. In most productions, Shylock torments Antonio by considering where to begin cutting, or by stroking the knife across Antonio's chest. Productions that want to make Shylock sympathetic sometimes introduce a moment of hesitation, as Shylock considers the enormity of what he is about to do. But either way, Shylock must eventually lunge at Antonio with the knife, whereupon he is suddenly stopped by Portia crying "Tarry a little: there is something else" (304). With good timing, the scene often can make the audience jump. Again, it is more dramatic if Portia is genuinely unsure what to do next. In some productions she is frantically flipping through legal textbooks, and finds a solution at just the right moment.

Portia's solution is to play Shylock at his own game. He has made a point of sticking to the letter of the law, so Portia decides to look closely at the wording of the bond. She realizes that the bond allows Shylock to cut "a pound of flesh," but says nothing about blood. And she further realizes that Venetian law prevents the shedding of blood. Thirdly, she realizes that Shylock must cut only a pound of flesh, nothing more, nothing less. She discovers that if Shylock fails to cut an exact pound of flesh without shedding blood, he can be executed and his goods confiscated.

This solution is based on playing with words, and bears no relation to any real legal practice. Indeed, a cynic would call it cheating. However, dramatically speaking, it is a perfect example of poetic justice. Shylock has been rigidly standing by the words of his bond; now Portia defeats him by being even more pedantic about the words. Almost immediately, the positions of the characters are reversed: Portia has the upper hand. Gratiano's cries of "O upright judge!" and "A second Daniel!" (316, 332, 339) echo Shylock's similar cries at 222–223 and 245—except now the Christians are eulogizing Portia, not Shylock.

Shylock realizes very quickly that he has lost. He still thinks he can escape, however. He asks to be given the money instead, and when that fails, Shylock tries to leave without taking anything. But again, his inflexible

stance is now counting against him; when he asks if he can just take the money, Portia tells him that he cannot, because he had earlier refused it (335–338).

Finally, Portia finds a fourth argument against Shylock. Venetian law allows a person to be prosecuted for conspiring the death of a Venetian citizen. But this law only applies to "aliens" (foreigners) like Shylock. Shylock's Jewishness is counting against him. Again, this is poetic justice. Shylock had been enjoying his feeling of power over the Christians, but now the position is reversed, and he is once more a member of the hated race, in the power of the Christians again.

The final piece of poetic justice is that Shylock, who had spurned "mercy" in favor of justice, now finds that his life depends on the mercy of the Duke (354–355, 362).

This final sequence of the trial scene demonstrates the power of mercy. Shylock must now beg for the thing he rejected. The Duke has clearly taken note of Portia's speech about mercy: he pardons Shylock from execution (367–368). This pardoning is an illustration of the power of mercy that Portia had described in lines 187–195.

However, Shylock protests that this is not mercy. By taking his money, they might as well have taken his life, because he cannot survive without money. As a usurer, the only way Shylock can make a living is by lending money, and if they take his money away from him, he cannot ply his trade any more. Some critics have said that this proves Shylock to be a symbol of the desire for money. However, recall that money is important to everybody, not least Antonio (in lines 266–271, Antonio says he would rather die than suffer a life of poverty). Merchants need money just as much as usurers, which is probably why Portia now turns to Antonio and asks him also to show mercy. Showing mercy toward Shylock is a very difficult thing for Antonio to do. After the terror and pain that Shylock had subjected Antonio to, it would be very difficult for him to forgive Shylock in any way. Yet, that is what Portia asks of him. When Antonio agrees to do so, the effect is therefore very powerful and demonstrates very convincingly the virtue of Portia's speech about mercy.

Antonio's solution is to insist that Shylock's money go to Lorenzo and Jessica when he dies. Again, this is poetic justice. The elopement, which had turned Shylock into a revenger, must now be consolidated with his own money. However, the final instance of poetic justice is more disturbing for a modern audience: the stipulation that Shylock must become a Christian. It is quite probable that the Elizabethan audience would not have found this offensive; indeed, they might have regarded it as a kindness, believing that conversion would save Shylock's soul. However, Shakespeare does direct us to feel *some* sympathy with Shylock, who has now been defeated in every way. His final exit has none of the energy and spirit with which he began. He simply says, "I am not well" (395), which demonstrates that he is not only not "content" as he had said earlier, but he is a completely broken man. Some actors try to turn this into a grand tragic exit (Laurence Olivier could be heard howling in the corridor outside after he left the stage), but the text seems to indicate a quiet, sad exit which is a fitting contrast with Shylock's earlier wicked exuberance.

This long scene ends with a sequence that sets up the final obstacle for the characters. Remember that Bassanio and Gratiano are still unaware that "Balthazar" and his clerk are really Portia and Nerissa in disguise. Shakespeare now uses their disguise in order to explore further the conflict between platonic love and sexual love.

The exploration takes the form of a test. Portia seems determined to find out how important Bassanio's love is for her. Shakespeare gives no precise reason for her actions, but most productions link it with Bassanio's statement in lines 281–286 that he would lay down Portia's life for Antonio. This sequence can be described as the final part of the subtle tug of love between Antonio and Portia that appears to underlie some of the action.

When Portia, still in disguise as "Balthazar," asks for the ring on Bassanio's hand as a reward for helping to save Antonio, she is testing him to see how much he values it. She is hoping that he will refuse to give it up, which at first he does. But Portia continues to ask for the ring, accusing Bassanio of merely being a cheapskate (443). When she exits, she is secure in the knowledge that Bassanio has passed the test, and does not value her love higher than that of Antonio.

But she is wrong. Bassanio changes his mind and sends the ring after "Balthazar." Bassanio sends the ring to Portia because Antonio manages to persuade him by using emotional blackmail. Antonio tells Bassanio to think of the work that "Balthazar" did to save Antonio—and to think of the love that Antonio has for him. Antonio believes that this should be valued above Portia's love (448–450). In addition, Antonio attacks Bassanio's masculine pride, implying that he should not be so weak as to obey his wife's commandments (448–450).

Thus, the scene ends not with complete happiness, but with an ominous sense that all is not yet well. Although Antonio is saved and Shylock has been punished, a new cloud has arisen: an awkward conflict between the two loves of Bassanio's life.

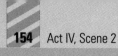

Act IV, Scene 2

Portia is saddened to learn that Bassanio was prepared to give away her wedding ring.

ACT IV, SCENE 2
Venice. A street.

[*Enter* PORTIA *and* NERISSA, *disguised as before.*]

Portia Inquire the Jew's house out, give him this
    deed,
And let him sign it. We'll away tonight
And be a day before our husbands home.
This deed will be well welcome to Lorenzo.

[*Enter* GRATIANO.]

Gratiano Fair sir, you are well o'erta'en.   5
My Lord Bassanio upon more advice
Hath sent you here this ring, and doth entreat
Your company at dinner.

Portia   That cannot be.
His ring I do accept most thankfully,
And so I pray you tell him. Furthermore,   10
I pray you show my youth old Shylock's house.

Gratiano That will I do.

Nerissa   Sir, I would speak with you.
[*Aside to* PORTIA] I'll see if I can get my husband's
    ring,
Which I did make him swear to keep for ever.

Portia [*aside to* NERISSA] Thou mayst, I warrant.
    We shall have old swearing   15
That they did give the rings away to men;
But we'll outface them, and outswear them too. —
Away, make haste! Thou know'st where I will tarry.

Nerissa Come, good sir, will you show me to this
    house? [*Exeunt.*]   20

NOTES

1.   *deed*: the deed of gift.

6.   *more advice*: further consideration.

15.   *old*: a great deal of.

17.   *outface them*: stare down; shame, silence them.

COMMENTARY

This short scene shows us the reactions of the women toward the apparent betrayal by their men. Portia is clearly shocked when she blurts out "That cannot be," (8) but characteristically recovers herself. Even so, the scene also indicates that the final denouement will be comic rather than tragic. Portia thinks about the blustering embarrassment that Bassanio and Gratiano will suffer when they are confronted with the absence of their rings. Rather than be sad, she decides to "outface them" (17); that is, to get the better of them by being cleverer than they are. Portia has proved in the trial scene that she is cleverer than anybody else in the play, and she intends to use her wit to prove her mastery once and for all.

Notes

THE MERCHANT OF VENICE

ACT V

Bassanio *Sweet Portia,*
> *If you did know to whom I gave the ring,*
> *If you did know for whom I gave the ring,*
> *And would conceive for what I gave the ring,*
> *And how unwillingly I left the ring,*
> *When naught would be accepted but the ring,*
> *You would abate the strength of your displeasure.*

Portia *If you had known the virtue of the ring,*
> *Or half her worthiness that gave the ring,*
> *Or your own honor to contain the ring,*
> *You would not then have parted with the ring.*

Act V, Scene 1

Lorenzo and Jessica talk about love beneath the moonlight; then the others return, and Portia questions Bassanio about the absence of his wedding ring, before revealing that she was the lawyer who took it.

ACT V, SCENE 1
Belmont. The avenue to Portia's house.

[*Enter* LORENZO *and* JESSICA.]

Lorenzo The moon shines bright. In such a night
   as this,
  When the sweet wind did gently kiss the trees
  And they did make no noise, in such a night
  Troilus methinks mounted the Troyan walls,
  And sighed his soul toward the Grecian tents   5
  Where Cressid lay that night.

Jessica   In such a night
  Did Thisbe fearfully o'ertrip the dew,
  And saw the lion's shadow ere himself,
  And ran dismayed away.

Lorenzo   In such a night
  Stood Dido with a willow in her hand   10
  Upon the wild sea banks, and waft her love
  To come again to Carthage.

Jessica   In such a night
  Medea gathered the enchanted herbs
  That did renew old Aeson.

Lorenzo   In such a night
  Did Jessica steal from the wealthy Jew,   15
  And with an unthrift love did run from Venice
  As far as Belmont.

Jessica   In such a night
  Did young Lorenzo swear he loved her well,
  Stealing her soul with many vows of faith,
  And ne'er a true one.   20

Lorenzo   In such a night
  Did pretty Jessica, like a little shrew,
  Slander her love, and he forgave it her.

NOTES

4–6. *Troilus . . . Cressid:* Troilus, the Trojan prince, was in love with Cressida, but she was sent as a hostage to the Greek camp, where she betrayed his love.

7. *Thisbe:* Pyramus and Thisbe were lovers who, forbidden by their parents to see each other, arranged to meet in a forest. Thisbe, frightened by a lion who mauled her cloak, ran away. On discovering the cloak, Pyramus assumed that Thisbe was dead and stabbed himself. Thisbe in turn killed herself upon discovering the body of Pyramus.

10. *Dido:* In Virgil's Aeneid, the Queen of Carthage who loved Aeneas. He abandoned her to sail for Italy.

willow: traditionally associated with forsaken lovers.

11. *waft:* waved.

13–14. *Medea . . . Aeson:* Medea helped Jason to win the Golden Fleece with her magic. She was able to restore the youth of his father, Aeson, with a brew of herbs. Later, Jason abandoned her.

16. *unthrift love:* i.e., Lorenzo.

Jessica I would out-night you, did nobody come;
But hark, I hear the footing of a man.

[*Enter* STEPHANO.]

Lorenzo Who comes so fast in silence of the night?   25

Stephano A friend.

Lorenzo A friend? What friend? Your name I
pray you, friend.

Stephano Stephano is my name, and I bring word
My mistress will before the break of day
Be here at Belmont. She doth stray about   30
By holy crosses where she kneels and prays
For happy wedlock hours.

Lorenzo   Who comes with her?

Stephano None but a holy hermit and her maid.
I pray you, is my master yet returned?

Lorenzo He is not, nor we have not heard from   35
him.
But go we in, I pray thee, Jessica,
And ceremoniously let us prepare
Some welcome for the mistress of the house.

[*Enter* LAUNCELOT.]

Launcelot Sola, sola! wo ha! ho sola, sola!

Lorenzo Who calls?   40

Launcelot Sola! Did you see Master Lorenzo?
Master Lorenzo! sola, sola!

Lorenzo Leave holloaing, man! Here.

Launcelot Sola! where? where?

Lorenzo Here!   45

Launcelot Tell him there's a post come from my
master, with his horn full of good news. My master
will be here ere morning. [*Exit.*]

Lorenzo Sweet soul, let's in, and there expect their
coming.
And yet no matter; why should we go in?   50
My friend Stephano, signify, I pray you,

23. *out-night you:* i.e., surpass you in the game of finding illustrations for in such a night.

31. *holy crosses:* wayside shrines marked with crosses.

39. *Sola . . . ha!:* Launcelot imitates the sound of a post horn, blown by a messenger arriving with news; see lines 46–47.

46. *post:* messenger.

51. *signify:* announce.

Within the house, your mistress is at hand,
And bring your music forth into the air

[*Exit* STEPHANO.]

How sweet the moonlight sleeps upon this bank!
Here will we sit and let the sounds of music   55
Creep in our ears; soft stillness and the night
Become the touches of sweet harmony.
Sit, Jessica. Look how the floor of heaven
Is thick inlaid with patens of bright gold.
There's not the smallest orb which thou behold'st   60
But in his motion like an angel sings,
Still quiring to the young-eyed cherubins;
Such harmony is in immortal souls,
But whilst this muddy vesture of decay
Doth grossly close it in, we cannot hear it.   65

[*Enter Musicians.*]

Come ho, and wake Diana with a hymn!
With sweetest touches pierce your mistress' ear
And draw her home with music. [*Play music.*]

Jessica I am never merry when I hear sweet music.

Lorenzo The reason is, your spirits are attentive.   70
For do but note a wild and wanton herd
Or race of youthful and unhandled colts
Fetching mad bounds, bellowing and neighing loud,
Which is the hot condition of their blood:
If they but hear perchance a trumpet sound,   75
Or any air of music touch their ears,
You shall perceive them make a mutual stand,
Their savage eyes turned to a modest gaze
By the sweet power of music. Therefore the poet
Did feign that Orpheus drew trees, stones, and   80
    floods;
Since naught so stockish, hard, and full of rage
But music for the time doth change his nature.
The man that hath no music in himself,
Nor is not moved with concord of sweet sounds,
Is fit for treasons, stratagems, and spoils;   85

53.	*music:* musicians; they probably descend from the upper stage and take up positions (at line 65) at the back of the main stage.
57.	*Become the touches:* befit the notes.
59.	*patens:* decorative metal plates.
62.	*Still quiring:* ever singing.
	young-eyed: the cherubim, according to Ezekiel 10:12, were endowed with keenness of vision above all other heavenly creatures.
64.	*muddy . . . decay:* the flesh; the harmony of heaven can only be heard by the angels and man's soul when it has left the body.
66.	*Diana:* here, the goddess of the moon.
70.	*spirits:* conscious mind.
	attentive: observant.
72.	*race:* herd.
77.	*mutual stand:* stand still together.
78.	*modest:* mild, innocent.
79.	*the poet:* Ovid; the story occurs in the Metamorphoses.
80.	*Orpheus:* in classical legend, the sound of Orpheus' lute made the rocks and trees of Mt. Olympus follow him.
81.	*stockish:* dull.
85.	*spoils:* plunders.

The motions of his spirit are dull as night,
And his affections dark as Erebus.
Let no such man be trusted. Mark the music.

[*Enter* PORTIA *and* NERISSA.]

Portia That light we see is burning in my hall;
How far that little candle throws his beams!   90
So shines a good deed in a naughty world.

Nerissa When the moon shone we did not see the
candle.

Portia So doth the greater glory dim the less.
A substitute shines brightly as a king
Until a king be by, and then his state   95
Empties itself, as doth an inland brook
Into the main of waters. Music! hark!

Nerissa It is your music, madam, of the house.

Portia Nothing is good, I see, without respect;
Methinks it sounds much sweeter than by day.   100

Nerissa Silence bestows that virtue on it, madam.

Portia The crow doth sing as sweetly as the lark
When neither is attended; and I think
The nightingale, if she should sing by day
When every goose is cackling, would be thought   105
No better a musician than the wren.
How many things by season seasoned are
To their right praise and true perfection!
Peace! [*Music ceases.*] How the moon sleeps with
Endymion,
And would not be awaked.   110

Lorenzo   That is the voice,
Or I am much deceived, of Portia.

Portia He knows me as the blind man knows the
cuckoo —
By the bad voice.

Lorenzo   Dear lady, welcome home.

86. *motions:* impulses.

87. *affections:* thoughts, feelings.

Erebus: in pagan mythology, a region near Hades, dwelling place of the dead.

91. *naughty:* wicked.

95. *his:* i.e., the substitute's.

state: position of dignity.

98. *your music:* your own musicians.

99. *without respect:* i.e., its goodness depends on circumstance.

103. *is attended:* i.e., accompanied by the other.

109. *Endymion:* a shepherd with whom the moon goddess fell in love. She came down to kiss him and caused him to sleep perpetually on the mountain.

Portia We have been praying for our husbands'
    welfare,
Which speed we hope the better for our words.   115
Are they returned?

Lorenzo   Madam, they are not yet,
But there is come a messenger before
To signify their coming.

Portia   Go in, Nerissa.
Give order to my servants that they take
No note at all of our being absent hence —   120
Nor you, Lorenzo — Jessica, nor you.

[*A tucket sounds.*]

Lorenzo Your husband is at hand; I hear his
    trumpet.
We are no telltales, madam; fear you not.

Portia This night methinks is but the daylight
    sick;
It looks a little paler. 'Tis a day   125
Such as the day is when the sun is hid.

[*Enter* BASSANIO, ANTONIO, GRATIANO, *and their
Followers.*]

Bassanio We should hold day with the Antipodes
If you would walk in absence of the sun.

Portia Let me give light, but let me not be light,
For a light wife doth make a heavy husband,   130
And never be Bassanio so for me.
But God sort all! You are welcome home, my lord.

Bassanio I thank you, madam. Give welcome to my
    friend.
This is the man, this is Antonio,
To whom I am so infinitely bound.   135

Portia You should in all sense be much bound to
    him,
For, as I hear, he was much bound for you.

Antonio No more than I am well acquitted of.

119–120. *take/ No note:* do not mention.

121. Stage direction "tucket": a short flourish of trumpets announcing an arrival.

127–128. *We . . . sun:* i.e., at night you give such illumination that we have day at the same time as those on the other side of the world; Bassanio carries on the sense of Portia's previous line.

129–130. *light:* (1) illumination, (2) wanton, loose.

130. *heavy:* sad, heavy in heart.

135. *bound:* i.e., in friendship and indebtedness.

138. *acquitted of:* released from.

Portia Sir, you are very welcome to our house.
It must appear in other ways than words;   140
Therefore I scant this breathing courtesy.

Gratiano [*to* NERISSA] By yonder moon I swear you
   do me wrong!
In faith, I gave it to the judge's clerk.
Would he were gelt that had it, for my part,
Since you do take it, love, so much at heart.   145

Portia A quarrel ho! Already! What's the matter?

Gratiano About a hoop of gold, a paltry ring
That she did give me, whose posy was
For all the world like cutler's poetry
Upon a knife — "Love me, and leave me not."   150

Nerissa What talk you of the posy or the value?
You swore to me when I did give it you
That you would wear it till your hour of death,
And that it should lie with you in your grave.
Though not for me, yet for your vehement oaths,   155
You should have been respective and have kept it.
Gave it a judge's clerk! No, God's my judge,
The clerk will ne'er wear hair on's face that had it!

Gratiano He will, an if he live to be a man.

Nerissa Ay, if a woman live to be a man.   160

Gratiano Now by this hand, I gave it to a youth,
A kind of boy, a little scrubbed boy
No higher than thyself, the judge's clerk,
A prating boy that begged it as a fee.
I could not for my heart deny it him.   165

Portia You were to blame — I must be plain with
   you —
To part so slightly with your wife's first gift,
A thing stuck on with oaths upon your finger
And so riveted with faith unto your flesh.
I gave my love a ring, and made him swear   170
Never to part with it; and here he stands.
I dare be sworn for him he would not leave it
Nor pluck it from his finger for the wealth
That the world masters. Now in faith, Gratiano,

141. *scant . . . courtesy:* cease well coming you with talk.

144. *gelt:* gelded.

148. *posy:* inscription inside a ring, often in verse.

149. *cutler:* a knife-grinder.

162. *scrubbed:* short.

164. *prating:* chattering, talkative.

172. *leave:* abandon.

174. *masters:* possesses.

You give your wife too unkind a cause of grief.   175
An 'twere to me, I should be mad at it.

176. *mad:* distracted to madness.

Bassanio [*aside*] Why, I were best to cut my left
    hand off
And swear I lost the ring defending it.

Gratiano My Lord Bassanio gave his ring away
Unto the judge that begged it, and indeed   180
Deserved it too; and then the boy, his clerk
That took some pains in writing, he begged mine;
And neither man nor master would take aught
But the two rings.

Portia   What ring gave you, my lord?
Not that, I hope, which you received of me.   185

Bassanio If I could add a lie unto a fault,
I would deny it; but you see my finger
Hath not the ring upon it — it is gone.

186. *fault:* error, misdeed.

Portia Even so void is your false heart of truth.
By heaven, I will ne'er come in your bed   190
Until I see the ring!

Nerissa   Nor I in yours
Till I again see mine!

Bassanio   Sweet Portia,
If you did know to whom I gave the ring,
If you did know for whom I gave the ring,
And would conceive for what I gave the ring,   195
And how unwillingly I left the ring
When naught would be accepted but the ring,
You would abate the strength of your displeasure.

Portia If you had known the virtue of the ring,
Or half her worthiness that gave the ring,   200
Or your own honor to contain the ring,
You would not then have parted with the ring.
What man is there so much unreasonable,
If you had pleased to have defended it
With any terms of zeal, wanted the modesty   205
To urge the thing held as a ceremony?
Nerissa teaches me what to believe;
I'll die for't but some woman had the ring!

199. *virtue:* power, importance.

201. *honor to contain:* honorable duty to keep.

205–206. *wanted . . . ceremony:* i.e., would so lack good sense
that he would demand something held as a precious
symbol.

208. *but . . . ring!:* if some woman didn't get the ring!

Bassanio No, by my honor, madam! By my soul
No woman had it, but a civil doctor,   210
Which did refuse three thousand ducats of me
And begged the ring, the which I did deny him,
And suffered him to go displeased away —
Even he that had held up the very life
Of my dear friend. What should I say, sweet lady?   215
I was enforced to send it after him.
I was beset with shame and courtesy.
My honor would not let ingratitude
So much besmear it. Pardon me, good lady!
For by these blessed candles of the night,   220
Had you been there I think you would have begged
The ring of me to give the worthy doctor.

Portia Let not that doctor e'er come near my house.
Since he hath got the jewel that I loved,
And that which you did swear to keep for me.   225
I will become as liberal as you;
I'll not deny him anything I have,
No, not my body nor my husband's bed.
Know him I shall, I am well sure of it.
Lie not a night from home; watch me like Argus.   230
If you do not, if I be left alone —
Now by mine honor which is yet mine own,
I'll have that doctor for my bedfellow.

Nerissa And I his clerk. Therefore be well advised
How you do leave me to mine own protection.   235

Gratiano Well, do you so. Let not me take him
     then!
For if I do, I'll mar the young clerk's pen.

Antonio I am th' unhappy subject of these
     quarrels.

Portia Sir, grieve not you; you are welcome not-
     withstanding.

Bassanio Portia, forgive me this enforced wrong,   240
And in the hearing of these many friends
I swear to thee, even by thine own fair eyes,
Wherein I see myself —

210. *civil doctor:* doctor of civil law.

213. *suffered:* allowed.

230. *Argus:* in classical myth, a giant with a hundred eyes.

236. *take:* catch.

240. *enforced wrong:* fault I was obliged to commit.

Portia   Mark you but that!
In both my eyes he doubly sees himself,
In each eye one. Swear by your double self,   245
And there's an oath of credit.

Bassanio   Nay, but hear me.
Pardon this fault, and by my soul I swear
I never more will break an oath with thee.

Antonio I once did lend my body for his wealth,
Which but for him that had your husband's ring   250
Had quite miscarried. I dare be bound again,
My soul upon the forfeit, that your lord
Will never more break faith advisedly.

Portia Then you shall be his surety. Give him this,
And bid him keep it better than the other.   255

Antonio Here, Lord Bassanio. Swear to keep this
     ring.

Bassanio By heaven, it is the same I gave the
     doctor!

Portia I had it of him. Pardon me, Bassanio,
For by this ring the doctor lay with me.

Nerissa And pardon me, my gentle Gratiano,   260
For that same scrubbed boy, the doctor's clerk,
In lieu of this last night did lie with me.

Gratiano Why, this is like the mending of highways
In summer, where the ways are fair enough.
What, are we cuckolds ere we have deserved it?   265

Portia Speak not so grossly. You are all amazed.
Here is a letter; read it at your leisure.
It comes from Padua from Bellario.
There you shall find that Portia was the doctor,
Nerissa there her clerk. Lorenzo here   270
Shall witness I set forth as soon as you,
And even but now returned — I have not yet
Entered my house. Antonio, you are welcome,
And I have better news in store for you
Than you expect. Unseal this letter soon;   275
There you shall find three of your argosies
Are richly come to harbor suddenly.

246. *oath of credit:* ironically said, since the oath is sworn by a double or hypocritical self.

253. *advisedly:* intentionally.

254. *surety:* guarantee.

262. *In lieu of this:* in return for this (hands him the ring).

265. *cuckolds:* men whose wives have betrayed them.

266. *grossly:* coarsely; Portia immediately puts Gratiano in his place.

amazed: lost in a maze.

You shall not know by what strange accident
I chanced on this letter.

Antonio   I am dumb!

Bassanio Were you the doctor, and I knew you not?   280

Gratiano Were you the clerk that is to make me
    cuckold?

Nerissa Ay, but the clerk that never means to do it,
Unless he live until he be a man.

Bassanio Sweet Doctor, you shall be my bedfellow.
When I am absent, then lie with my wife.   285

Antonio Sweet lady, you have given me life and
    living!
For here I read for certain that my ships
Are safely come to road.

Portia   How now, Lorenzo?
My clerk hath some good comforts too for you.

Nerissa Ay, and I'll give them him without a fee.   290
There do I give to you and Jessica.
From the rich Jew, a special deed of gift,
After his death, of all he dies possessed of.

Lorenzo Fair ladies, you drop manna in the way
Of starved people.   295

Portia   It is almost morning,
And yet I am sure you are not satisfied
Of these events at full. Let us go in,
And charge us there upon inter'gatories,
And we will answer all things faithfully.

Gratiano Let it be so. The first inter'gatory   300
That my Nerissa shall be sworn on is,
Whether till the next night she had rather stay,
Or go to bed now, being two hours to day.
But were the day come, I should wish it dark
Till I were couching with the doctor's clerk   305
Well, while I live I'll fear no other thing
So sore as keeping safe Nerissa's ring. [*Exeunt.*]

288. *road:* roadstead, anchorage.

296–297. *not . . . full:* not fully satisfied with the explanation of these events.

298. *charge . . . inter'gatories:* a legal phrase meaning take an oath to answer interrogation.

302. *stay:* wait.

307. *sore:* acutely.

COMMENTARY

It is night in Belmont. The original performances of this play in Elizabethan theatres would have taken place in broad daylight, in a theatre open to the sky. There was no way the theatre company could have "adjusted" the lighting, because the sun provided the only light. If a scene was set at night, the playwright had to create the *idea* of night in the audience's minds by using the power of language. That is what happens here. The beautiful language creates images of night that paint the scene in the audience's minds. You can find other examples of this technique in *A Midsummer Night's Dream* and *Macbeth*.

The dialogue between Lorenzo and Jessica is beautiful but unsettling. They describe themselves alongside the stories of other romantic couples of the past. But the stories they refer to are inappropriate. The love between Troilus and Cressida (2–6) was doomed when Cressida betrayed Troilus; Pyramus and Thisbe were tragic lovers who died (6–9); Dido waited in Carthage for her lover to return (9–12), but he betrayed her; and Medea (12–14) was abandoned by her lover, Jason.

Shakespeare expected his audience to recognize these stories and the tragic sadness that they evoke. Yet he places them into the mouths of newlywed lovers. Why does he do this?

Some have suggested that Lorenzo and Jessica have fallen out of love and are arguing. This may seem to be the case when Jessica accuses Lorenzo of winning her with false vows. But in III.5.84–91, they seemed to be the sort of couple who enjoyed "winding each other up." A better explanation is that Shakespeare is finely balancing idealism and realism. When Jessica and Lorenzo elope, Gratiano and Solanio undermine our belief in their romance by saying that men become bored with women after they have married them (II.6.5–19). Jessica and Lorenzo have therefore always been associated with a "realistic" view of love, which acknowledges its darker side. Here, in the perfect land of Belmont (where even Gratiano surprised himself by falling in love), Lorenzo and Jessica look up into the stars and see the harmony of the heavens (54–65). Yet the key line comes at lines 64–65. The "muddy vesture of decay" is the human body, which "closes in" the soul. If the soul were free from the body, it could appreciate the harmony of the heavens. But trapped within a body, which has sexual desires, things aren't as simple as they could be. In this way, Shakespeare idealizes the beauty and harmony of the universe, while acknowledging the complicated reality of human behavior and suggesting that love, while beautiful, can be filled with sadness as well.

When Launcelot barges into the scene, we see another symbol of the "flesh." No one could better be described as a "muddy vesture of decay" than the greedy, lazy Launcelot. Indeed, Launcelot's incongruous entrance may be the stimulus for Lorenzo to talk about the conflict between the soul and the body.

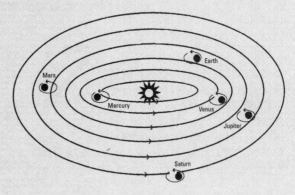

The Renaissance universe, made up of rotating spheres.

The conversation between Lorenzo and Jessica moves on to some beautiful speeches about music. In the first, Lorenzo describes the music of the spheres (54–65). This idea originated in Ancient Greece and continued to the Renaissance. Before the birth of modern astronomy, people believed that the universe was comprised of rotating crystal spheres that carried the stars and planets on their paths. As the spheres rotated, they rubbed against each other, and created a beautifully harmonious sound. But human beings, living on the earth, have heard the sound so much that they no longer hear it. The "music of the spheres" theory suggests that there is a beautiful, higher harmony operating "behind" our lives, even though we cannot appreciate it. The idea is illustrated by the music that begins to play in line 68. It should be beautiful and harmonious to complement Lorenzo's speech.

Jessica's last line in the play is "I am never merry when I hear sweet music" (69). Some people have taken this to mean that Jessica is depressed and upset at having betrayed her father. But if you look at Lorenzo's reply, you can see that Jessica means the music makes her thoughtful rather than merry. Lorenzo says this is because her mind is alert and that music can bring about tranquillity, even to a herd of stampeding horses (70–79).

When Lorenzo claims that "The man that hath no music in himself . . . Is fit for treasons, stratagems, and spoils" (83–85), the audience may well remember Shylock, who ordered Jessica to shut the windows against the sounds of the musicians outside (II.5.28–36). By extension, Lorenzo links Shylock with "disharmony." The implication is that Shylock's defeat has restored tranquillity.

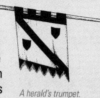

A herald's trumpet.

A similar theme is talked of by Portia and Nerissa when they enter. Portia describes how beautiful things are only beautiful when compared with something else. By implication this refers to herself, because her claim that the distant shining candle looks like "a good deed in a naughty world" (91) makes us think of Portia's behavior in Venice, where she was like an angel of mercy in the "realistic" city.

Note that Bassanio's entrance is heralded by a fanfare of trumpets (122). Usually, such an honor would be accorded only to a king or a lord. But having married Portia, Bassanio has become the lord of Belmont and is therefore justified in entering with some pomp and ceremony.

The entrance of Bassanio, Gratiano, and Antonio causes a complex set of emotions on the stage. The men are relieved and happy. As far as they are concerned, their adventures are over; Antonio is safe, and they can return home to their wives, who have been patiently waiting for them. They do not realize that Portia was the lawyer who saved the day.

Portia's emotions are far more complex. Some actresses play her as unhappy and depressed that Bassanio was prepared to give away his wedding ring. Others play her as relishing the situation, treating the event

as a joke, and looking forward to observing Bassanio's embarrassment. Either way, we must keep in mind that Portia is *acting* during the ensuing dialogue. She is covering up her true feelings in order to find the best way of confronting Bassanio.

The "quarrel" between Gratiano and Nerissa is a meatier and more overtly comic precursor to Bassanio and Portia's. Gratiano exposes himself as a fool almost immediately, when he swears an oath "By yonder moon" (142). This is a common joke in Renaissance drama; swearing by the moon is deceptive because the moon changes shape every night.

Gratiano is in big trouble, because his wife is (pretending to be) convinced that he gave the ring to another woman. Gratiano's embarrassed protest that he actually gave it to "a little scrubbed boy . . . that begged it as a fee" (162) hardly helps matters, because it makes him look even more ridiculous. Nerissa is clearly enjoying herself as she torments her flustered husband. We can see this when she uses an amusing piece of dramatic irony (*dramatic irony* is a moment in which the audience knows something that one of the characters doesn't). When Gratiano talks of the clerk growing up to be a man, Nerissa, still pretending to be suspicious about another woman, says "Ay, if a woman live to be a man" (160). The joke, of course, is that the clerk was Nerissa, who did indeed "live to be a man." We can imagine Nerissa winking at the audience or at Portia as she speaks the line.

In general, the audience probably takes Portia's confrontation of Bassanio more seriously than it does the confrontation between Nerissa and Gratiano. This is not to say that the sequence isn't funny—there is a lot of humor in the sequence—but the language used by Portia is much more powerful and moving, so that the action is raised onto an altogether more serious level.

Portia's speech in lines 166–176 articulates the importance of what they are talking about. Her description of the ring being "stuck on" Gratiano's finger "with oaths" and "riveted with faith" onto his flesh is a powerful image of the sanctity of marriage. It is a type of image that describes an intellectual concept in physical terms, so that the concept of fidelity to one's partner becomes a physical image of a ring welded to the husband's finger.

The humor of the sequence comes from the behavior of the two men, who behave like naughty schoolboys in trouble with the headmistress. Bassanio's appalled embarrassment ("Why I were best to cut my left hand off / And swear I lost the ring defending it," lines 176–177) never fails to get a laugh, and the same is true of Gratiano's childish means of deflecting attention from himself; pointing at Bassanio he protests, "My lord Bassanio gave *his* ring away . . ." (179), at which point Portia turns to her husband with a menacing stare.

Even funnier is Bassanio's flustered attempt to justify what he has done (192–198). The way he keeps repeating the word "ring" shows that he is struggling for words in the face of stern glares from the two women. Portia's reply parodies his speech and ends in accusing Bassanio of giving the ring to another woman.

Worth considering is what Jessica is doing during this sequence. One may think she has nothing to do in this part of the scene. But some productions have tried to make the audience remember that the events of this scene have similarities with Jessica's story. When Jessica eloped with Lorenzo and went on a spending spree in Genoa, she too gave away a ring. It was Shylock's ring, given to him by his wife when they were courting (III.1.118–123). Some productions make it clear that Jessica remembers her action, and feels guilty about it, because Shylock's ring must have meant as much to him as Portia's did to her. It is not certain whether Shakespeare intended for the audience to remember this fact during the scene—there is certainly nothing in the text to suggest it. But the bizarre fact that Jessica swapped the ring for a monkey, coupled with Shylock's moment of sadness when he thinks about the ring, and the unusual phrase "I would not have given it for a wilderness of monkeys" (122–123) may indicate that Shakespeare intended the scene to stick in the audience's minds.

Portia now begins a new method of humiliating Bassanio. She tells him that if he has given away their wedding ring to the doctor, as far as she is concerned, the doctor is now her husband. She tells the astonished Bassanio that she will sleep with the doctor, and "not deny him anything I have" (227). In this sequence, the fun comes, once more, through dramatic irony. The audience knows much more about the situation than Bassanio and Gratiano. They know that the "doctor" was really Portia herself. This means that the words that Portia speaks have a double meaning. They mean one thing to her and to the audience, but to Bassanio and Gratiano they mean another. When Portia says, "I'll have that doctor for my bedfellow" (233), the audience knows that this is a harmless thing to say, because Portia *herself* is the doctor. But of course, Bassanio doesn't know this, and great humor can be achieved through the look of horror on his face as he hears this news.

In this scene, Portia's cleverness becomes evident once more. The scene is entertaining because Portia's brilliant wit enables her to distort everything that Bassanio says. Even when he tries to swear "by thine own fair eyes / Wherein I see myself . . ." (242–243), Portia twists his meaning; she reminds him that she has *two* eyes, each of which contains his reflection, and this "double self" (245) symbolizes the fact that he is a deceiver. No matter what he does, Portia manages to baffle and outwit poor Bassanio.

Portia is reveling in the power that her cleverness gives her. But by this point, the audience is probably sympathizing with Bassanio's humiliation, and Portia decides to put him out of his misery. In most productions, there is a long pause between line 255 and line 256, as Bassanio stares at the ring in astonishment, and as the truth gradually dawns on him.

The few lines that Bassanio is given to speak in the remainder of the play do not make him look very intelligent. There seems to be an implication that Bassanio's respect for his wife should increase if he is to have any hope of surviving in the real world. The scene demonstrates that although Bassanio is technically the "master of the house," Portia is the brains of the team.

The final part of the play ties up some loose ends. Portia gives to Lorenzo and Jessica Shylock's will, which promises that all his wealth will pass to them (288–295). Then Portia gives Antonio a letter in which it

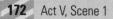

is revealed that three of his ships were safe after all; Antonio is no longer bankrupt. Some critics have called this a clumsy piece of plotting, and they are right. How did Portia come by this letter? And how does she know what is written in it if it is sealed? However, it is clear that Shakespeare is perfectly aware of this clumsiness. When Portia says "You shall not know by what strange accident / I chanced on this letter" (278–279), we can see that Shakespeare had no interest in thinking of a realistic reason for Portia's obtaining of the letter. Any long-winded explanation would have spoiled the flow of the drama, so Shakespeare just deflects it with a cheeky wink at the audience.

The play ends in happiness. Jessica and Lorenzo leave the stage, followed by Portia and Bassanio, and the stage is left to the earthier Gratiano and Nerissa who exit with a crude joke. In some productions, however, the ending is not as simple as that. Directors have focused on two complications. The first complication is Jessica. In productions that try to portray Shylock as sympathetic, Jessica is often shown to be having second thoughts, and in some productions she even walks offstage without Lorenzo, as if to return to her father. Of course, there is no warrant for this in the text, but some directors have felt that Jessica's silence can be used in this fashion. The second complication is Antonio. At the end of the play, the couples walk off arm-in-arm, but Antonio must leave alone. Some productions deliberately highlight the fact that Antonio is left without a partner at the end. The only person he had ever loved was Bassanio, but Bassanio is arm-in-arm with Portia. We will never know whether Antonio's single status was highlighted in Shakespeare's original productions.

Why would directors want to complicate the apparently simple harmony of the ending? Because *The Merchant of Venice* is not a simple play. Although it is full of laughter and love, it is also full of horror and sadness. The play has deliberately set up an idealized world in Belmont, alongside a realistic world in Venice. Although Bassanio and Portia will now live out their lives in Belmont, the world of Venice still exists, where money rules everything and Shylock pines for his daughter. Many people believe that a reminder of the darker side of life is important in this play. They argue that Shakespeare deliberately included in the ending Antonio's lack of a partner, and perhaps also Jessica's silence, in order to complicate the simplicity of the ending, and to leave us with a reminder that harmony does not exist for everyone.

Notes

Notes

The Merchant of Venice
CLIFFSCOMPLETE REVIEW

Use this CliffsComplete Review to gauge what you've learned and to build confidence in your understanding of the original text. After you work through the review questions, the problem-solving exercises, and the suggested activities, you're well on your way to understanding and appreciating the works of William Shakespeare.

IDENTIFY THE QUOTATION

Identify the following quotations by answering these questions:

* Who is the speaker of the quote?
* What does it reveal about the speaker's character?
* What does it tell us about other characters within the play?
* Where does it occur within the play?
* What does it show us about the themes of the play?
* What significant imagery do you see in the quote, and how do these images relate to the overall imagery of the play?

1. The brain may devise laws for the blood, but a hot temper leaps o'er a cold decree; such a hare is madness the youth to skip o'er the meshes of good counsel the cripple. But this reasoning is not in the fashion to choose me a husband.

2. Who riseth from a feast
   With that keen appetite that he sits down?
   Where is the horse that doth untread again
   His tedious measures with the unbated fire
   That he did pace them first? All things that are
   Are with more spirit chased than enjoyed.

3. So may the outward shows be least themselves;
   The world is still deceived with ornament.

4. The quality of mercy is not strained;
   It droppeth as the gentle rain from heaven
   Upon the place beneath. It is twice blest;
   It blesseth him that gives and him that takes.
   'Tis mightiest in the mightiest; it becomes
   The throned monarch better than his crown.

5. Hath not a Jew eyes? Hath not a Jew hands, organs, dimensions, senses, affections, passions?

6. My Lord Bassanio, let him have the ring.
   Let his deservings and my love withal
   Be valued 'gainst your wife's commandment.

7. If thou wilt lend this money, lend it not
   As to thy friends; for when did friendship take
   A breed of barren metal of his friend?

8. Why, all the boys in Venice follow him,
   Crying, His stones, his daughter and his ducats.

9. Out upon her! Thou torturest me, Tubal. It was my turquoise. I had it of Leah when I was a bachelor. I would not have given it for a wilderness of monkeys.

10. Such harmony is in immortal souls,
    But whilst this muddy vesture of decay
    Doth grossly close it in we cannot hear it.

TRUE/FALSE

1. T F   Jessica steals money from Shylock.

2. T F   Portia refuses to submit to the casket test.

3. T F   Bassanio compares Portia to the Golden Fleece.

4. T F   Shylock's wife once gave him a ring.

5. T F   Antonio is Jewish.

6. T F   Shylock wins the trial.

7. T F   Gratiano marries Jessica.

8. T F   Morocco chooses the golden casket.

9. T F   There is a death's head in the silver casket.

10. T F   According to the song, fancy is engendered in the eyes.

11. T F   Portia takes on the name of Balthazar when she disguises herself.

12. T F   Shylock is legally entitled to take a pound of flesh from Antonio.

13. T F   Jessica and Lorenzo are left in charge of Portia's house when she leaves.

14. T F   Old Gobbo is deaf.

15. T F   Launcelot got a Moorish woman pregnant.

MULTIPLE CHOICE

1. Does Shylock
   a. Borrow money from Bassanio
   b. Lend money to Bassanio
   c. Lend money to Antonio

2. Which of the following characters does *not* get married at the end of the play?
   a. Portia
   b. Gratiano
   c. Antonio
   d. Jessica

3. Which of these concepts does Portia describe as the most important principle in the courtroom scene?
   a. Mercy
   b. Justice
   c. Money

4. Who designed the casket test?
   a. Portia
   b. Portia's father
   c. Portia's mother

5. Where do Lorenzo and Jessica escape to?
   a. Belmont, then back to Venice.
   b. Genoa, then on to Belmont.
   c. Belmont, then on to Genoa.

6. Launcelot is:
   a. Shylock's servant who defects to Bassanio
   b. Bassanio's servant who defects to Antonio
   c. Antonio's servant who defects to Shylock

7. What is the 3,000 ducats?
   a. The money Jessica steals from Shylock
   b. The forfeit on Shylock's bond
   c. The money Antonio and Bassanio borrow from Shylock

8. How does Tubal help Shylock?
   a. He searches for Jessica
   b. He lends him money
   c. He tries to prevent Jessica from leaving

9. What is Bassanio's occupation described as in the text?

    a. A merchant and a traveler

    b. A soldier and a scholar

    c. An idle lord

10. Which of the female characters disguise themselves as boys during the course of the play?

    a. None of them

    b. Portia and Nerissa

    c. All of them

11. Antonio says "In sooth, I know not why I am so sad," to

    a. Bassanio and Gratiano

    b. Shylock and Jessica

    c. Solanio and Salerio

12. Which character is the "fool"?

    a. Launcelot

    b. Antonio

    c. Old Gobbo

13. What does Jessica swap her father's ring for?

    a. A parakeet

    b. A stoat

    c. A monkey

14. "Balthazar" asks Bassanio for:

    a. A loan

    b. His ring

    c. A monkey

15. What does Shylock bring with him to the courtroom?

    a. A knife and scales

    b. Leah's ring

    c. 3,000 ducats

FILL IN THE BLANK

1. Launcelot Gobbo and Jessica both run away from _____.

2. Antonio loses all his money because _____.

3. Bassanio, Gratiano, and Jessica all give away a _____.

4. Shylock demands _____ as the penalty for nonpayment of his loan.

5. Lorenzo tells Jessica about the music of the _____.

6. The Prince of _____ boasts about his exploits in the wars.

7. Shylock leaves Jessica alone when he visits _____'s house for dinner.

8. _____ is made a prisoner when he becomes bankrupt.

9. The Prince of Arragon chooses the _____ casket.

10. Gratiano marries _____.

DISCUSSION

Use the following questions to generate discussion:

1. Despite accusations of racism, *The Merchant of Venice* continues to be performed across the world. Do you think this is right, or is the play unacceptable for a modern audience? Give reasons for your answer.

2. To what extent does Portia conform to conventional Renaissance ideas about how a woman should behave?

3. It has been suggested that *The Merchant of Venice* depicts characters exerting different types of control or "bondage" over each other. What examples can you find to support this claim? Do the characters escape from their "bondage"?

4. Is Bassanio an uncomplicated and somewhat bland romantic hero? Give reasons for your answer.

5. Do you read *The Merchant of Venice* as a vindication of Christian teaching? Discuss, with reference to Renaissance opinions, not modern ones.

6. In your opinion, which character in the play is the most obsessed with money? Consider the question carefully and give reasons for your answer.

7. Which does the play depict as more important: friendship or love? What do you think we are supposed to conclude about friendship and love at the end?

8. Do you think that Jessica is portrayed as an admirable character?

9. Some people find the character of Launcelot Gobbo annoying, unfunny, and irrelevant to the plot. How would you argue against this view?

10. There are three rings in the play, belonging to Bassanio, Gratiano, and Shylock. Comment on what happens to these rings, their importance to the plot, and their relevance to the issues discussed in the play.

IDENTIFYING PLAY ELEMENTS

Find examples of the following elements in the text of *The Merchant of Venice*:

* Dramatic irony
* Rhyming couplets
* Comic monologues
* "Choric" voices
* Dialogue
* Asides to the audience
* Classical allusion
* Hyperbole
* Metaphor
* Suspense

ACTIVITIES

The following activities can springboard you into further discussions and projects:

1. Find two videos of *The Merchant of Venice* (or find one video and see another performance in the theatre). Compare the way different productions handle the same scene.

   Useful scenes to compare might be the following:

   a. Act I, Scene 3, in which Shylock appears for the first time. How do the actors differ in their portrayals of Shylock, and why do you think they make the decisions they do in terms of their portrayal of the character?

   b. Act IV, Scene 1, in which Portia and Shylock interact. Compare the way Portia and Shylock react to each other. How do the actors portray the relationship between Portia and Shylock?

2. Watch a theatre or video production of *The Merchant of Venice*. Try to think about its depiction of the issues raised in the play, such as the following:

a. How are the issues of racism handled in the production?

b. How is the relationship between Antonio, Bassanio, and Portia portrayed?

c. Is the production romantic or cynical in its attitude?

d. Whose side are you on in the trial scene?

3. *The Merchant of Venice* is a play that can very easily be divided into contrasting ideas, such as Christians versus Jews, friendship versus romantic love, realism versus idealism, Venice versus Belmont, earned money versus inherited money. For each of these topics, create a chart that lists the characters most associated with the contrasting ideas.

4. Use a library and/or the Internet to find out more about the play's historical background. Put together an illustrated booklet to convey to other people the information you find. Examples of subjects that you could research include: Jewish people in Renaissance England; the status of women in Renaissance society; or love in Renaissance fiction.

A good starting place is **www.daphne. palomar.edu/shakespeare**. Many Shakespeare sites can be found on the Web, as well as sites devoted to Renaissance history, which you can find by using a search engine. Also look in the history and Shakespeare sections of your library.

5. Design a Web site to present information about *The Merchant of Venice*. Find an appropriate structure by which to organize it. For example, you could include a separate page for each character, or a "Venice" page and a "Belmont" page. Find images on the Web with which to decorate your page and information with which to fill it.

6. Put Shylock on trial for the second time. He is charged with attempted murder. The defense counsel is demanding leniency. Draw up a case for the defense and a case for the prosecution. Then stage the trial in the classroom. Who will win?

7. Design the sets for a big-budget stage or film version of *The Merchant of Venice*. Design settings for Venice and for Belmont. How will they differ? Will you use modern or traditional settings? Will the settings be realistic or symbolic? Give reasons for your decisions.

8. Imagine that you have been commissioned to direct a production of *The Merchant of Venice*, in which the action will be updated to the present day. Design costumes that you think could be worn by modern-day equivalents of Shylock, Bassanio, Antonio, Gratiano, Portia, Launcelot, and Jessica. Explain why you've chosen these costumes. Are there some characters for whom you cannot find a modern equivalent? If so, explain why.

9. With a group, rehearse and perform a short scene from *The Merchant of Venice*. Use a few rehearsals to figure out where the characters are standing in relation to others; how the characters move during the scene; which parts are intended to be funny. Examples of scenes you might want to try are:

a. Act II, Scene 9 (the Prince of Arragon). This scene can be very amusing in performance; try to find the places where Arragon's pomposity becomes funny, and where it is deflated. Also think about how the other characters are reacting during the scene.

b. Act III, Scene 1 (Shylock wants revenge). Use this scene to think about how the audience's emotions are manipulated; where does Shylock seem evil, and where does he seem sympathetic? Think about how the actor should change his acting style to reflect these shifts of sympathy.

10. Read the opening dialogue of Act V, Scene 1, and use a library or the Internet to research the Classical stories to which Lorenzo and Jessica refer (Troilus and Cressida, Pyramus and Thisbe, Dido and Aeneas, Jason and Medea). Try to write up the stories in a short and simple form. Find their similarities, and then write down how they are similar to and different from the stories of Bassanio and Portia, and Lorenzo and Jessica.

ANSWERS

Identify the Quotation

1. Speaker: Portia; Person spoken to: Nerissa; Location: Act I, Scene 2

2. Speaker: Gratiano; Person spoken to: Salerio; Location: Act II, Scene 6

3. Speaker: Bassanio; Person spoken to: Portia; Location: Act III, Scene 2

4. Speaker: Portia; Person spoken to: Shylock; Location: Act IV, Scene 1

5. Speaker: Shylock; Persons spoken to: Salerio and Solanio; Location: Act III, Scene 1

6. Speaker: Antonio; Person spoken to: Bassanio; Location: Act IV, Scene 1

7. Speaker: Antonio; Person spoken to: Shylock; Location: Act I, Scene 3

8. Speaker: Salerio; Person spoken to: Solanio; Location: Act II, Scene 8

9. Speaker: Shylock; Person spoken to: Tubal; Location: Act III, Scene 1

10. Speaker: Lorenzo; Person spoken to: himself; Location: Act V, Scene 1

True/False

1. True; 2. False; 3. True; 4. True; 5. False; 6. False; 7. False; 8. True; 9. False; 10. True; 11. True; 12. False; 13. True; 14. False; 15. True

Multiple Choice

1. c; 2. c; 3. a; 4. b; 5. b; 6. a; 7. c; 8. a; 9. b; 10. c; 11. c; 12. a; 13. c; 14. b; 15. a

Fill in the Blanks

1. Shylock; 2. his ships sink; 3. ring; 4. a pound of flesh; 5. spheres; 6. Morocco; 7. Bassanio's; 8. Antonio; 9. silver; 10. Nerissa

The Merchant of Venice

CLIFFSCOMPLETE RESOURCE CENTER

The learning doesn't need to stop here. CliffsComplete Resource Center shows you the best of the best: great links to information in print, on film, and online. And the following aren't all the great resources available to you; visit **www.cliffsnotes.com** for tips on reading literature, writing papers, giving presentations, locating other resources, and testing your knowledge.

BOOKS

Brockbank, Philip, ed. *Players of Shakespeare: Essays in Shakespearean Performance*. New York: Cambridge University Press, 1985.

Jackson, Russell and Robert Smallwood, eds. *Players of Shakespeare 2: Further Essays in Shakespearean Performance*. New York: Cambridge University Press, 1988.

These books are collections of essays by actors from the Royal Shakespeare Company, in which they describe their experience of acting a particular role. The first volume includes Patrick Stewart on playing Shylock and Sinead Cusack on playing Portia. The second volume includes Ian McDiarmid on Shylock.

Coyle, Martin, ed. *The Merchant of Venice, William Shakespeare*. New York: St. Martin's Press, 1998.

This book is aimed at more advanced students. It is a collection of modern critical essays, which explore the play's historical and cultural background.

Doyle, John and Ray Lischner. *Shakespeare For Dummies*. Foster City, California: IDG Books Worldwide, Inc., 1999.

This guide to Shakespeare's plays and poetry provides summaries and scorecards for keeping track of who's who in a given play, as well as painless introductions to language, imagery, and other often intimidating subjects.

Gross, John J. Shylock: *Four Hundred Years in the Life of a Legend*. London: Chatto & Windus, 1992.

This book describes the different ways in which the character of Shylock has been interpreted by actors and critics. The first chapter is especially useful because it assesses Shakespeare's portrayal of Shylock and the questions of anti-Semitism. The final chapter explores modern ideas about Shylock.

Holmer, Joan Ozark. *The Merchant of Venice: Choice, Hazard, and Consequence*. New York: St. Martin's Press, 1995.

This book will be of use to more advanced students. It is a thorough exploration of all aspects of the play. Using the index well can give you many interesting insights into the play.

Leggatt, Alexander. *Shakespeare's Comedy of Love*. London: Methuen, 1974.

This book attempts to study each of Shakespeare's romantic comedies on its own terms. It finds that *The Merchant of Venice* is an experiment in writing a comedy that explores the dark side of life.

Overton, Bill. *The Merchant of Venice*. Atlantic High-
lands, New Jersey: Humanities Press International, 1987.

This book is split into two halves. The first half
discusses the play on the page, the second analyzes
stage and television productions.

Wells, Stanley. *Shakespeare: The Poet and His Plays*.
London: Methuen, 1997.

This book is a very good introduction to Shakespeare's plays. The section on *The Merchant of Venice*
describes the ways in which theatre productions can
find different meanings. The book is a revision of
a previous edition, entitled *Shakespeare: A Dramatic Life*.

Wilders, John, ed. *Shakespeare: The Merchant of
Venice: A Casebook*. Nashville: Aurora Publishers, 1970.

This is a collection of essays by various scholars
from the eighteenth century to the present day. They
discuss all aspects of the play.

INTERNET

Mr. William Shakespeare and the Internet
(**daphne.palomar.edu/shakespeare/**)
This is an excellent place to begin searching for
Shakespeare Web sites. It contains hundreds of links
organized into different subsections. You can find
links to criticism of *Merchant* at **daphne.
palomar.edu/shakespeare/playcriticism. htm#merchant.**

The London Globe's Web Site (**www.rdg.ac.uk/globe/**)
Contains information about Elizabethan staging
techniques, and a "virtual reality" guided tour of
the reconstructed Globe Theatre in London. It
also contains reviews of a production of *The
Merchant of Venice* that was staged there.

Other virtual reality tours of Shakespeare's
Globe:

**sterling.holycross.edu/departments/theatre/wrynders/globe/
globe.htm**

virtual.clemson.edu/caah/shakespr/vrglobe/tourst.htm

Online hypertext editions of *The Merchant of
Venice*:

the-tech.mit.edu/shakespeare.html

www.hypermedic.com/style/shakespeare/merchant.htm

Hypertext editions can be an improvement on
paper editions, because they are filled with links that
can connect you swiftly with further information.
However, they are not always as easy to read as paper
editions (and you can't carry them in your coat
pocket).

Shakespeare and Anti-Semitism: The Question of
Shylock (**www.geocities.com/athens/acropolis /7221/**)
This site provides information on Jews in
Renaissance England, and argues that *The Merchant
of Venice* is anti-Semitic. This is a useful site, but you
should consider the arguments *against* the authors'
case, because there are several issues that he does not
consider, such as how Shakespeare portrays
Christians.

FILMS

Three versions of *The Merchant of Venice* are
available on video. Unfortunately, none of them does
the play justice in terms of entertainment value. Even
so, performances are always useful for giving life to
the bare words on the page. The most valuable exercise is to watch two versions and compare the way
they stage different scenes.

Renaissance Classics: The Merchant of Venice. Dir. Jonathan Miller. Polygram Video, Ltd. 1973.

This film is based on a production at the National Theatre, in London. It is set in 1890s Venice and is a heavily cut interpretation, which portrays Shylock as more sympathetic than the Christians. The production is rather slow, but Laurence Olivier's clever portrayal of Shylock is well worth seeing.

BBC Shakespeare: The Merchant of Venice. BBC Enterprises, Ltd. 1980.

This production is set in the Renaissance. It solves the racism question by making both Jews and Christians look bad. This film is useful because it presents the entirety of the play, without cutting a line.

Channel 4 Education: The Merchant of Venice. Channel 4, 1996.

The best *Merchant* available on video. The acting is strong, with Bob Peck playing Shylock as a villain with sympathetic qualities.

OTHER MEDIA

Arkangel Complete Shakespeare: The Merchant of Venice. Dir. Clive Brill. Penguin, 1998.

Sound recordings are useful, because hearing actors speak the lines gives meaning to the words. Read the play as you listen, because telling the characters apart in a sound-only production can be difficult.

The Merchant of Venice

CLIFFSCOMPLETE READING GROUP DISCUSSION GUIDE

Use the following questions and topics to enhance your reading group discussions. The discussion can help get you thinking — and hopefully talking — about Shakespeare in a whole new way!

DISCUSSION QUESTIONS

1. Although *The Merchant of Venice* is a comedy, some scenes and subjects in the play feel as if they come from a more serious, issues-oriented drama — perhaps even a tragedy. How funny is *The Merchant of Venice?* What are the pros and cons of using comedy to deal with serious topics? How thin is the line between comedy and tragedy?

2. *The Merchant of Venice* takes places in two unique worlds — Venice and Belmont. What worth do these two different worlds place on money? On the rights of women? On the importance of law and order? Does Shakespeare favor one world over the other? Do you?

3. In a way, Venetian society has imposed several labels on Shylock: *Jew, usurer,* and *alien* to name just three. How do these labels limit Shylock? Which of these labels is most damaging to Shylock? Are any of the labels unfair? Would Shylock be as fascinating a character if Shakespeare had made him only a usurer and an alien? Only a Jew and an alien?

4. Some historians contend that Shakespeare's dramatization of Shylock led Globe Theatre patrons to order the execution of Rodrigo Lopez, a Portuguese Jew who served as Queen Elizabeth's personal physician. What does this action say about the power of the play? Of theatre? Can you think of other instances when theatrical productions (or any media performance for that matter) aroused similar passion from an audience? Was the passion based on rational truth or irrational reactions?

5. One of the earliest realistic, more sympathetic portrayals of Shylock was by a famous black Shakespearean actor. Ira Aldridge (1806 – 1867) performed throughout Europe in numerous Shakespearean roles — including King Lear, Othello, and Shylock — to critical and popular praise. What qualities might a black actor bring to the role of Shylock? What challenges would an audience have in accepting a black actor playing the role of Shylock? What similarities do you see in the portrayal of Jews and blacks in other theatrical works, films, television show, books, or popular song?

6. The characters of Portia and Nerissa are popular examples of Shakespeare's *breeches heroines* — female characters who masquerade as boys. Some scholars describe breeches heroines as characters who *use deception as a path toward freedom.* In what ways is this description appropriate for Portia? For Nerissa? What else do they use deception for? When is deception justified?

7. From Shakespeare's day through the eighteenth century, most theatrical costuming was primitive. For example, the character of Shylock always wore a red wig and large, fake nose. How would this costuming affect your understanding of the play? What aspects of the play and the character of Shylock would be highlighted with this type of costuming? What aspects of the play might be lost? Could a present-day production costume Shylock in such a manner?

8. *The Merchant of Venice* features numerous supporting characters. Why did Shakespeare include the characters of Salerio? Solanio? Launcelot? Old Gobbo? Tubal? What do these characters add to the play? How would the play be different if you took away each of these characters?

9. Many films and stage productions of Shakespeare's plays have been set in different time periods and locations other than those specified by Shakespeare in his original writing. For example, productions of *Romeo and Juliet* have been set in Victorian England, 1920s Chicago gangster world, and even outer space. What other time periods or locations can you envision for a production of *The Merchant of Venice?* Which scenes and lines would you need to cut or rewrite in order to make the play work in another time period or location?

10. One recent stage production of *The Merchant of Venice* set the play in a World War II Nazi concentration camp. Actors were costumed as Jewish interns in the camp or as Nazi officers. What are the strengths of staging *The Merchant of Venice* in this manner? What issues in the play do these radical staging choices highlight? What weaknesses does this type of staging bring to the play?

Index

continued

M

continued

continued

Notes

Notes

Notes

Notes

Notes

Notes